Pros & Cons
A Debater's Handbook

SIXTEENTH EDITION BY
MICHAEL D. JACOBSON

Routledge & Kegan Paul
London, Henley & Boston

First edition by J. B. Askew
published in 1896
Sixteenth edition revised by Michael D. Jacobson
published in 1977
by Routledge & Kegan Paul Ltd
39 Store Street, London WC1E 7DD;
Broadway House, Newtown Road,
Henley-on-Thames, Oxon RG9 1EN;
and 9 Park Street, Boston,
Mass. 02108, USA

Set in Monotype Plantin
and printed in Great Britain by
Cox & Wyman Ltd, London,
Reading & Fakenham

British Library Cataloguing in Publication Data

Jacobson, Michael D

Pros & Cons : a debater's handbook – 16th ed.

1. Social policy
I. Title
300   HN17.5

ISBN 0–7100–8525–7
ISBN 0–7100–8526–5 Pbk

Contents

▼

Preface to the sixteenth edition

Pros & Cons provides material for debates on a wide range of controversial questions of permanent or topical interest. The arguments for and against appear in adjacent columns, numbered point by point, so that each Pro corresponds as far as possible with the Con of the same number.

For the sake of convenience, the debating subjects are arranged in alphabetical order, even though this entails the separation of some subjects which are relevant to each other. However, ample cross-references are given – within the text and in the Index – to related themes.

In covering such a broad spectrum of political, social, industrial, educational and other complex issues, the views expressed or information given cannot always be comprehensive; but it is intended that they should offer the debater guidelines which are capable of expansion, if wished, or which may suggest further points for development.

The extent of changes in the social and moral climate during the past decade or so could hardly be illustrated more graphically than by a comparison of the debates in this and the previous edition of *Pros & Cons*. This is the sixteenth revised edition since the book was first published in 1896; the last appeared in 1965, and it must be doubted whether so large a volume of modifications and entirely new matter has ever been necessary before, between any two of the previous successive editions.

Since 1965, the arguments over whether Britain should join the European Common Market have passed into history – and, with them, those on athletics for women, decimal coinage, the legalisation of abortion, equal pay for equal work, and several more once heated controversies. Instead of Capital Punishment, Abolition Of, the debate now is on whether it should be restored. Raising the school-leaving age has somersaulted similarly, as an issue, into the fors and againsts of lowering it again.

In the interim, many new topics have assumed increasing public importance and have duly been incorporated for the first time. Among them: pollution and various other aspects of the environmental problem; commercial radio; a number of constitutional questions such as the calls for Britain to have a coalition government and a written constitution; the future of private medicine; terrorism; and Women's Lib (not yet founded as a movement when the last edition was published but now forming the longest individual debate out of all the new subjects which have been added).

Of the 'traditional' debating themes retained, e.g. advertising and vivisection, nearly all have required extensive revision and bringing up to date. Even while this latest edition was in course of preparation, the pace of events and the ceaseless flow of fresh legislation entailed radical modifications – not only of particular arguments but of several subjects as a whole.

The reviser wishes to express his special thanks, for suggestions and help received, to Christopher Bishop, Christopher Davalle, D.A. Orton, P.D.B., S.M.J. and G.J.J.

M. D. J.

Pros & Cons

Advertising, Public Control and Taxation of

Pro: (1) The case for public control is demonstrated above all by the general lack of trust in advertising now evident. Only new legislation, and the creation of a State-backed controlling body with 'teeth' to impose penalties on offenders, will ease the present widespread public suspicion of advertising – notably as regards its cost, waste of man-power and material, and the belief that too many advertisements, if not actually dishonest, are downright misleading. The fact that the Advertising Standards Authority launched a national campaign, inviting members of the public to send in complaints if they saw a Press, poster, cinema or direct mail advertisement which they believed to have broken the Code, was a clear recognition of the likelihood that such contraventions are still to be found.

(2) The expense of advertising adds greatly to overall production costs and thus to the prices of goods or services when they reach the public. Too much money is spent on advertising, in relation to the scale of any benefits it may bring in making products known or giving people information they genuinely wish or need to acquire.

(3) Much of the huge sum devoted to advertising each year is

Con: (1) The standards set by the present British Code of Advertising Practice are already the highest in the world; most of the other European countries, in fact, have been studying it with a view to adopting it for themselves. Within the industry, controls to ensure that advertisements are 'legal, decent, honest and truthful' are exercised by several bodies, with the Advertising Standards Authority at the top. The system is voluntary but has enormous moral weight. Other professions, like the law and medicine, are also governed by themselves, internally, and experience has proved that a voluntary system of this nature is more effective than formal legislation, which almost always leaves large loopholes.

(2) Businessmen are always seeking the lowest costs they can find. For example, they decide to buy their own lorries, for delivering their goods, only if they believe this is cheaper and more efficient than using the railways or other means of public transport. Equally, they would not spend a penny on advertising unless they felt it did an essential job in helping to increase the sale of their products – nor would they spend a penny more than they deemed necessary for the purpose.

(3) Under the principle of

unnecessary and could be used more fruitfully to bring down prices. There is particular public resentment at the mass advertising for rival brands of products like petrol or detergents – which, most people suspect, are so similar in character as to be virtually indistinguishable except in their packaging. Another wasteful practice is the 'prestige' advertising placed by big companies whose names are so familiar that, in reality, people no longer need even occasional reminders of them. In some cases, too, the products advertised are so specialised that it seems pointless to tell the general public about them in this way. The only material return from such advertisements, one may deduce, is that the companies concerned can claim the cost against tax. In effect, therefore, the practice denies revenue to the Exchequer.

(4) The advertising industry employs an undue number of people, a large proportion of whom could be put to better and more constructive use in other fields.

(5) Advertising is, by its very nature, a subterfuge – the head of a leading British advertising agency once described himself as being 'in the myth-making business'. Although blatant lying in advertisements has become much less common, not only because of the Code but because it is counter-productive once detected, advertisers still believe nevertheless that it is legitimate to mislead people, without actually telling them lies. And people *are* misled, through being persuaded to buy products which may well be good of their kind but which they don't really need. This almost amoral attitude among advertisers should, clearly, be subjected to much more rigorous restriction and control, through new legislation.

(6) The Press depends for its very survival on its income from ad-

'economies of scale', advertising may actually lead to lower prices: the better a product becomes known and the bigger its sales volume, the more chance there is of bringing down its unit cost. Petrol companies gain much of their custom because motorists come to recognise that garages selling a particular brand usually have a higher standard of service than others – the implicit object of the advertising; detergent manufacturers insist that their products *do* differ, whatever some people may imagine. In relation to the size of their businesses, anyway, their spending on advertising is quite small. Indeed, the total level of advertising expenditure in Britain annually represents only about 2 per cent of the Gross National Product. Even in the USA, the world's most advertising-conscious nation, it is no more than some $3\frac{1}{2}$ per cent of the GNP.

(4) The industry does not make a large use of labour. In 1975, the total number of people employed in all the advertising agencies in Britain (including secretaries and accountants, etc.) was only about 15,000.

(5) Visiting a factory, one may see chemists or scientists producing some new, anonymous liquid, developed to fulfil a particular function or meet a specific need. They have created it, but that's where their job ends. They have no idea how to sell it; except, perhaps, for a long technical name, they don't even know what to call it. That is where an advertising agency comes in, by creating a personality for the product. It is a perfectly valid task – no matter whether the liquid concerned happens to be, say, a new stain-remover, lawn-mower lubricant or even some new, life-saving medicine. Advertisers create symbols, sell ideas and associations, and thereby bring awareness of a product to people who will be glad to make use

vertisements. Most British newspapers have to rely on advertising for about 50 per cent of their revenues. Those papers which fail to attract sufficient advertisements face the prospect either of closing down or, perhaps, of continuing to exist only through the financial buttressing of another, healthier newspaper in the same 'stable'. (For example, the *Guardian* would probably not have survived without its support from the highly profitable *Manchester Evening News*.) This is a lamentable state of affairs, and it opens the door to all sorts of pressures from advertisers. Years ago, it was quite common for newspapers to be threatened with the withdrawal of advertising if they published stories the advertiser didn't like. While such threats are now almost unheard of (except, perhaps, on some small local papers), and journalists would in any case strongly resist that kind of blackmail, there are other, subtler pressures which are even more harmful. The bigger a newspaper's circulation, the more it can charge for its advertising space. Popular papers therefore have a compulsion to get a bigger audience – as, indeed, do commercial TV and radio companies – and they try to acquire it, all too often, by lowering their editorial standards: hence their resort to pin-ups, sex stories and other superficialities which, they believe, appeal to mass tastes. This pernicious struggle to gain more readers, in order to get more advertising, at higher rates, would be unnecessary if each paper had a fair share of all the advertising available. The only way to achieve that would be to channel the advertising through a central, officially-established body, responsible for ensuring its equitable allocation. Such a measure would not merely save a number of worthwhile publications from extinction but help to

of it. The advertising industry knows better than anyone the importance of public trust in advertisements, because lack of it means a loss of advertising effectiveness which can cost clients millions; apart from their social responsibility, therefore, it is in advertisers' own best commercial interests that advertising should be both as trustworthy and as trusted as possible. They remain convinced that the industry itself can achieve this more surely than could any form of governmental control.

(6) Far from decrying the importance of advertising to newspapers, we should recognise it as being one of the ways we get a free Press. It is an essential pillar not only for a newspaper's solvency but for its very independence. Without advertisements, the full economic price per copy that newspapers had to charge their readers would be so high, compared with the present levels, that their circulations would be extremely limited. Advertising, therefore, performs a useful social function, in addition to its own purpose, since it enables a much larger number and wider variety of newspapers to reach the public than would be possible without it. No form of State control has yet been devised which would improve matters, in this field, without interfering unwarrantably with other aspects of a newspaper's work. Various Government Departments are themselves among the biggest individual advertisers; like any private advertiser, they buy space in publications which are the most 'cost effective', i.e. which provide the largest audience for a given sum of money, irrespective of whether or not they approve of the policies of the publication concerned. If a governmental body were given responsibility for allocating all advertising, it might well be more

raise editorial standards in others. Proposals of this nature, in fact, have already been discussed in Parliament.

(7) Some publications do already survive healthily without advertisements. The French humorous weekly *Le Canard Enchaîné* is a case in point. Soviet newspapers, too, had no advertising for years and still contain very little. Accordingly, querying the basic assumption that advertising is essential to the Press in Western countries, one parallel suggestion mooted in Britain is that newspapers' financial security (and thus their existence) should be assured instead by means of a Government subsidy. This would have no 'strings' attached, as regards editorial control, and would presumably be along the lines of the system for the BBC, which receives its money from the State but remains completely autonomous, free to decide its policies and attitudes without Government interference.

(8) The Press is only one of many aspects of advertising marked by abuses which require remedying by stricter public control. Among examples: the defacement of the countryside by huge billboards along the trunk roads; and the apparently unrestricted rash of neon signs, flashing lights and other such illuminated advertisements in the towns, which are usually ugly and may even be positively dangerous when they obscure or clash with road and traffic signs. Deceptive packaging, phoney price reductions and 'gifts', and the excessive use of children in TV commercials to persuade mothers to buy foods or other products they don't really need, are further menaces to the housewife in particular. Perhaps the most dangerous development in recent years is subliminal advertising, whereby the 'message' is implanted in people's minds without

likely to threaten a reduction in the share-out to newspapers of which it disapproved. It is public opinion, not the influence of advertisers, which newspapers consider when deciding their attitudes to given issues. In 1956, two leading British national papers showed heavy circulation losses, within a month, when they opposed Britain's participation in the Suez invasion. That was solely the pressure of public opinion – and it proves that Government control would be both unnecessary and irrelevant.

(7) The examples given opposite are special cases. Russian newspapers did not have advertising originally because the Soviet economy at the time put little or no emphasis on consumer goods; but their level of advertising in recent years has been increasing steadily (even though they still tend to talk of 'realisation of a schedule' rather than 'selling'). A Government subsidy, however well-meaning, would have several drawbacks; not the least is that, ultimately, the responsibility for handing out the money would rest with a small committee set up for the purpose – and that committee, even if it did not mean to, would be bound to exercise an influence on editorial content, because newspapers would depend so heavily on its largesse.

(8) The advertising industry itself has instituted a whole series of 'watch-dog' bodies, at different levels, to ensure that the consumer is not misled by what an advertiser says or by any promises he makes about his products. Not a single TV commercial can be transmitted in Britain until several such bodies have scrutinised it at each stage – from the original script up to the final film. In Britain, the authorities already impose considerable restrictions on the nature, number, size and siting of street advertisements; these controls have avoided the

them being consciously aware of it.

(9) The case for specific taxation on advertising makes sense on several different grounds. It would reinforce the effectiveness and authority of the reforms proposed above. In these days of high taxation, it is an appropriate and fully justifiable new source of Government revenue. It would reduce the volume of unnecessary or dubious advertisements and thereby serve the cause of worthwhile advertising. Above all, it could be introduced very simply, through VAT. At present, advertising is 'zero-rated' for VAT, which means that it pays no tax in practice but is *not* actually exempt. The Chancellor of the Exchequer, therefore, could change that zero-rating to the standard 8 per cent, or whatever other rate he decided, by a simple stroke of the pen – and without need for any new Act of Parliament. A Press baron who had a leading part in founding one of the regional independent television companies in Britain once described commercial TV as 'a licence to print money'. If the profits of those who hold the commercial television franchises were not so excessive, they would have less temptation to put on so many programmes appealing to the lowest common denominator.

hideous jumble of roadside advertising seen in the USA and, indeed, have greatly improved the situation even in this country, compared with that between the wars. In packaging and all other aspects affecting household shopping, new measures of consumer protection are being introduced all the time, and advertisers automatically conform to them. As for subliminal advertising, it is no longer likely to be used, because it is not considered to be effective. Even if someone did try it, the Advertising Standards Authority does not approve of the method and would ask the advertiser to halt it – and that 'request' would certainly be obeyed.

(9) Apart from the fact that companies are already hit by Corporation Tax and other forms of taxation, a direct tax on their advertising would have one serious outcome: it would increase marketing costs and thus, inevitably, result in higher prices to the consumer. The suggestion that taxing advertisements would reduce the amount of commercially unnecessary advertising does not hold water; contrary to popular myth, companies do not advertise for fun. Even under VAT, the burden would be inequitable; it would fall most heavily on companies whose products are subject to the greatest degree of competition (e.g. detergents, confectionery and toiletries); it would also tend to penalise large advertisements, whereas 'small ads' are, in fact, proportionately much less cost-effective and so more wasteful. Proposals for the taxation of advertising were first made as long ago as 1947, but were rejected by the Labour Government at that time because the measures were seen to be both unfair and impracticable. No new proposals have yet been devised which overcome those objections.

'Amateur' Sports:
Can Britain Retain Any?

Pro: (1) Nobody would suggest that the old, snobbish distinction between amateurs and professionals in sport – stemming from the class-conscious pre-First World War days, when young middle- or upper-class sportsmen had private incomes which permitted them to devote all their time to a sport, without receiving payment – is either feasible or desirable any longer. But the amateur spirit of playing a game for its own sake, not for any financial rewards, has a great deal to commend it. Our national life would be infinitely poorer if it were to disappear entirely, even just from the top echelons of sport.

(2) Most people welcomed the ending of 'shamateurism' in sports like tennis and the best grades of (previously) amateur soccer, where top players maintained their supposedly non-professional status by receiving unduly high expenses and other clandestine benefits. That was hypocrisy well dispensed with. However, there are still sports in which virtually all the participants, including those at the highest international levels, remain true amateurs – athletics and Rugby Union are two cases in point. Such sports preserve their special qualities because of the absence of commercialism, and they would lose their present public support without those qualities.

(3) The world's greatest sporting event, the Olympic Games, enshrines the amateur ideal that what matters is not winning but taking part. Yet nobody could suggest that this lowers the standards of performance; indeed, there is always a

Con: (1) Few spectacles were more degrading than the practice – in cricket, for example – of having separate gates from the pavilion on to the pitch for amateurs and professionals. It took even longer to abolish the stupid tradition that England's cricket captain had to be an amateur, despite the fact that he was in charge of professionals who were usually much more skilful than himself. Such attitudes, happily, now belong to history, and it is recognised universally that top-class sport, when it has the character of public entertainment, must offer spectators the best standards possible. To get the best, you have to pay for it.

(2) That it took so long to end 'shamateurism' demonstrates the basic dishonesty of trying to maintain a concept which only a tiny minority of wealthy people could now uphold without deception. The acceptance of professionals in all sports would be to the benefit of amateurs, rather than the contrary. It would raise standards of performance generally and, without in any way affecting the popularity of a sport or the enjoyment of amateurs practising it in their spare time, would serve as an incentive for those wishing to strive for representative honours. All professionals were amateurs once. Relative to the size of their respective followings in Britain, ordinary (professional) Rugby League matches regularly draw much bigger crowds than do (amateur) Rugby Union matches. Moreover, the plain truth is that even amateur athletics has not remained without a degree of

plethora of new world records at every Games. Although some countries may flout the Olympic spirit, treating the event as an opportunity to enhance national prestige, even this cannot overcome the essential benefit of the Games – the sight of many hundreds of young people, from scores of different countries, getting to know and understand each other a little better, in completely friendly rivalry. Whatever governments may think, the young people themselves know that it is an honour merely to have been selected for the Games – and no matter if they don't get beyond the first heat!

(4) Professional sport could not exist without the infinitely bigger foundation of amateur sport below it. The professionals would not attract the large crowds they need unless amateurs had created public interest in the sport in the first place.

'shamateurism' among some of the top international performers.

(3) The ideal was all very well in the leisured days when Baron Coubertin re-created the Olympic Games in 1896, but nowadays it is more honoured in the breach than the observance. Many countries set out blatantly to gain prestige through their athletes' achievements at the Games. To that end, they provide likely prospects with well-paid but undemanding jobs and other facilities which, if difficult to prove as contravening the letter of the law, are clearly contrary to its spirit. (The athletics scholarships provided by some American universities are not much better.) In some sports at the Games, like football, our own amateurs find themselves playing teams whose members are professionals in all but name. If the amateur–professional concept were ended once and for all, it could well be to the advantage of the Olympic Games – and not only by restoring standards of honesty. For one thing, governments would be less inclined to use the Games (as some of them have in recent years) for purposes of political blackmail.

(4) Even if truly amateur sport could continue to exist, which is questionable, its ultimate survival would still depend on the ever-higher standards and public interest secured by professional sport.

(See also *School Sport, Compulsory.*)

Anarchism

(Anarchism, as a political philosophy, opposes any form of established government or imposed authority and is summed up by the belief that 'every man should be his own government, his own law, his own church'. Holding that each community should run its affairs by voluntary, co-operative means, it shares Communism's ultimate goal of a classless society but differs from Communism in rejecting control by the State or any other organised authorities such as political parties or trade unions.)

Pro: (1) Universal suffrage and representative institutions do not prevent governments from being as hostile to liberty as aristocracies or monarchies were in the past. Only the abolition of governments and of all compulsory associations can secure the right of liberty, because people who make it their profession to control others will always be tyrannical in practice, however well-meaning they may be in principle.

(2) Voluntary association has always accomplished much more than is commonly recognised. One can always refuse to work with, or for, those who have failed to act honourably. Men are social beings and behave socially, except when prevented by anti-social institutions.

(3) There can be no real liberty as long as a constant check is imposed from without on the actions of the individual.

(4) Anarchism won large-scale support in Spain, before the civil war; far from being just a theory, it proved extremely efficient and had many achievements to its credit.

(5) If adopted, anarchism would not mean disorder. The mere fact that it has not been tried out recently is not a valid argument against it.

Con: (1) Government is necessary to prevent a minority of fanatical, self-seeking or wicked people from exploiting the common man. If as many abuses as possible are prevented, it is better to risk occasional oppression by governmental control than to run the greater risk of private tyranny and violence. Most people do not want the trouble of managing their own communal affairs. Some degree of uniform behaviour and of controls over the individual, within generally accepted limits, is necessary for the development of social life and civilisation.

(2) Boycotts, strikes and refusal to co-operate are just as much instruments of coercion as fines and imprisonment. Most of the important so-called voluntary associations, in this context, rest either on some government's coercive resources or on equally coercive conditions.

(3) 'Liberty' is equivocal. Liberty to do good is desirable, not liberty to do evil. But it often depends on the point of view as to which is which.

(4) While the Spanish Anarchists taught peasants to read and worked to form self-governing groups of workers in industry and agriculture, they resorted to widespread murder and violence to try to achieve their political aims. No end can justify such means.

(5) Institutions are a necessity for any form of social life. Without them, there would be chaos.

Animals, Rights of

Pro: (1) Most forward-thinking countries recognise that animals do have rights – in particular, those according them the 'restricted freedom' to live a natural life, in harmony with the perpetual requirements of the community.

(2) The rights of animals have

Con: (1) The treatment of animals must be related to the needs of mankind. We should be kind to animals for the sake of our self-respect and for material considerations (e.g. conservation), not because they have any specific rights of their own accord.

long been recognised by thinkers, e.g. Bentham, and emphasised by some religions, e.g. Buddhism.

(3) It is absurd to make a distinction between 'domestic' and other animals, whereby the former are given more protection than the latter from hunting excesses and the infliction of pain.

(4) The lack of recognition of these rights tends to encourage greater cruelties under the pretext of scientific research, the provision of food, and so on.

(5) Animals (if left to themselves) live their own lives fitly, killing for food only and not for pleasure, which is more than can be said for man. Like man himself, they form part of nature's scheme of evolution: each has a crucial role in the ecological chain.

(6) It is nonsense to assert, as some people do, that rights can be allowed to exist only if they are reciprocal. Otherwise, what claims could lunatics or infants have on our protection?

(7) The feeling of community among all sentient creatures is clearly desirable – and mutually beneficial.

(2) These theories are connected with mysticism, vegetarianism, etc., which have little or no bearing on the matter for the majority of people who do not subscribe to such specialist views.

(3) We protect domestic animals because they are valuable to us (either materially or emotionally), and not because they have a special claim on us.

(4) The alleged cruelties of vivisection have been much exaggerated. The benefits to mankind, from the use of animals in controlled scientific research, have been beyond measure. Man is entitled to ensure his own survival, at the expense of animals if necessary.

(5) Sometimes man has to be protected from animals which would kill him either by violence or by eating up his food supplies. Animals show small consideration for other species.

(6) Solidarity between members of the same species is natural and necessary. It is not so between members of different species.

(7) This feeling would be all on one side, and in practice would often mean placing man's interests second to those of animals.

(See also *Vivisection and Experiments on Animals*.)

Armaments, Limitation of Conventional

Pro: (1) Swollen armaments encourage militant nationalism, and often misplaced pride, in the countries which maintain them. At the same time, they create distrust and fear among other nations, leading them to increase their armaments in turn. In this mad race, each nation's defensive measures become interpreted by its neighbours as preparations for aggression.

Con: (1) Armaments are not a cause but a symptom of the causes which bring about war. Preparedness for war is natural only in a country which has a definite war programme.

(2) It is exceptionally difficult to bring about any effective limitation of conventional forces and armaments because qualitative reckonings are more important than quantitative. This has been the big problem for NATO and the Warsaw

(2) Experience has shown that schedules of disarmament are possible. Even with nuclear weapons, the Soviet Union and the USA have made some progress towards agreement to reduce their stockpiles. The limitation of conventional armaments, with a corresponding reduction in the size of armies, would lessen the danger of local wars – which always risk becoming bigger conflicts.

(3) The Geneva disarmament conference has served a useful purpose in forcing its participants to lay their cards on the table and in fostering an atmosphere of greater frankness. Its imperfections are admitted but, though ignored by some powers, it is generally recognised as a forum which it is essential to maintain.

(4) The burden of armaments is heavy in all countries and crushing in some. If it could be removed, trade would have a chance to improve, taxation would be lessened and all countries would become more prosperous.

(5) Large armies and navies involve the existence of a large class of professional military men, who are naturally prone to warlike ambitions.

(6) Disarmament on a large scale would secure at any rate a considerable delay before war was resorted to, and the time taken to raise a nation to the pitch of warlike efficiency would give the forces of peace a better chance of prevailing.

(Some) Disarmament by one country (without waiting for agreement from others) would be a courageous step which would prove that country's good faith and help to break down the atmosphere of distrust.

Pact powers, in their negotiations for mutual and balanced force reductions. In any case, America and the Soviet Union have given priority – quite rightly – to the much graver threat of nuclear arms.

(3) Without the participation of two of the world's nuclear powers, China and France, the Geneva disarmament conference is worthless. It has become a mere ritual and continues only because, politically, none of the major UN powers dares to take the responsibility of admitting the fact.

(4) One lesson war has taught all countries is that, unless armaments are kept up-to-date and in sufficient stock, a war can easily go in favour of the aggressor in the early days and be prolonged, if not lost altogether.

(5) In the most powerful countries especially, the professional soldier is essentially peaceable. Trained for war, he wants to prevent it from happening. The fomenters of modern war are the civilians.

(6) It is impossible to disarm any modern country, because armament is co-extensive with the country's organised knowledge and resources. Unilateral disarmament is a Utopian idea. It would merely be regarded as a sign of weakness by other countries.

(See also *Nuclear Weapons: Should They Be Banned Completely?*)

Birth Control: Voluntary or Compulsory?

Pro: (1) Left to the operations of nature, men, like plants and animals, tend to outrun the supplies available to satisfy their wants. Fierce competition and destruction of the weaker is the usual way of meeting the difficulty, but this is a wasteful method and not in accord with man's increasing mastery over nature. For centuries, man has been learning and practising the control of nature's productivity in the plant and animal worlds, yet the application of such principles to man himself is still hardly out of the elementary stages. Between now and early in the next century, the world's population will have doubled – to 8,000 million by the year 2010, it is estimated. But the Earth's natural resources are finite and such huge population growth will make shortages of food and raw materials inevitable. It is urgently necessary that birth control education and facilities should become universal. The only arguable point is whether these should be voluntary or compulsory.

(2) The wider provision of reliable medical advice on birth control has not been followed by the upsurge of immorality that the prophets of gloom predicted. There is now a strong movement in favour of allowing birth control even in the Roman Catholic Church, many of whose adherents already practise it.

(3) In more and more countries, abortion is now legal (under specified conditions, the most common being those cases when birth would be dangerous to the mother's health). Many of these operations could have been avoided by the wise use of birth control. There is no evidence, in general, that birth control does any harm to those who practise it or to their potential fertility. In

Con: (1) The imposition of world-wide birth control programmes, as a means of easing pressure on natural resources, would put the cart before the horse (quite apart from any moral objections). The danger of food shortages, apart from special causes, has arisen in the past from large-scale devastation due to war, from inadequate knowledge locally, and also partially from the artificial restrictions resulting from financial difficulties and manipulations. But any shortages could be overcome – or avoided – by proper international co-operation (as already seen in part through the UN Food and Agricultural Organisation). Science and technology have made such progress that an increase in supplies at least proportionate to population could be effected without difficulty.

(2) To check the birth rate artificially is immoral. It is rankly disobedient to the teaching of the Roman Catholic Church and, indeed, of many other religions. The motive of limitation is nearly always selfish, fundamentally.

(3) From the huge demand for abortions, since their legalisation, it is obvious that only a relatively small proportion of them are really necessary, on strictly medical grounds. Birth control has been used too often to avoid imagined risks for purely selfish reasons. Furthermore, there are indications that the continued practice of birth control actually reduces fertility. Even the Pill, supposedly 'safe', has made some women permanently infertile – and has been blamed for occasional deaths by thrombosis. When birth control is used to prevent child-bearing altogether, women are denying themselves the exercise of their natural functions. It is well established medically that,

fact, the contrary has been proved by the population increases in the advanced countries since the last world war. The law still controls methods which might be harmful if wrongly applied. For instance, the Pill can be obtained only on medical prescription to ensure women get the type most suitable for them (as regards oestrogen, etc.).

(4) Birth control is used mainly to limit, and not to avoid, child-bearing. In Western countries, the rise in the standard of living of the poorer classes has coincided with the decrease in the size of families, and they no longer regard their children from a largely economic point of view. It is only in some developing nations, such as India, that peasant parents still regard having a large number of children as an insurance – a means of adding to the family's earning power and of safeguarding the parents' keep in their old age. But massive family planning campaigns are gradually succeeding in cutting the annual birth rate in such countries, even so.

(5) With attitudes towards women's position in society now becoming more enlightened, their freedom to practise birth control is among those rights which are already widely accepted as fundamental. Many women are no longer content to spend the most active years of their adult lives solely in bearing and rearing children; they wish to play their full part in the life of the community, which usually requires more spare time than traditional family ties would allow them; such women should have the practical means of deciding for themselves on the extent of family responsibilities they are willing to accept.

(6) The spread of birth control education and facilities, with official encouragement, has not only helped to eradicate dubious, hole-in-the-

in most cases, child-bearing has a beneficial effect on a woman's mental and physical health.

(4) The desire for small families often springs from less worthy motives than regard for the welfare of the children. Many selfish people decide against having children merely because they don't want to cut back on expensive enjoyments like foreign holidays. Such people frequently offer proof that the retention of material amenities, at that price, may well be outweighed by the loss of spiritual values. In the poorest countries, the prime need is not family planning but the achievement of higher economic standards – and that's where concerted international action should mostly be directed. The Chinese, with more inhabitants than any other nation, insist that this presents no problems because, whatever the growth in the population, the country's economic growth has been at an even higher rate.

(5) To suggest that birth control gives women more freedom to widen their horizons, socially or intellectually, just isn't true. Only a relative minority of women show any real interest in the life and welfare of the community at large. Of those who do take an active role, very few manage to combine their public and private responsibilities without difficulty (or without some loss on one side or the other). For the average mother of a small family, with no other interests, extra spare time is rarely of any particular benefit. Some, feeling lonely, may enter industry – for the sake of the companionship as much as for the extra cash – but this will often be to the detriment of what remains of family life.

(6) The almost unrestricted availability of birth control appliances (even the Pill, from complaisant doctors) is encouraging

corner sources which existed formerly but has made people franker and more honest in their approach to the whole subject of sex. Except, perhaps, for the greater Press publicity it receives, sexual immorality is no greater today than in past ages when birth control was unknown.

immorality in the young and already leading many of them to reject the concepts of a society founded on the family and monogamic marriage – essential cornerstones of Western civilisation.

(See also the next article.)

Birth Rate, High

Pro: (1) A country's prosperity is bound up with the size of its working population. It cannot be developed, nor its economy carried on adequately, with too small a population. That is why some of the oldest and largest Commonwealth countries, such as Australia and Canada, were only partly developed until relatively recently, when intensified campaigns to encourage immigration gradually alleviated their shortage of manpower.

(2) Modern methods of production and scientific improvements in agriculture make it possible to support larger populations than our ancestors ever imagined. Britain's population has increased fourfold in the last century; the average standard of living of her people, particularly the poorer classes, has risen beyond measure in that time.

(3) Populations cannot be reduced harmoniously at all levels, unless by emigration on an enormous scale. A low birth rate really means a gradual decrease in the number of young people and a corresponding increase in the old. For instance, it has been estimated that, by the end of the century, Britain will probably have as many people over 65 as under 15. That will mean a decrease in the manpower available for industry – as already seen in West Germany, where, with insufficient men of her

Con: (1) Most nations should be striving for lower, not higher birth rates. It's true that countries like Australia and Canada still have many resources which they are only just beginning to exploit, as well as wide open spaces able to take huge populations. But with the world's total population expected to double within the next 30 years, it is anything but certain that our resources will be sufficient by then, which could well mean increasing shortages of food supplies and raw materials, greater health hazards, fewer job opportunities, lower educational and living standards.

(2) The wealthier nations, which consume a much higher proportion of the world's resources than anyone else, have long benefited unfairly from the poor but heavily populated countries' huge pool of cheap labour. For our common survival, a more equitable situation is essential. Britain herself, despite her huge rise in agricultural production since 1939, is still quite unable to feed her own population. Economically and environmentally, she would probably be most viable and self-sufficient with a population one-quarter its present size.

(3) The expectation of life has risen by more than 20 years in the last century or two, and the prospect is already not too far distant of

own, the post-war 'economic miracle' could not have been achieved without bringing in millions of 'guest workers' from other, poorer countries.

(4) A falling birth rate is one sign of an increasing sense of insecurity among the people. The world-wide wars and economic depressions of the last sixty years are responsible for this; although a temporary increase in the birth rate is a common wartime phenomenon, such rates are not normally reached again in times of peace. (Up to 1974, Britain's recent birth rate had been declining by up to 7 per cent annually; over the ensuing year, the country's population became 'static' – neither up nor down in total.)

(5) The vast majority of families in Britain today have two children at the most (and the proportion of single-child families shows a steady increase). Such children are usually at a disadvantage in life compared with children from large families, who have undergone the salutary discipline of having to consider other people's needs and to share in their joys and occupations. Infantile mortality has been very much lessened by modern science, and hardships to the parents can be alleviated by society, though no action by society should interfere with the individual's discharge of his duty.

(6) A large population is necessary from a military point of view. No country can reckon to defend itself successfully if it has a stationary or falling population. In war, numbers are always a decisive factor.

(7) If the morale of society were good and purely artificial hindrances to family life were removed, much recent social legislation would have been unnecessary and parents would be willing and able to cope with the tasks of raising more children than they intend to have at present. The

people working fewer days a week and retiring at an earlier age (having learned to put their extra leisure time to worthwhile use). Modern technical advances – e.g. automation – make possible a vastly increased production at the cost of much less human effort; here again, therefore, the long-term trend will not be towards a bigger labour force but effectively towards a smaller, more highly trained one.

(4) Who can blame young couples if, in face of the nuclear threat, pollution and other adverse conditions in the world today, they decide to restrict their families to only one or two children at the most (or even to have none at all)? In fact, a lower birth rate may well be a positive, not a negative development. Britain, one of the world's most densely populated industrial countries, has been nearing saturation point; halting her population growth will be beneficial rather than otherwise.

(5) A high birth rate is always accompanied by a high death rate and, despite medical advances, by an increased level of invalidism in mothers. In present circumstances, few parents can support a large family properly. Overcrowding is one of the chief factors contributing to child mortality and inferior health. Quality is more necessary than quantity. The theory that children in large families are better balanced socially, and more self-reliant, simply does not stand up to closer examination. In any case, even single children get plenty of companionship in school and elsewhere.

(6) Numbers are not necessarily decisive in war; victory is more likely to depend on a sufficiency of weapons and a high level of industrial production generally. But even if numbers were decisive, a good deal might be said against conducting life from the military standpoint alone.

housing shortage will not be a permanent problem, and progressive local authorities have already begun to make provision, in their housing schemes, for the accommodation of larger families.

(7) It is impossible to organise society satisfactorily if the proportion of children is unduly large. For instance, the improvements indicated in the crucial 1944 Education Act proved largely unworkable owing to the fluctuations in the child population and the tremendous amount of money and labour required. Recent educational programmes have had to be cut back, because the cost of maintaining them had become prohibitive, and the standard is falling steadily.

(See also the preceding article.)

Bishops:
Should They Be Excluded from the House of Lords?

Pro: (1) Bishops have quite enough to do in looking after their dioceses. They are rarely fitted by circumstances or temperament to be legislators and, as a body, have an unfortunate history in this capacity.

(2) When the bishops were temporal powers, their presence in the House of Lords was necessary and natural. Today, their original status and duties have gone; the country holds many faiths and no faith. Their presence occasions resentment among those who are not members of the Established Church. It is a further infringement of the democratic principle that members of a legislature should be elected.

(3) Religion should have no place in politics. It appears to give no sure guidance in the problems before Government. Now that the Church has a much larger measure of self-government than it used to have, the bishops' defence of its interests in the Lords is no longer necessary.

Con: (1) Being independent of party, the bishops do very useful work as guardians of the interests of religion and the Church. They can take a statesmanlike view of public policy. As the clergy are not allowed to sit in the Commons, the bishops are all the more needed in the Lords.

(2) Long before the creation of life rather than hereditary peerages became the general practice, bishops were among the few Lords who sat by virtue of merit and not by accident of birth. The bishops' continued presence, therefore, is sound political science.

(3) Their exclusion would mean a further divorce between religion and politics. Most English people are religious, and the Church of England is still the State Church and the one which best represents the national feeling.

(See also *Disestablishment of the Church of England*; *Lords, Reform of the House of.*)

Blood Sports
(i.e. Hunting and Shooting)

Pro: (1) Sport is one of the best elements in our national life, tending to keep the race healthy and to maintain the idea that physical strength and endurance are qualities worth trying to achieve.

(2) There is comparatively little cruelty about blood sports. Certainly, most members of the British sporting class are very knowledgeable about animals and abhor conduct that is unnecessarily cruel to them.

(3) In many ways, sport counteracts the evil effects of city life by bringing man closer to nature and to an observation of her ways. This is especially the case with shooting and fishing.

(4) The keen sportsman does not mind undergoing discomfort in pursuit of sport, and this calls out in him the power of sacrificing the present to the future, one of the signs of man's superiority over all other creatures.

(5) Sport encourages development of the powers of observation, of quick calculation and of rapid decision.

(6) The chief objections to sport are made by so-called humanitarians who claim that animals should be regarded as existing for their own ends. Man's treatment of animals must be related to his own needs – and most particularly as regards those which provide him with food, such as fish and game birds, or which are pests or positively harmful, such as foxes. (See *Animals, Rights of.*)

(7) Sport has been an element in the spread of civilisation and in giving us a knowledge of unexplored parts of the world. It has given to the British that roving spirit which has

Con: (1) Such sports are not national, as they are practised by only a limited section of the community. Games like football and cricket promote the qualities of physical health and endurance more effectively.

(2) Blood sports involve great cruelty and demoralise the sportsman because they foster a too ready acquiescence in the infliction of pain. This is proved by the way the classes given to blood sports governed Britain when they were in power and by the ferocity with which they treat intruders, e.g. poachers.

(3) Most of the men who have advanced our knowledge of nature have been either hunters for a living or naturalists. Youth hostels and the Scout movement have done far more than blood sports to give young people from the cities knowledge of and access to nature.

(4) Sport is made the excuse and occasion for luxury. Most industrial occupations involve far more hardship.

(5) The powers of observation, etc., can be cultivated without any need to kill other creatures in the process.

(6) There can be no justification for treating animals as if they existed only to serve man's ends. Animals must be seen to have rights of their own before man can really advance in his knowledge of nature. Sport is a most inefficient method of exterminating noxious animals – and, in fact, sometimes deliberately preserves them. The unpopularity with sportsmen of farmers who shoot foxes is sufficient commentary on the usefulness of fox-hunting.

(7) Compared with such motives

placed them in the forefront of the world's pioneering nations. Big-game hunters have been of great benefit to tribal communities in protecting them from dangerous wild animals.

(8) Hunting with horses plays an important part in improving their breed and maintaining a proper supply.

(9) The abolition of blood sports would cause hardship or distress among many hard-working classes of the community. The popularity of hunting is proved by the large crowds that gather to watch a meet.

(10) The rearing of game birds, for the shooting season, not only provides employment for many people in rural areas but has helped to preserve species of birds which, if left unprotected in nature, would have been threatened with extinction. Moreover, the organisation of the sport, allied to the birds' flying abilities and acquired cunning, ensures that a good proportion of the birds avoid being shot. One need merely point out that, in terms of numbers, the principal species concerned – grouse, pheasant and partridge – are all thriving.

as trade, adventure and social conscience, sport has played a negligible part in spreading civilisation. The sportsman in the tropics has been of very varying value in the past; he has imperilled the survival of the tiger, as a species, and was only just stopped from doing the same to elephants.

(8) The needs of agriculture and horse-racing will ensure adequate supplies of horses, and improvements in the breed, much more certainly.

(9) Sport is enormously wasteful. Hunters arrogate to themselves the right to ride over ploughed fields, destroy fences and generally disorganise farm economy. Many farmers regard hunts as an unmitigated nuisance, though the continued feudal nature of much of our rural society tends to keep their objections muted.

(10) It is hard to imagine anything more unspeakable than the practice of rearing creatures, in protected conditions, for the sole purpose of shooting at them later. (Likewise the custom of keeping a stag captive with the object of hunting it periodically.) The claim that gamebird species' survival would otherwise have been threatened can hardly hold water when, at some big 'shoots', hundreds of birds are killed in a single day. Even the protagonists of this alleged sport have never tried to pretend that food requirements explain such slaughter. As for providing jobs, the number of gamekeepers and others in full-time employment for this purpose is, in fact, quite minimal.

The 'Brain Drain'

Pro: (1) More than 4,500,000 Britons, most of them aged under 35, have left to settle in other countries since the last world war.

Con: (1) The argument is not against emigration, nor even against temporary departure for jobs abroad; it concerns the loss of highly skilled

From a peak of just under 300,000 a year in 1965, the exodus levelled out to some 200,000 annually over the next decade – though a renewed upturn was anticipated from 1975 onwards, as a result of the economic crisis. Most of the emigrants say that they decided on the move in order to seek a higher standard of living, a warmer climate, or a better future for their children; some also talk of wanting better facilities for their work than they can get in Britain. A proportion of those leaving, either permanently or for a number of years, are men with professional or other specialist qualifications – doctors, scientists, engineers, etc. It is these who have been classed as the 'Brain Drain' in British newspapers, which express growing concern at their loss to the country. But the greatest cause for concern should be the unsatisfactory conditions here which led them to wish to depart. Regrettable though the 'Brain Drain' may be, it will not stop as long as such men feel unfulfilled by their life and work in their native country. Nor, without remedying such conditions, have we any right to bar it or impose special restrictions on it. It would be an injustice for these 'brains' to be denied rights which are open to everyone else.

(2) Among the biggest individual groups represented in the 'Brain Drain' are doctors and nurses, fed up with conditions under the National Health Service. Overworked, subject to bureaucratic restrictions, limited in their maximum earnings so that their standard of living has dropped compared with that of people with equivalent incomes even 10 years ago, it is small wonder that the much higher rewards and better working conditions available in other countries should attract them. Another big 'Brain Drain' group consists of

people who have mostly been trained for their qualifications at the State's expense and then leave the country – often soon after qualifying – without giving Britain a fair return for the money spent on them. It would be only common sense, and entirely just, if young people whose education was paid for by the taxpayers had to undertake to work here for a certain minimum period after acquiring their professional, scientific or technical qualifications. A period of, say, 3–4 years would not be unreasonable. There are precedents; several other countries impose retrictions of this nature, without anyone objecting. (One or two have even gone to the length of demanding that would-be emigrants, of high skill, pay back the cost of their education before being allowed to leave; but that remedy is doubtless too drastic to be acceptable in Britain.) At another level, Commonwealth countries which granted 'assisted passages' to British emigrants – enabling them to pay as little as £10 for journeys normally costing several hundred pounds – imposed as a condition that the beneficiaries, on arrival, should remain in their selected job for not less than a year or 18 months. Again, nobody saw anything wrong with that.

(2) From the catalogue of woes opposite, anyone would think that people working in such fields, in Britain, always have to put up with antiquated methods and inadequate facilities – whereas, in medical research, the peaceful uses of nuclear energy, some aspects of automation, aeronautical engineering and many other specialised fields, we are actually the most advanced nation in Europe. Nobody would claim that this is consistently the case; and it is true that, through adverse economic circumstances in recent years, our living standards and incomes have,

scientists and research workers who are offered far superior facilities for research, etc., than they can hope to obtain in Britain. This often applies as well to skilled industrial workers, who are drawn by the prospect of having more up-to-date processes and equipment at their disposal in jobs offered to them abroad. Who can blame any of these people for wanting more job satisfaction than they can get here?

(3) People may deplore the fact that there is always an upsurge in emigration enquiries whenever Britain has an unusually hard winter, a prolonged strike, a heavy rise in taxation or a big increase in unemployment. But there is no justification for condemning those who wish to escape such conditions and are sufficiently energetic and adventurous to do so.

(4) Britain willingly accepts the large number of foreign doctors and nurses now working here – in effect, a 'Brain Drain' in reverse. They are not simply replacements, because there are many more than we lose to emigration among our own people in the field; and, without these reinforcements from abroad, many of our hospitals would have to close. Conclusion: we cannot expect to 'have our cake and eat it'.

(5) Most people talking about the 'Brain Drain' think implicitly that it applies mainly to the USA and to the more thriving Commonwealth countries (particularly since the atter have ended their previous large-scale immigration policies and now advertise only for people with the particular working qualifications they most need). But Britain's membership of the EEC will change the picture. Common Market policies provide for freedom of labour, i.e. for workers from one member-country to find jobs in another. In time, we can expect that an increasing number of our professionals and

overall, fallen behind those of several other European countries, at present. But people with a vocation, whether professional or technical, should be in the forefront of the fight to overcome these problems. Leaving aside the question of patriotism and duty to one's fellow-citizens, though these are not without relevance, the best way to get the living standards and working facilities they want is to stay here and create the conditions which make those improvements possible. That, surely, is the most rewarding challenge of all.

(3) That confuses the point under discussion with emigration as a whole. A desire to escape from adverse conditions at home contributed to the pioneering spirit which led to Britain's greatness in the days of her empire-building. Nowadays, it could be held that emigration has certain advantages environmentally, by abating the pressures of over-population. But the nation cannot afford to lose large numbers of its best brains before it has had some return from them. When you prune a rose-bush, you dispense with some of its surplus growth – you don't cut off any of its roots.

(4) If reasonable limits were placed on the number of highly qualified people allowed to emigrate each year, we would not need to rely on foreign recruits to such an extent. Without disparaging the contribution made by foreign doctors and nurses, which has generally been of great value, it must be said nevertheless that they are not always trained so well as our own people and several authoritative bodies have expressed fears of a possible consequent lowering of standards.

(5) The EEC policy over labour movements applies almost solely – in practice, if not in theory – to those semi-skilled or unskilled workers who are most needed to reinforce

other skilled people will be attracted by the idea of settling in another European country.

the skilled labour pool in the heavily industrialised countries like West Germany. If there were a sudden attempted influx of large numbers of professionals or other highly paid people, taking good jobs away from a country's own nationals, we'd soon see the shutters go up!

(See also *Immigration: Should The Present Restrictions Be Lifted?*)

British Commonwealth:
Is It a Reality?

Pro: (1) The Commonwealth has absorbed most of the nations which were formerly part of the British Empire. This fact is a tribute to the principle of achieving independence by consent which has been practised by Britain, and a proof that the Commonwealth as an entity has a useful function.

(2) The friendly relations which exist between Britain and the other members of the Commonwealth are an example to the world. The help of the mother country was readily available to all the new African and Asian countries, and was gratefully accepted by them, in coping with the problem of building a nation.

(3) The old-established Dominions, settled largely by people of British stock, are firmly linked to Britain by emotional as well as economic ties, as their support in times of war has demonstrated. Canada prefers Britain to absorption by the USA, and New Zealand and Australia are even closer. New Zealand is more or less dependent on Britain economically. South Africa left the Commonwealth for special reasons, and in any case had less of an emotional tie since the majority of its white population is not of

Con: (1) The British Empire was assembled from a haphazard series of conquests and had no discernible pattern, either strategic or economic. On the contrary, its defence was a strategic liability. All that is left now is a series of islands and small territories scattered about the world. The Commonwealth which succeeded it is bound together by the force of inertia alone and, in the course of time, is bound to disintegrate.

(2) While the new nations accepted British help, they were at pains to make it clear that they did not feel in any way bound by British policies. Some of them lean more towards links with countries which have never been in the Commonwealth.

(3) Canada has had no vital economic dependence on Britain for many years past. Australia has turned more towards the USA in recent years, and is also building up her political and economic links within her own Far East theatre – a policy which New Zealand is beginning to follow. South Africa felt able to exist without the Commonwealth altogether, and has not suffered any ill-effects.

British but of (Dutch) Boer descent.

(4) Britain bequeathed her parliamentary system to the new nations, many of whose future leaders were educated in Britain and learned to respect British institutions. The older Dominions all carried the home traditions of parliamentary democracy into their new lives.

(5) The present loose arrangement is most suitable, especially while the relations and balance of the member countries are still fluid. None of them, with their varying needs and ways of life, would wish to be bound in detail by inflexible decisions. The healthy existence of a community with such unrestricting and impalpable bonds could be a pointer to the rest of the world for the groupings of the future. However wide their individual differences, in practice, the Commonwealth members share fundamental beliefs in democracy, racial equality and tolerance which other nations might well copy. The recent proposals for the wealthier Commonwealth nations to take more concerted action to aid the developing members are a further case in point.

(6) The viability of the Commonwealth is amply proved by the fact that other Commonwealth countries backed Britain's membership of the EEC, and its reaffirmation in the 1975 referendum, recognising the realities of Britain's best future interests. At the same time, the renegotiated terms of British entry take due account of her continued relationships with her Commonwealth partners.

(4) The Dominion Parliaments were profoundly modified and many are now closer to the American model. While India perhaps achieved something resembling the British form of government (before the 1975 state of emergency, at any rate), experience in the new African countries does not suggest that they have absorbed the traditions of parliamentary democracy or even that these traditions are best suited to them – as witness those African countries which now practise one-party politics.

(5) One of the principal ties stemmed, traditionally, from the fact that the British monarch also fulfilled that role separately for each member country: but this has much less meaning now that so many of the Commonwealth nations have become republics. Equally, recent meetings of the constituent countries have demonstrated that Britain is no longer the dominant partner. There might be some point in a Commonwealth Federation – if this were compatible with Britain's membership of the EEC. But otherwise the Commonwealth as at present constituted is an anachronism.

(6) Despite the lip service paid to Commonwealth consultation, Britain's decision to 'go into Europe' was taken unilaterally. The older partners were strong enough to begin establishing alternative trading links; the still developing members could only hope to derive benefits from the Common Market through their association with Britain. Either way, though, none of the other partners was given any real choice in the matter.

(See also the preceding article; *Internationalism*; *United States of Europe*.)

Broadcasting, Public Control of

Pro: (1) Broadcasting, sound and television, is possibly the most potent method of propaganda and education. Its influence is so pervasive that the service cannot be left with safety to private concerns; some form of public control, and indeed of management, is essential. The BBC, which is established by government charter and gets its finance from licence fees, but provides its public service autonomously, free of government intervention, is regarded by many other countries as a near perfect model.

(2) Commercial television has lowered the standard of the programmes. Public control, as exercised in Britain by the BBC, enables all tastes to be catered for in some measure, whereas a commercialised service tends to pander to the lowest, and the more serious talks, classical music and educational broadcasts all suffer. No privately owned broadcasting service would have initiated Radio 3, for example. The BBC has accomplished much in raising the general level of the public taste, particularly in music and drama, and in stimulating a thirst for knowledge. The schools broadcasts are models of their kind. Freedom of speech is more likely to be preserved by an impartial authority than under the control of vested interests through sponsored programmes.

(3) Technical advances, such as world-wide communications satellites and the European link-up, indicate a need for a greater measure of international control rather than allowing the air to be thrown open to unrestricted competition.

(4) Television, particularly, is in need of public control. The low standards of the majority of

Con: (1) Because of its power of manufacturing opinion, broadcasting ought not to be the subject of government control, much less of public management. The inevitable result of such control is that programmes are biased in favour of the current government viewpoint, minority bodies and views are given little or no hearing, and live controversial subjects are often suppressed from discussion. A notable example of all these drawbacks has been provided by French TV and radio under the rigid government control imposed by the Gaullists.

(2) Public control is in effect a form of dictatorship by persons who, as in the BBC in Britain, are virtually inaccessible to the public. In the BBC, a 'civil service' attitude prevailed which resulted all too frequently in lack of enterprise. It was only under the stimulus of competition from the livelier independent TV programmes that the BBC brightened its own offerings. Commercial television provides a wide variety of programmes, mostly good of their kind. On both commercial TV and radio, freedom of speech, in the form of open discussion of controversial subjects, fares no worse than under the BBC.

(3) The alternative to public or quasi-public control and management is not unrestricted competition but regulated competition under private management. This already exists in Britain, where the private companies in both commercial TV and commercial radio are still subject to the regulations of their own centralised authority and sponsors do not control programmes, as in the USA.

(4) Standards of taste in the USA are different from ours generally and

programmes in the USA show the depths of taste to which TV can descend when left in private hands.

fears that our commercial programmes might descend to such levels have not been realised. While many popular American TV programmes are shown here, there is an official limit on the proportion which may be screened – and the quantity has in any case declined over the years.

(See also *Commercial Radio: Should It Be Abolished?*)

Cabinet Government

Pro: (1) Under Cabinet Government, the more important Ministers are supreme in their respective departments and at the same time benefit from their colleagues' advice and support.

(2) By giving each government department a chief of wide outlook and experience, the prejudices of permanent civil service officials in that department are counterbalanced.

(3) The House of Commons does not exercise direct authority over government departments, but it does have ultimate control over the system, through the power of dismissing Ministers.

(4) The Cabinet connects the executive with the legislative branch of government and protects the departments from hasty and disastrous interference by Parliament.

(5) A complexity of affairs can only be managed by a small and united group; hence the success of our system. The business of the Cabinet is to formulate a general policy as the outcome of calm discussion. The temperamental differences among its members are sufficient to prevent its becoming a rigid machine.

Con: (1) The joint responsibility implicit in Cabinet Government often compels Ministers to give a colleague indiscriminate support and to compromise over the interests of their own departments.

(2) Permanent officials inevitably dominate the inexperienced and harassed Minister. In the eyes of senior civil servants, a 'good' Minister is one who always follows their advice.

(3) Cabinet Government has reduced the House of Commons to impotence. In practice, the House does not dismiss either Ministries or Ministers. Because of the Cabinet system, an attack on one department has the often-unwanted effect of an attack on the whole Government.

(4) It subordinates administration to the political vagaries of a few men, who are both inexpert and primarily concerned with the fortunes of their party. Departments should have permanent heads directly responsible to Parliament.

(5) Once established, a Cabinet, provided it remains unanimous, has all the power and the characteristics of an oligarchy. Most Cabinets play for safety for themselves.

(See also *Coalition Government*; *Party Government*; *Written Constitution*.)

Calendar Reform

Pro: (1) Our present calendar, devised by Pope Gregory XIII in 1582, is both inconvenient and illogical. It was a correction of the Julian Calendar drawn up by Julius Caesar in 46 BC, which reckoned the length of a year as 365¼ days, whereas it is actually 365.2422 days. But its irregular and arbitrary division of the year into months of uneven length could easily be improved upon. Various associations exist with the object of bringing about such reform, and it would not be difficult to arrange for international action. The matter was under consideration by the League of Nations in the 1930s, and about 200 different proposals were investigated.

(2) There are definite advantages in such a tidying up, and several excellent schemes have been put forward. The simplest was one suggested by a Yugoslav who would abolish weeks and months altogether, and distinguish the date only by number. Thus one might make an appointment for 11 a.m. on the 159th. Leap Year, according to this plan, would merely stop at the 366th day instead of the 365th.

(3) In spite of British conservatism, some such scheme is bound to come sooner or later. The principal improvement needed is a perpetual calendar that remains unchanged year after year. There are two main schools of thought – the equal months school, and the equal quarters school. British reformers largely incline to the latter, and Americans, exemplified by the International Fixed Calendar Association, to the former.

(4) It is generally agreed nowadays that a perpetual calendar would have great advantages in business

Con: (1) The Gregorian Calendar has been used satisfactorily for nearly four centuries. The only people who wish to change it are a handful of cranks, who would find themselves in a very small minority if any of their schemes were taken seriously. The whole civilised world would be thrown out of gear by such a change and would gain in compensation nothing but a rearrangement or re-shuffling of names and days. The calendar might look a little better to people who set logical tidiness before practical convenience, but there would be no real advantage whatever.

(2) Such a scheme would be of little value unless universally adopted. Great Britain, of all countries, is least likely to agree to it. We waited 170 years before accepting the Gregorian Calendar and began to use it long after the rest of Europe had fallen into line.

(3) Similar schemes have been put forward before and have met with no lasting success, since they gave no fundamental advantage. The French Revolution Calendar, introduced in 1793, had twelve equal months of thirty days, each subdivided into ten-day weeks, or decades. The year was completed by five national holidays. The months were named according to their traditional weather – Brumaire, Frimaire, Nivôse, Pluviôse and so forth. This calendar was abandoned in 1806. Russia in 1929 abolished Saturday and Sunday in favour of a five-day week, but the final result has been merely an arrangement comparable to our own. During the Fascist regime, Italy introduced a system which counted years from the beginning of the regime instead of the birth of Christ, but the change

and accounting. Such a one is the international fixed calendar, advocated mainly by the International Fixed Calendar League. This calendar has thirteen months, each of twenty-eight days, and a New Year's day which comes between 28 December, the last day of one year, and 1 January, the beginning of the next. The thirteenth month, named Sol, comes between June and July, and in Leap Year an extra day is inserted between June and Sol, which would be a general holiday. The advantage of this scheme, which has won an increasing measure of support, is that the same date always falls on the same day of the week.

(5) There are already business concerns which have successfully worked the thirteenth-month system, e.g., Kodak. Many companies in France pay monthly salaries on the basis of a thirteenth month, added to payments at the beginning of December (and thus a welcome bonus before Christmas).

(6) There is a clear public demand for a fixed Easter, which makes itself heard every year as that holiday comes round. According to the British scheme (usually known as the Desborough plan), not only would the date of Easter be fixed but other important social fixtures, such as August Bank Holiday and school and university terms, could also be standardised.

had no effect on everyday life in the country.

(4) Because of deep-seated superstition, number 13 is widely unpopular. An unofficial committee on calendar reform has already considered this scheme and has described the 13-month year as 'definitely repugnant to British feeling'. Moreover, it has several disadvantages for business purposes. The number 13 is difficult to divide by and impossible to divide into. Neither the quarters nor the half-year would contain a whole number of months; a quarter would consist of three and a quarter months. Thirteen monthly balancings, stock-takings, and payments would increase trouble and complicate business.

(5) The exception does not prove the rule. If there were any general desire for calendar reform, we should hear more about it.

(6) There is still a considerable body of opinion, especially religious opinion, opposed to a fixed Easter. And those religious bodies which approve a fixed Easter would show great divergence of views about how and when it should be fixed. If school and university terms were permanently stabilised, the gradual public acceptance of the need for the staggering of holidays would inevitably be jeopardised.

Capital Punishment, Restoration of

Pro: (1) Experience since its first experimental abolition has proved that capital punishment is a stern, though regrettable, necessity. Without it, our lives and property have become less secure and crimes of violence have increased. In the present unsettled state of the world,

Con: (1) The death penalty is an anachronism in the modern penal code. It is a relic of an age when all punishments were savage and vindictive, and will be regarded by our successors with the same horror with which we now look upon the hanging of little children for theft.

its restoration is becoming more, not less, necessary. The police say that, now criminals do not have to fear hanging, the numbers who carry guns when committing robberies or other crimes have risen enormously.

(2) Capital punishment should be used to rid society of its enemies, instead of keeping them for the remainder of their lives as a perpetual charge upon the public purse. Some of the countries which had virtually ceased to carry out capital punishment, e.g. France, have since found it necessary to draw back from its complete legal abolition.

(3) The reformation and re-education of some types of criminal may be possible, but a hardened murderer is beyond hope of reform. Are we to allow such men, ready to kill without compunction not once but several times, to live and return to society as a source of danger to their fellows on the expiry of their sentences (for even a life sentence may in practice amount to little more than ten years)?

(4) If there is the slightest doubt in the minds of the jury, a verdict of guilty is not returned. Despite public concern over the possibility of mistakes, only one wrongful conviction and execution (that of Timothy Evans) is known out of the many thousands of murder cases in Britain since the last world war.

(5) Discrimination between degrees of homicide, and the possibility of returning a verdict of manslaughter, gives juries plenty of opportunity for clemency. Insane murderers are never executed. It might be argued that the majority of murderers are insane – temporarily, anyway – and that there is a case for revising the present somewhat restricted legal definition of insanity. But the prospect of facing the supreme penalty, not just a long jail sentence, is the only way to deal

Up to the early part of the nineteenth century, the death penalty could be, and was, inflicted for more than 200 different offences. Hanging is now recognised to be a revolting and cruel punishment. Its abolition was a major step towards our claim to be more civilised.

(2) Capital punishment is not an effective deterrent. In fact, the statistics of crime in all countries prove that violent punishment does not tend to bring about a decrease in violent crime. In spite of the death penalty, the average number of murders in Britain each year remained almost stationary for half a century – and there has been no appreciable change either way since capital punishment was abolished.

(3) Out of about thirty countries that have abolished the death penalty, not one has reported any increase in murders, and several have reported decreases. A penal code based on the idea of education and reformation of the offender is far more likely to reduce the amount of crime.

(4) The death sentence is irrevocable. A mistake once made cannot be put right. Even a single mistake, among no matter how many thousands of cases, is one too many for a civilised society to chance.

(5) Murderers did sometimes escape all legal punishment because the jury refused to convict, but this has become less likely now there is no death penalty. In many cases, death sentences were passed as an empty and cruel formality, when there was no intention of carrying them out. Very few of the murders committed really are premeditated. Up to 80 per cent are committed by people who are found to be insane – and no threatened penalty is likely to deter a lunatic – while in the great majority of those cases in which the murderer is held to be sane, the crime is committed under the

with the clearly threatening rise in the proportion of hardened killers and those who murder in the course of other crimes. A life sentence is in some ways even more cruel than a death sentence, and there have been some convicted murderers who would actually have preferred the latter.

(6) That many people habitually signed petitions seeking clemency for convicted murderers was often merely the result of mass suggestion or hysteria – due, it may be, to newspaper propaganda. It proved nothing.

(7) The State has a duty to its people to act harshly, if need be, to help preserve the good order of society.

temporary stress of violent passion or anger. That such people had to be condemned for premeditated murder, under the previous law, was a travesty of justice.

(6) That thousands were always eager to sign petitions for reprieve, even in cases where murder was definitely proved, shows how deep is the feeling that infliction of the death penalty is against the conscience of civilised man.

(7) Whether by the State or by an individual, the plain fact remains that the destruction of human life is a crime.

Censorship

Pro: (1) The purpose of enlightened censorship is to protect the public, and especially to prevent young people from being exposed to films, plays or books which centre on violence, pornography or other harmful aspects of life which they are not old enough to understand.

(2) The British Board of Film Censors is quite inadequate. Although operating as an independent, self-supporting body, its income consists of fees from distributors when they submit a film for a rating – and it necessarily has one eye on the financial commitments of the film industry. Under the present system, too, its authority is lessened by the fact that its decisions can be overruled. Even when it bans films, local authorities have the power to license them for showing in their own areas. And vice versa. The classification of films is merely an invitation to young people to evade the regulations. This state of affairs is the more deplorable since the

Con: (1) It is for the parents and guardians of young people to protect them from damaging influences, or alternatively to influence and educate them so that the effect is minimised. A policy of censorship would deprive children of much in the works of Shakespeare, Chaucer and many other great writers.

(2) According to the type of audience for which they are considered suitable, films are now rated as U, A, AA or X (meaning, respectively: may be seen by anyone; ditto, but parents are advised that the film contains adult material; no one under 14; no one under 18). These classifications give adequate guidance to cinemagoers and make any other form of supervision unnecessary.

(3) The people of Asia and Africa have had many opportunities of checking their impressions of Europeans and Americans in recent years and are by no means so unsophisticated as in the early years of the

majority of cinemagoers today are young people.

(3) The cinema is still popular in places not yet reached by television and particularly in Asia and Africa. Already, untold harm has been done by the caricatures of European and American life shown in films which should have been censored at source.

(4) Television programmes should be more firmly controlled. Violence is depicted too often even in children's programmes – and to a yet greater extent in programmes screened at times when children are still likely to see them.

(5) The Lord Chamberlain's role as theatrical censor was ended in 1968. But his office was manned by cultured and experienced people, and previously the best sort of manager had welcomed their censorship of stage productions as a protection. In latter years, this censorship was usually confined to occasional lines or situations, and no serious subject was denied a hearing altogether.

(6) There is a strong case for censorship of books and so-called 'comics' which appeal to the semi-literate. At present, anyone can air his sick fancies or unsavoury experiences in print and exercise a depraving influence while stopping short of actionable obscenity. In the absence of any guidance, it is left to booksellers, librarians and the police to proscribe works in the light of their own experience and knowledge of literature. This is unfair both to them and to serious authors.

cinema. Many of the film-shows exported are of a better type and often have to compete with home products nowadays.

(4) It is unrealistic to try to shield children from the facts of aggression and violence altogether. The moral outlook of most television programmes is healthy and, indeed, the main objection to many television programmes is rather that of triviality.

(5) The best managers, the best playwrights and the best actors were against censorship and, up to 1968, were almost the only people still suffering from it. The Lord Chamberlain's function of censorship began as a political one and remained excessively Establishment-minded (e.g. forbidding portrayals of living or recent royalty). His office banned Hochhuth's *The Soldiers*. It even ordered the deletion of a revue sketch about the sinking of the Royal Barge, despite the fact that no royalty was seen in person – and that the sketch had already been shown on television!

(6) Most of the 'comics' in question are American and can be controlled by import regulations, if necessary. It is quite wrong for librarians and others to exercise a private censorship. If a book is to be called in question, it is better that this should be done publicly in the courts, where balanced views on it can be aired and works of merit can receive fair criticism. Most evil influences are lessened by the fresh air of publicity. Few of our most respected classics would escape the censor, and any risk would be preferable to the stultification which results from censorship as applied in Eire or the Soviet Union.

Channel Tunnel:
Should The Project Be Restored?

Pro: (1) Despite governmental concern about the rising costs of the project at a time of inflation and general economic crisis, the fundamental case for a Channel Tunnel has not altered. Now that Britain has committed herself to Europe, that case is, in fact, stronger than ever. The Tunnel would make communication with the Continent much easier and would be the only means of relieving the burden on other services (e.g. harbours and ferries) from the vastly increased flow of cross-Channel freight and passenger traffic expected in the 1980s.

(2) Britain's cancellation of the project in January 1975 was premature. It was announced only two weeks before the completion of new plans for a profitable rail link between London and the Tunnel – an essential part of the project. These plans would have saved at least £100 million on the original proposals, yet still have assured enough capacity for the traffic expected when the Tunnel opened. If the Government had waited just six months before cancelling, it would have had the benefit not only of this new rail link scheme but of one and a quarter miles of fully lined pilot tunnel, with all the priceless practical experience gained from building it. The private companies involved in building the Tunnel assert that, although they were willing to make fresh proposals to keep the project going for this, the Government refused to negotiate.

(3) British Rail regarded the Tunnel as the mainstay of its future profitability. Both the French authorities, at one end, and Kent County Council (the local authority

Con: (1) From an estimate of £846 million in January 1973, costs had soared so high that, by the time Britain backed out two years later, the Government calculated that the total cost of the project would be £1,200 million – and some other estimates put it as high as £2,000 million. The Tunnel would have been the biggest single industrial undertaking for generations; at a time of economic crisis, the Government could justifiably have been accused of irresponsibility if it had diverted such a huge proportion of the country's over-stretched resources to a single scheme.

(2) Britain has not cancelled the project for ever and a day. The Environment Secretary, in announcing the decision in the Commons, did not rule out the possibility that the Tunnel might still be built in his lifetime (he was then 56). All the plans and existing works are to be preserved 'in the best possible state' in case the scheme is revived 'when circumstances are more propitious'. One factor contributing to the decision was the Government's claim that the private companies involved in the project had put forward unacceptable terms, aimed at covering themselves against delays.

(3) The harbour boards, ferry companies and all others concerned with conventional cross-Channel transport (other than rail links) say firmly that they will have little or no difficulty in handling the increase in traffic that has been forecast. The ferries, for instance, insist that, with their existing fleets and the larger vessels already on order, they will need only half the total number of ships which the Tunnel planners

at the British end of the Tunnel), were keen to carry on. The full implications – and costs – of meeting future cross-Channel traffic needs by conventional means have not yet been worked out.

(4) The French, who had already ratified the Channel Tunnel Treaty which Britain abandoned, regard the cancellation as having been motivated by political and not simply economic reasons. It proved, in their view, that the British Prime Minister attached more importance to the unity of the Labour Party and was prepared to sacrifice Franco-British relations to the insularity and 'Francophobia' of his party's left-wingers.

(5) The importance which the Continent attaches to the Tunnel project, not simply as a symbol confirming Britain's new role in Europe, but above all for its practical benefits, is proved by the prompt discussions among other Common Market members (after the cancellation) about possible ways for more European governments to help with the financing of the scheme.

had said would be required to cope with the traffic.

(4) The subsequent result of Britain's Common Market referendum disproves any suggestion that the Left Wing had the least influence on the Tunnel decision. It was taken solely on valid economic grounds, in accordance with provisions for abandonment written into the treaty (unlike the Concorde agreement). The French Government itself was known to be divided over the real need for the Tunnel, particularly since the oil crisis had raised doubts as to whether the increased capacity to handle cross-Channel traffic, on the scale provided by the Tunnel, would be required quite so soon.

(5) Since the furore in the first few days after Britain's decision was announced, no more seems to have been heard about this cost-sharing idea.

Christendom, Reunion of

Pro: (1) The ideal of Christian reunion is both desirable and necessary if the churches are to stem the present-day flood of scepticism and indifference, or to deal properly with contemporary social problems. It will also be the only solution, in the long term, if the Church is to make any real impression on the non-Christian world.

(2) Minor differences should be sunk or natural allowances made. The Anglican and Methodist Churches have already come within sight of agreement along the road to integration, with churches planned for both forms of worship. Although

Con: (1) However desirable, the ideal cannot be realised. Any proposals put forward or supported by the Church of Rome would mean simply the absorption of other churches. There are at present such strong antagonisms between the various sects that we can only wait and try to heal the internal dissensions existing in each body.

(2) The failure to secure ratification of the Anglican-Methodist proposals, even though the gap between these churches is among the narrowest of all, shows how deep-seated are the fundamental objections. Undenominational Chris-

the proposals have been rejected at the moment, there are many people on each side who are still working for them to be accepted and are hopeful that they will be in the foreseeable future.

(3) Modern thought is less interested in theological problems than in the ethical side of religion. Many non-believers could be attracted to the churches if they were to produce a united programme of social reform, based on such views as could be agreed between all sects – and there have been notable advances recently in this direction.

tianity would inevitably be colourless and therefore of less value. Few would accept it, least of all the Roman Catholic Church.

(3) Good works are not the whole of Christianity. Sceptics would still prefer to dispense with the theological doctrines, and people of religions other than Christianity are not impressed by them. But Christianity is concerned with the world after death as much as with this one, and few sects would be prepared to risk eternal error by sacrificing what they believe to be the truth in the interests of temporary earthly advantage.

Christian Socialism

Pro: (1) Christ's teaching applies quite as much to life in this world as to a future life, and is intimately concerned with teaching us to obtain and realise justice on earth. Many sayings in the Gospels which are taken to refer to a future life apply even more surely to this one. The Socialist theory of the Brotherhood of Man is a natural complement of the belief in the Fatherhood of God.

(2) The early Church undoubtedly laid down standards of conduct, even inculcating communism, for its members. The medieval Church took the greatest pains to arrive at ethical principles for the conduct of life and commerce and industry, including such ideas as the Just Price and the condemnation of usury. Monastic communities tend to be communistic in spirit and often in practice. Many of the Protestant sects since that day have shown a strong interest in the problems of social life and organisation, and the new democratic spirit abroad in Europe after the last world war led to the formation of Christian Socialist

Con: (1) Christianity and Socialism have no connection. Whereas the Socialist declares that the individual's chief aim is happiness in this life, Christianity teaches that the greatest happiness will be found in the life after death. This world is merely a preparation for the next, and we should live for the Kingdom of Heaven before all else. Socialism has no interest in the other world and has a purely naturalistic theory of morals. The results are to be seen in the Soviet Union and other places where Socialism has had its fling.

(2) Christ's teaching applies to general principles of individual conduct. He lived in a society where modern Socialism was undreamed of and indeed inconceivable. Any communistic organisation of Church bodies was a temporary measure used for the defence of the Church against barbarism or for the establishment of Christian communities in new countries. The leaders of the Catholic Church, and many others today, see in Socialism and Communism an enemy of religious doctrine. Most Christian Socialist or

or Democrat parties in most countries.

(3) If the Church is to regain its hold on mankind, it must identify itself with the highest aspirations of humanity, even if they sometimes appear from outside its borders.

Christian Democrat parties have found it necessary to abandon bit by bit the Socialistic programmes with which they began, in order to preserve intact the domination of the Christian idea.

(3) No religion has ever won the day by rashly embracing the passing doctrines of the moment. What else is Socialism, historically?

(See also the next article.)

The Churches:
Should They Take Part in Politics?

Pro: (1) The churches, as representing the idealist element in the community, are bound to share in its most vital activities, which necessarily involve political questions. When they become directly involved in politics – as, for instance, in Spain, where many ordinary priests have sided with the workers in protests against the regime (often in defiance of their own bishops) – it has usually resulted in their moral authority being enhanced, not lessened.

(2) The Christian churches have in the past played great roles in times of crisis. They have a body of ethics and traditions which binds them morally to follow precept with practice and to oppose actively the abuses of the times.

(3) Although church-people may very well differ in their views, it is possible for them to present common policies in accordance with Christian teaching and to exert influence, on this basis, for the problems of the day to be handled in a humane and Christian way.

(4) Because of their independence of political parties, churchmen of all denominations have been able to take a courageous stand on such questions as nuclear warfare and on

Con: (1) The churches are concerned with religion and private morals. They should remain outside the arena of political controversy and limit themselves to presenting ideals on which all people of good will may draw for inspiration and guidance. They have no business to lay down rulings in political matters which necessarily admit of different points of view.

(2) The churches in the past have nearly always been equated with reaction. Despite the increased number of bishops holding liberal or 'progressive' views, in recent years, the main body of church-people and of church government remain highly conservative, and there is no reason to suppose they will be any different in the future.

(3) Members of the churches hold conflicting but equally sincere conceptions of the proper principles of the community's actions and organisation; active intervention in politics by the churches would therefore bring about disastrous quarrels, with serious damage to the cause of religion.

(4) No Government could take the pronouncements of church dignitaries as really representing the feelings of their religious followers

racial and other issues involving human rights.

on non-religious matters. People who clamour for the churches to enter politics are almost always those who expect it to favour Socialistic tendencies.

(See also the preceding article; *Bishops: Should They Be Excluded from the House of Lords?*)

Civil Disobedience

Pro: (1) In view of the increasingly undemocratic nature of representative government, and in the absence of any really effective provision for the ordinary public to express dissatisfaction with its conduct of major issues during a government's term of office, civil disobedience is justified as a measure of protest.

(2) Not everybody is willing or able to take the risks involved, but those who do are representing many more of their fellow-sufferers. Civil disobedience has the element of self-sacrifice which is absent from normal forms of protest, and thus adds cogency to a protest.

(3) In India, it did a great deal by proving the devotion and determination of the people to secure independence. Anywhere that the people are suffering under unjust laws, it is justified. We approved not only of civil disobedience but even of terrorism by people resisting oppression in occupied Europe during the last world war. In Northern Ireland more recently, the form of civil disobedience represented by the so-called 'workers' strike', which brought an end to the power-sharing Assembly, showed how strongly it can work; whatever one's views about the merits of the issue, the fact remains that the protest succeeded because a sizeable part of the population supported it.

(4) The police in Britain are generally tolerant, especially where,

Con: (1) Dissatisfaction with the government can be expressed through by-elections, through the organs of popular opinion, and through the action of Members of Parliament (who can be spurred on by opinion in their constituencies), without disrupting the administration of government.

(2) It is a form of coercion by a minority and is therefore undemocratic. It is displeasing to most people, who object to the disruption of law and order whatever their views on the question at issue. The effects are quickly forgotten, and it is useless as a protest unless it is practised continually and by a majority of the population.

(3) Indian independence was finally secured by her contribution to the war effort in 1939–45, by her strong financial position in relation to Britain and, above all, by the inevitable course of history generally. Other new nations have gained independence without it. War conditions are a special case. So are those in Northern Ireland, where, for anyone not inflamed by sectarian passions, the outcome of the 'workers' strike' can only be regarded as a highly regrettable and retrograde step.

(4) It has a brutalising effect on the police through its provocative nature, and itself easily passes into violence. The Doukhobors in Canada and the British suffragettes resorted

as in the case of nuclear disarmament, there is no great argument on the issue. Civil disobedience is generally resorted to by people who are pacific by nature and in intention.

(5) Refusal to pay taxes for the pursuing of policies of which one disapproves involves no violence or provocation and is a completely altruistic method of protest.

at once to arson and destruction generally when they perceived the ineffectiveness of civil disobedience.

(5) It is impracticable to try to separate taxes into their components and achieves nothing but the satisfaction of an individual conscience.

Classics (Latin and Greek) in Education

Pro: (1) The Latin and Greek Classics represent the most important and vital part of our inheritance from the past, both in literature and in social institutions. They have been a great, sometimes the sole, source of inspiration to most of our leaders and teachers of eminence, past and present. Their study need not preclude the proper study of other subjects.

(2) Their literatures have a more permanent value than the generally ephemeral products of contemporary nations, which constitute the staple reading of nearly all students of modern languages except specialists.

(3) The study of the Classics has great disciplinary value, and the prolonged period through which they have been studied and taught has brought the teaching of them to a high level.

(4) Latin and Greek are fine instruments for the expression of human thought. They enshrine the works of the picked intelligences of two great peoples, from whom we still have much to learn. A great deal of their value is lost if they are read only in translations.

(5) Most of the masters of English style have had the Classics as the foundation of their education.

(6) The Classics are a reminder of other values and other achievements, and so prevent mankind

Con: (1) They represent only part of our cultural inheritance. Ancient Egypt, the Middle Ages, and more recent times are quite as important, and are more interesting because less hackneyed. The study of prehistoric and primitive man is of more moment than that of Greece and Rome, which were half-barbarous, half-civilised. Statesmen reared on the Classics have often been ignorant, unprincipled and stupid.

(2) Proper education in other subjects is neglected through lack of time, e.g., modern foreign languages, in which the Englishman is usually woefully deficient.

(3) The disciplinary value of German or Russian syntax is equally great and the practical value incomparably greater. The study of mathematics and science instils habits of logical thought, mental accuracy and regard for truth much more effectively.

(4) 'Classics in Education' usually means Latin crammed for a few years, dropped and forgotten. Greek, much the better language and literature, is less frequently studied. Both are clumsy and undeveloped languages, far inferior in grammar, syntax, and vocabulary to English. Not more than half a score of Latin authors (apart from medieval writers, whom the Classicist very rarely reads) are worth reading, and

from undue pride in modern scientific and industrial triumphs. These latter are not of much cultural value. Modern life, scientific, industrial, and mechanical, is not satisfying to the artistic aspirations of man, who has had a vastly different environment through almost all his existence; nor are man's recent triumphs over matter likely to create moral and aesthetic values suited to his essential needs and nature. Greece and Rome represent the more permanent values in life.

no more than a dozen Greeks, though these are much superior. Their chief merits are visible in translation, and the time saved could be spent on the rich literatures of Europe.

(5) Many masters of English prose have had no such education, and the multitude of bad writers who have studied the Classics for years shows that the benefits are most uncertain.

(6) Modern life is founded on science and technology. Only by concentrating on these, and by treating all problems in the light of current needs and organised knowledge, can we expect to maintain or reach a satisfactory condition. The value of history in relation to current problems diminishes in proportion to its remoteness. Greek and Roman civilisation rested on slavery; ours rests on science.

Closed Shop

Pro: (1) The working classes have had to struggle continuously to gain improvements in their wages and working conditions and a reasonable standard of living. Their weapon has been collective bargaining and the unity of their organisations, the trade unions. The closed shop, where only members of specified unions are admitted to employment, is the logical next step in the consolidation and safeguarding of what they have so far achieved.

(2) The principle of the open shop enables unscrupulous employers to introduce new, untrained or semi-trained personnel into industry. This is unfair to those who have had to pass through the stage of apprenticeship and burdens an industry with people who know nothing of its traditions and customs – people, moreover, who may well be prepared to accept lower rates of pay,

Con: (1) While the right of workers to organise for collective bargaining is accepted, in their capacity as producers they are only one section of the community and should not have the right to impose their will on the others. Freedom of conscience is a fundamental right which is being attacked every day in modern society. No man should be deprived of employment because he is unwilling to pledge himself to action which might cause suffering to the community as a whole.

(2) The requirement that only members of an approved trade union should be employed in any industry unduly restricts the freedom of workers to change their occupations and stifles initiative in industry. Such restrictions are unfair to the community and hamper its progress, especially today when new processes and machines have often

if the employers can get away with it.

(3) Temporary relaxations could always be permitted to cope with special circumstances, such as war and other emergencies, provided that the general principle is preserved and the unions are consulted.

(4) If all the workers in an industry, including clerical, administrative and professional workers, are not organised in trade unions, strike-breaking becomes easy and union organisation as a weapon for bargaining is rendered useless. The recent actions by doctors and nurses, in withdrawing their labour as a protest, shows that professional work is not incompatible with the use of the strike weapon.

(5) Employers have done their best, within the legal limits now allowed them, to combine and exclude competitors from their operations. Employees have no less right to act in this way. Those workers in industries which have already achieved the closed shop are only doing what other sections of workers would do if they had sufficient organised strength.

replaced the craftsmanship required in the old days.

(Some) The 100 per cent shop, where new entrants to an industry are required to belong to a trade union during their employment only, would meet the requirements of unity in action without destroying flexibility in industry.

(3) The closed shop system is unworkable where large numbers of new workers are suddenly required, as in the engineering industry in wartime. It then comes into direct conflict with crucial national interests.

(4) Several types of professional work are not amenable to trade union organisation, such as that of welfare and medical workers or people responsible for safety precautions. Even those that have been 'organised' are divided among a number of unions, without much cohesion of aims, and would not accept closed shop conditions.

(5) Workers in closed shops have been able to gain huge concessions, out of all proportion to those of their fellow workers and at the expense of the community as a whole.

(See also *Trade Unions: Should Their Powers Be Restricted?*)

Coalition Government

Pro: (1) In time of war, Britain accepts readily enough that a coalition government is the best, perhaps the only way to get full national support for whatever measures may be necessary and to ensure that the widest possible range of talent is available. The country's present economic troubles represent just as much of an emergency, and the same criteria should apply. This was recognised by the Liberal Party at the second 1974 election, when, with the prospect that it might

Con: (1) It is relatively easy to sink party differences in wartime, when winning the war is all that matters and every other political issue is subordinated to that one vital objective. But no British coalition in peace-time has ever been a real success – as witness the poor record of the National Governments of the 1930s. The theory that the parties could come together for one agreed programme to deal with an emergency situation, like the economic crisis, would be proved un-

emerge holding the balance of power, its leaders said they would not enter a coalition with one or other of the major parties but only a broadly-based national government formed from all of them. Several individual Tory and Labour MPs have since spoken out in favour of such a coalition, in present circumstances.

(2) Coalitions have worked successfully in Belgium, the Netherlands and several other European countries, for many years. Nobody could claim that the first two, in particular, have lacked necessary reforms or otherwise suffered; they are among the most prosperous nations in Europe.

(3) In countries which have quite a number of political parties represented in Parliament, but with the main party groupings fairly evenly balanced, it sometimes takes several weeks or more to agree on a new coalition. Yet this can have its advantages. For, in the process of forming a coalition government which will have majority support, the issues which matter most to a country are thrown up more clearly and subsequently receive more priority than they might otherwise have done.

(4) By their nature, coalition governments usually last only a few years, at the most, before a reshuffle is necessary. But this need not matter greatly, provided there is continuity of administration – as shown by France under the 4th Republic. At that time, coalition governments were considered the only way to prevent the Communists from coming to power. Despite all the political confusion caused by the rapid succession of these coalitions, the broad lines of government did not change much. Whatever the Gaullists may say, moreover, it was during the 'chaotic' 4th Republic that the foundations were laid for

workable quite quickly; party differences on other issues are too ingrained. On the other hand, the major parties are frequently in broad agreement over several really important policies (for example, the lack of Tory opposition to the Labour Government's anti-inflation measures in 1975). So, despite a show of differences over detail, the basic policies on these key matters are effectively bilateral, anyway – thus avoiding any need for a coalition, with all its unwanted compromises.

(2) On the contrary, some European countries have suffered a good deal from the inability of any one of their political parties to win an overall majority. A prime example is Italy, which, for this reason, has had nothing but coalition governments since the last world war – with the result that each in turn, through fear of the political consequences or inability to achieve agreement among the coalition partners, failed to carry out reforms that were overdue years ago.

(3) Can it seriously be suggested that delays of this nature are not harmful? As for throwing up the key issues, no single party forming a government would have won its overall majority unless the biggest proportion of the electorate felt that it had got its priorities right.

(4) The French 4th Republic became notorious for its ever-changing governments because of the chief drawback to all coalition systems: the fact that parties shirk from their responsibility to carry out unpopular measures – if need be, engineering the overthrow of the government and the emergence of a reshuffled coalition in which they still participate but another party has to take the main responsibility for the unpopular measures concerned. It lessens the confidence and trust of other countries when a

industrialisation, the EEC, and many other factors in the re-establishment of French stability and prosperity which came to fruition after General de Gaulle's resumption of power in 1958.

(5) When different parties accept membership in a coalition government, they *ipso facto* accept the need to refrain for the time being from demands which their partners regard as too controversial. Equally, though, they will not join a coalition unless demands they consider to be irreducible are included in the programme which all the partners agree as their common platform. A coalition government's initial policies, therefore, reflect each of its member-party's views – and each has equal responsibility for them.

(6) Each major political party is itself a coalition. The British Conservative and Labour parties, the American Republicans and Democrats – all have their own left-wing, centre and right-wing strands of opinion, under the broad party umbrella. But, whatever their internal disagreements, that does not prevent them from reaching a consensus on the policies which their party should put to the voters at election times and which duly reflect that party's fundamental attitudes. By the same token, coalition governments formed by a number of parties can be just as effective politically.

nation is subject to such continual government changes. Even though one may criticise some of de Gaulle's methods, none of the foundations supposedly laid under the 4th Republic would have been effective without the political stability he brought about.

(5) If a majority party is in power and its government makes a mistake, that party has to take the blame. In coalition governments, one party has the opportunity to blame another more easily – and will almost always do so.

(6) That most big parties are themselves coalitions is true enough – but irrelevant. It has no bearing on the efficacy or otherwise of coalition governments, as such. The essential difference is that a party, after thrashing out its internal arguments, does not merely hope that members of varying views will accept the ensuing proposals for a limited period, anyway; once it has published its election manifesto, detailing the measures and reforms it plans to carry out, those proposals are advocated by all its candidates during the electoral campaign – and, if the party wins power on the strength of its manifesto, its MPs accept that that is the programme the whole party has undertaken to put into effect. Coalition governments inevitably lack this unity in the long term. Worse still, coalitions are usually formed as a result of post-electoral deadlock – which means that they are set up without consulting or involving the voters and, likewise, that the compromise programme agreed by the coalition parties will not have been submitted to the electorate.

(See also *Party Government*.)

Co-Education

Pro: (1) The mixing of the sexes in education is natural, practical and economical. It was formerly prevalent in Scotland, is in vogue in the United States of America, and has been adopted in several private and most State-aided schools in this country.

(2) The feminine mind gains from association with boys and men, and the masculine from association with girls and women. The character develops more rapidly and shyness diminishes. Competition is greater between the sexes than between rivals of the same sex, so that higher standards of achievement are reached.

(3) False masculinity was a temporary phenomenon which arose during the struggle of women for emancipation. It now tends to be found only in girls educated in girls' schools. In co-educational schools, it is completely absent; the relation between the sexes falls into a more natural pattern, and the only loss is, perhaps, the ultra-sentimental chivalry which is in any case a survival from the days of women's subjection.

(4) The presence of both sexes together is a wholesome factor in institutions. In all communities where one sex is segregated, e.g., schools, colleges, monasteries, convents, etc., it is more likely that various evils will flourish; women tend to become hysterical, men to acquire unnatural vices, and the whole atmosphere is morbid. In colleges and universities, the presence of women raises the general tone both ethically and academically.

(5) Marriages made after co-educational experience are best. If the man and woman have known each other as fellow-students, a

Con: (1) It is not convenient for the two sexes to be educated together. Many subjects are necessary for one sex which are not suitable for the other. Some subjects cannot be taught in the presence of both sexes without embarrassment on the part of teacher and class. Co-education tends to diminish the chivalry that is largely the product of early separate education. Co-educational schools in England in the past produced a sizeable proportion of cranks.

(2) The feminine mind assumes masculine characters which are only a hindrance in later life and which actually repel men, while some boys become effeminate and so are disliked by both their own and the other sex. Competition in any form between the sexes should be discouraged. Shyness is a natural stage in the development of youth, which wears off in the course of family life and ordinary social communication.

(3) It has been found that, far from raising the status of women, co-education tends to result in their being relegated to second place and pushed into the careers which have always been considered as belonging to women. The best academic records among women have been achieved by those educated in single-sex schools. Although co-education may be of benefit to the mediocre, it does not favour those of outstanding ability.

(4) Co-educational institutions provide conditions conducive to a low tone, and serious evils might result. Enforced associations of the sexes at adolescence is likely, in some cases, to make permanent the slight aversion from the other sex that sometimes exists at that period;

surer basis is given for married life than that gained from purely social acquaintance. If they have moved among others of the opposite sex on equal terms, each will have a better appreciation of the qualities and make a fairer judgment of the short-comings of the other.

(6) Co-education is general in primary schools, and in small schools in rural areas has been so for many years.

(7) In nearly all branches of life, women are becoming more and more the colleagues of men or their rivals on equal terms. They are equally competent as teachers, members of committees, administrators, doctors and research workers. In mixed schools, a greater proportion of headships should be thrown open to them; at present, the most that all but a very few of them have achieved is a kind of assistantship. If it is absurd to think of a woman as head in a school containing boys, it is absurd for a man to be head in one containing girls. Men and women should be placed on the same professional level of conditions and pay.

(8) Co-education enables investigation to be made into the different characters of boys and girls, the different environment and subjects they may need. It offers a field for wide varieties of research that may provide solutions for many of the problems now vexing both education and society.

(9) Most schools are inadequately staffed; many have insufficient material and equipment. The necessary improvements would cost less if provided for co-educational schools than if they still had to be duplicated for separate schools for boys and girls.

in many other cases, it brings about the premature 'growing up' which is so lamentable a feature of Western life today.

(5) The history of marriage in the USA does not encourage expectations of much advantage from co-education. Nor has the growth of co-education in this country caused any increase in the number of successful marriages. Genuine love (as opposed to temporary infatuation) still needs an element of romance, which is destroyed by too much familiarity between the sexes.

(6) Quite young children may well be educated together; but after they are 9 or 10 years old, boys should be taught by men and girls by women. They need separate training to suit the different rates of physical, intellectual and emotional growth. The two sexes can thereafter mix quite enough in family and social life.

(7) Though men and women may co-operate successfully in their work, children above primary school age usually have a tendency to shy away from the other sex, for some years. One sex gains its experience in a different way and interprets it differently from the other. It can be guided through this stage of life only by someone who has traversed the same path. In single-sex schools, women are more likely to attain the leading positions and responsibilities they desire, as headmistresses and principals.

(8) Such investigations can be pursued with each sex separately. Co-education might perhaps follow – but it should certainly not precede – the conclusions reached by this kind of research.

(9) Mixed schools are more expensive to run than those for one sex only.

(See also *Public Schools*; *Women's Liberation*.)

Collectivism

Pro: (1) The narrow conception of the State's function as confined to securing order and liberty for person and property is quite antiquated. Economic pressure of every sort, price fluctuations as well as unemployment, sweated labour as well as land monopoly, work more injury to the mass of citizens than any amount of 'normal' crime. The economically weak must be protected from the economically strong. Therefore, the State must reorganise the vital productive and distributive processes in the interests of the community.

(2) It is no more iniquitous to order the economic actions of citizens than to conscribe their persons for war; yet many anti-collectivists approve the latter.

(3) Private capitalism has achieved much, but not enough. It has developed vast power, yet the lightening of the burden of human labour has come only from the pressure of the workers. Capitalism directs enterprise into profit-making rather than into socially desirable channels. Modern capital depends almost entirely on manipulations of credit by bankers and financiers. The present situation shows the inadequacy of capitalism.

(4) Collectivism is necessary if Britain is to husband her comparatively small natural resources and hold her own in international commerce. Postwar experience suggests that tariffs, quotas, subsidies and the like do not suffice to maintain Britain's economic prosperity, and that salvation is to be found only in a greater measure of collectivism and direction of the national economy.

(5) The Government during the last world war, although largely

Con: (1) The function of the State is to govern, not to trade. It should keep order and maintain the conditions of liberty. The State is a purely political institution, designed to protect the national independence, the rights of persons and the rights of property. If it steps outside these limits, it does wrong and will inevitably cause trouble.

(2) Collectivism implies monopoly. The rights of the individual to trade and dispose of his capital are attacked; collectivism thus offends the principles of justice. War is an exceptional episode in the life of a society and justifies exceptional measures.

(3) The justification of private enterprise is its results. It has built up modern industry, with its vast achievements and its vast possibilities. Wealth has been increased many times over. The ends of the earth have been developed and made to yield their riches. A civilisation undreamed of has been erected, and mankind is better off than ever before.

(4) Foreign trade depends above all on private enterprise. Collectivism would mean ruin of this trade, which is essential to Britain's economy. All the good alleged to be derived from collectivism could be obtained by protection in the form of tariffs or subsidies or other incentives to producers.

(5) Governments have proved just as guilty of waste and inefficiency as any private body. For example, army supplies have been dumped in large quantities and left to rot, good farming land has been taken over and destroyed, and government departments have built up ever-larger clerical and administrative staffs – encroaching on housing,

composed of people politically opposed to collectivism, was forced to
exercise more and more control over
industry and sometimes to take over
factories and firms in order to save
the country from the effects of their
inefficiency. The Ministries of Food
and Agriculture controlled the import and production of food, with
notable benefit to the public, and
saved the country from the worst
evils of food shortage. Recent
'rescues' of large industrial enterprises by the State have provided
individual proof that, on a broader
plane, the need continues to this day.

(6) Under private enterprise,
profits are the only incentive, the
object of all industrial activity.
This does not necessarily produce
efficiency; in fact, under privately
run monopolies, it has often led to
the restriction of production and the
suppression of inventions which
might have encroached on the
markets for outmoded goods.

(7) Centralisation effects enormous
economies. Privately owned coal
seams, for example, were incompletely exploited because of the need
to maintain barriers between properties underground. The only other way
of abolishing wasteful competition is
by anti-social trustification; but
whenever a monopoly is attained
by capitalists, they have no further
motive for efficiency, since within
wide limits they can secure constant
profits from an indifferent service
highly priced. Private enterprise in
practice always tends towards
monopoly, and the choice nowadays
lies between a monopoly operated
for the benefit of a few shareholders
and one operated for the good of the
whole community.

(8) Government departments are
administered successfully. Despite
traditional grumbles about the
failings of Britain's nationalised
industries, they are in fact run more
efficiently than comparably huge

industrial buildings and productive
manpower. That Britain's rate of
inflation in the mid-1970s has been
higher than that of any other
European country is largely attributed to excessive Government
spending.

(6) The success of commercial
undertakings depends largely on
elasticity and breadth of view, and on
their competence to make prompt
decisions and take wise risks. State
officials are notoriously cautious
and unenterprising. They fear
responsibility and resist innovation.
Collectivism would mean hordes of
bureaucrats with vested interests
and conservative minds.

(7) Centralised monopoly is not
so efficient as decentralised competition. It abrogates the interplay
of supply and demand. It is also
relatively less efficient after the unit
of management exceeds a certain
size. The advantages that are claimed
for it are obtainable by voluntary
agreements between various firms.
Near-monopolies are rarely successful in practice, from their own point
of view, for they never succeed in
eliminating all competitors.

(8) The constitution of the
machinery of government, with its
fretwork of divided responsibilities,
its political influences and intrigues,
is unsuited to administer commercial
undertakings. There is no satisfactory means of appealing against a
Government monopoly, and the
Ministers and Government departments concerned are all too rarely
prepared to amend their decisions to
meet the complaints of aggrieved
individuals. The State telephones
in Britain are less efficient than the
privately owned telephones of the
USA, and State-owned railways and
other nationalised industries are
chronically insolvent (and were so
long before the present world
economic and inflationary problems
arose).

undertakings in other countries. Their basic difficulties are due to their financial structure, which takes no account of their function as public services, and to the heavy financial commitments with which they were saddled initially.

(9) Much of the rottenness in political and national life is due to the influence of private capitalist forces which, while repudiating State interference (on behalf of the community) at their expense, seeks to secure State interference on their own behalf at the community's expense. There is no doubt that international commercial interests are as powerful in modifying government policy as are strategical or ethical considerations.

(10) People are more willing to work efficiently for the State, as the organ of the community, than for individuals or companies whose first concern is profit, gained through a system of which unemployment is a necessary feature and where maximum production brings economic crises. The feats of production achieved by miners since nationalisation could never have been approached under capitalism. The serious loss of manpower to the industry has been arrested by the incentive of collective enterprise.

(11) Aggravated by the current international inflation, the gap between wages and profits, and the consequent bad distribution of goods and fluctuations of purchasing power, are the chief evils at present. Collectivism would remedy them.

(Some) Domination by bondholders is by no means an inevitable feature of collective systems. On the contrary, their aim is the service of the community. Payment of doles to bondholders does not imply control by them of the country's industrial and financial policy.

(9) Business men are the backbone of the nation. They are the most vitally interested in its welfare and shoulder most of the responsibility for securing it.

(10) Although there are some exceptions, the great majority of workers in nationalised industries have not worked for the State with greater efficiency than they did before. On the contrary, rather. Experience indicates, moreover, that 'collectivised' workers will use their political power to extort the most favourable conditions, just as much as they use their industrial strength under private enterprise.

(11) The gap between wages and profits, which is justified by the increased risk taken by the capitalist, is being continually narrowed by taxation and the provision of costly social welfare schemes.

(Some) The chief problem of industrialism is the wage system, which collectivism does not solve. Collectivism may easily mean the servile state in which the mass of the workers toil, under good conditions maybe, for a minority of State bondholders.

(See also *Co-operation*; *Co-partnership in Industry*.)

Commercial Radio:
Should It Be Abolished?

Pro: (1) Commercial radio was established at the behest, mainly, of advertising interests who saw it as yet another means of making money. Its inception was legalised by the former Conservative Government in what seemed more than anything a re-affirmation of the party's traditional belief in free enterprise rather than on the merits of the case. Tory MPs themselves had been subjected to prolonged lobbying by protagonists of commercial radio. In the event, the innovation has been a failure. It has added nothing to the cultural life of the nation, has made no innovations of note (except, perhaps, for the almost non-stop playing of pop records), and has been an unnecessary and unjustifiable expense in the present adverse economic period – and probably in any other period, for that matter.

(2) Most, if not all, of the commercial radios have failed to attract the volume of advertising which they need if they are to be financially viable. What advertising they do receive has simply reduced the level of advertisements in other outlets like newspapers, thus compounding the problems of other media. It is highly debatable, in any case, whether any kind of radio 'commercials' should ever have been allowed in the first place. What with commercial TV and the rest, we are submerged in such a flood of advertising that the preservation of one form of communication from its influence would surely have been a blessing. No wonder so many people stick to BBC radio!

(3) The same flaws which have marked the first generation of independent television are clearly

Con: (1) Although commercial radio in Britain is still in its infancy and has yet to become generally profitable to its backers, the claim that there was a demand for it has already been abundantly proved. One reason for the objections to it by Establishment-minded antagonists is that it has won an increasingly large audience away from the BBC's local radios, which are usually less enterprising and varied in their programmes. In short, commercial radio has justified itself by demonstrating that it fulfils a need. The unique character of the London Broadcasting Company, one of London's two commercial radio services, which puts its emphasis entirely on news coverage, is an experiment of which any country in the world would be proud.

(2) There are some kinds of advertisement for which sound is a particularly good medium. That commercial radios provide an inexpensive outlet for local businessmen in their own areas, particularly those for whom national advertising would be unnecessary or too costly, is obvious. In addition, they offer a day-to-day immediacy which can rarely be matched by the local weekly newspapers which serve many provincial areas. The level of advertising has fallen in all media during the country's present economic difficulties; yet several commercial radios are already getting a higher level than they had anticipated at this early stage – and they will get much more when the economy recovers.

(3) Commercial radio in Britain is free of undesirable influences because it echoes the pattern of our commer-

evident in commercial radio as well. To win more advertisers, it is necessary to show them large audience figures; and that results in lower standards, with the programme organisers pandering to what they suppose to be 'mass' tastes – cheap music, interminable 'phone-ins', cretinous competitions, and the like. All right, it's not always as bad as that; wallpaper music has its place, and local traffic reports are useful. But it was sheer capitalist self-indulgence to set up commercial radio for the purpose. The BBC's network of local radio stations – which would have been even more comprehensive if the Government had got its priorities right and allowed the BBC more money to carry out the original plans – would have been perfectly adequate to meet all genuine needs of the communities it serves. It can still do so; and, what's more, without commercialism and without basing its programmes on the lowest common denominator.

cial TV programmes, whereby advertisers are not allowed to have any influence on or control of the programme content. Advertising is restricted to certain specified periods and we do not suffer the experience of American listeners, with a 'commercial' breaking into the middle of a piece of music or, excruciatingly, a split-second before an important climax in the plot of a play. Nor do we suffer the results of the US system of sponsorship, under which the nature of programmes is dictated by the advertisers paying for them. Anyone who has had to listen to an average day's American commercial radio will know how fortunate we are! One consequence of the British system is that the intellectual and cultural standards of many of our programmes are a good deal higher than opponents of commercial radio give them credit for.

(See also *Broadcasting, Public Control of.*)

Common Currency

Pro: (1) A common currency, freely usable in every country (or at least, initially, in a number of countries agreeing to it), would facilitate international trade, travel, and many other aspects of relationships between nations. Countries would still be able to use their own currencies as well, internally, and most would doubtless wish to do so – though it's probable that, over the years, the common currency would gradually supersede them.

(2) The world nowadays is moving more and more towards thinking in international rather than national terms. A common currency, the

Con: (1) It is a Utopian ideal, quite unworkable in present monetary conditions (or any in the foreseeable future). An immediately insuperable stumbling-block is that, as many of the national currencies are 'floating' and their exchange rates thus vary from day to day, it would be impossible to fix a standard value between the common currency and all the others.

(2) A common currency would only be possible, if at all, in conditions of complete economic and financial stability between the participating countries. Otherwise, its valuation would have to be

regulation of which would necessitate close international co-operation, would greatly encourage this trend and eventually be an essential ingredient of it.

(3) Bodies like the International Monetary Fund already make use of units of account which, although not 'real' money in a tangible sense, have much the same effect as a common currency among the participants. Similarly, under the Common Market's agricultural policy, there are make-believe units like the so-called 'green pound' for fixing the level of payments, etc. If artificial currencies like these are used successfully for book-keeping purposes, it would surely not be all that difficult to transform them into the real thing.

(4) The introduction of a common currency among members of the EEC is one of the key steps foreshadowed under the Treaty of Rome.

variable, from one country to the next. Instead of contributing to stability, therefore, it would merely aggravate all the present complications. There is already very close co-operation between financial experts of many countries (e.g. the International Monetary Fund); none has ever championed the advisability of a common currency.

(3) Devices which are feasible on paper, to simplify accounting procedures, would not be acceptable in practice for everyday purposes. The units of account used by some international bodies are subject to most of the same disabilities suffered by real currencies (as witness the 20 per cent devaluation of the 'green pound' in 1975, made necessary by the effects of inflation). But the chief objection to the idea of a common currency, perhaps, is that it ignores the extremely strong attachment which each country feels towards its own currency, as part of its national heritage and identity. As an example, General de Gaulle's introduction of the 'new' franc, whereby 1,000 became 10 (but without radically changing the appearance of the money), proved to be one of the most important symbols of the re-establishment of French prosperity.

(4) It is one of the Common Market provisions which, because of the practical difficulties, the member-nations recognise as unachievable for years yet.

(See also *Internationalism*; *United States of Europe*.)

Comprehensive Schools

Pro: (1) It is now generally admitted that the tripartite system of secondary education inaugurated by the 1944 Education Act has broken down. More and more

Con: (1) Whatever may be said about selection at 11 years of age, some kind of selection or streaming is essential if the best use is to be made of all levels of intellect.

authorities have abandoned the system of selection at 11 years of age, or have modified it in an attempt to make it more efficient. At the time of the Education Act, too much faith was placed in crude intelligence testing; it has since been discovered that the intelligence quotient is not a static thing but can be altered by environment or nurture.

(2) Secondary modern schools, which were supposed to liberate the less academically-minded from the tyranny of examinations and give them a worthwhile general education, have failed conspicuously in their purpose. The less enterprising have become dreary places in which to mark time until working life begins, and the better ones, under pressure from both parents and employers, have introduced examinations. The fact that some children have passed these, under great handicaps compared with the grammar school child, and gone on to higher education, is a proof of the folly of selection at 11 years.

(3) In spite of the hopes expressed in 1944, grammar schools have kept their superior social status, and assignment to the modern schools carries a sense of failure which itself acts as a bar to achievement. Grammar schools perpetuate the class division which has always been a curse in this country and is now being increasingly recognised as a bar to technological and scientific progress.

(4) The grammar and direct-grant schools have not unnaturally led the campaign against comprehensive schools, since they feel their own existence to be threatened. But there is no intrinsic reason why those public and direct-grant schools which merit it should not continue to exist – although, as the excellence of the comprehensive system becomes clearer, they must expect to dwindle in numbers.

Experience in other countries where comprehensive schooling is the rule has shown this; in the United States, many parents are turning to private schools where streaming is the rule. Some kind of discrimination, however disguised, is inevitable even in a comprehensive school.

(2) One advantage of the 'modern' school is that it allows children to reach the peak of their performance without being overshadowed by their more academically ambitious fellows. Transfers to grammar schools can correct any errors made at the initial selection, and some authorities have colleges of further education where public examinations can be taken. Alternatively, selection could be made at a later age, when abilities and ambitions become clearer.

(3) The remedy for class distinctions between schools is to make the modern schools what they were meant to be, by the expenditure of more time, thought and money, rather than to condemn non-academic children to a form of education to which they are wholly unsuited. If the artificial distinction between technical and modern schools were abolished, the standard of achievement and technical education in non-grammar schools could be raised. Only in this way can the meritocracy be prevented from succeeding the aristocracy.

(4) The direct-grant schools, which are to a certain degree comprehensive, and some of the older-established grammar schools, have built up high reputations for the excellence of their teaching. They have given many brilliant children the chance to develop at a pace suited to them, without upsetting the balance in the ordinary grammar schools. Private schools are free to develop, and to experiment away from the tyranny of examination and curricular conformity, and have in the past pioneered many

(5) With proper organisation, there is no reason for the more brilliant children to suffer. They would benefit from the extra equipment and libraries needed for advanced work, which existing schools are often too small to provide. Socially, contact with less academically minded children would give them a broader view of life.

(6) The curriculum of a comprehensive school can be much broader in scope than that of any of the older types of secondary school. Complaints about over-specialisation in grammar schools are often made by educationists, and a turn to broader education is a feature of university reform.

(7) Though most (but not all) of the earlier comprehensive schools were large, this is not generally necessary or inevitable; in any case, a system of houses and tutoring does much – as in the larger public schools – to mitigate the effects of size.

(8) Both grammar and modern school teachers tend to be influenced by fears for the future of their profession, but both have much to contribute to education in a comprehensive school, be they graduate teachers or those who have gone straight to teacher training colleges for special training in education. If present trends continue, with the standard and status of teacher training raised and with such training made compulsory for graduates, any differences felt to exist at present will soon disappear.

(9) Whatever the merits of previous systems, there is no doubt that education in this country is not producing enough people with higher education, and that a large reserve of talent is left unused. The universal establishment is a first step towards a general reassessment of our educational needs.

changes which are now generally accepted. It would be suicidal to destroy this store of educational experience and wisdom.

(5) The history of comprehensive schools elsewhere suggests that they do not cater adequately for the brilliant child. The atmosphere of a school where only half the pupils take their education seriously is not conducive to serious study, and academic achievement is likely to be less highly regarded than athletic prowess, as in all but the best public schools. As sixth forms are becoming larger everywhere, the problem of size will soon be solved.

(6) Revision of university entrance requirements would at once cure over-specialisation in grammar schools. At present, it applies equally to the academic streams in a comprehensive school.

(7) One great objection to the comprehensive school is its size, which is fatal to the corporate feeling without which a school cannot prosper. Teachers seldom meet the headmaster, staff meetings take up a disproportionate amount of time, and timetables are complicated, while the group life of the children lacks stability.

(8) Many teachers have misgivings about the comprehensive system. The carefully built up structure of incentives would be destroyed, especially for secondary modern school teachers, whose special experience in the more difficult kind of teaching is still likely to rank lower in esteem than academic qualification, despite the latest reforms. Many valuable members of the profession would drift away if they no longer saw any chance of reaching the top.

(9) The present system of teaching, leading to university and technological training for some and apprenticeships and special training for others, has developed out of

educational need and can be made to produce a society in which no one is without some skill. Extension and improvement of the present system is better than the imposition of a system of unproved efficacy.

(See also *Co-Education*; *Public Schools*.)

Co-operation:
Compared with Capitalism

Pro: (1) Co-operation, by substituting for the self-interest of an individual or a small group of individuals the interest of the whole community of workers, puts each worker in a position of being, in a sense, his own master, and secures a higher standard of work from him, since he receives his proportionate share of the proceeds in full.

(2) The commercial policy is regulated by the advice of those immediately interested in its success. Unlike capitalism, co-operation does not primarily aim at profits; accordingly, while monetary balances have their due place, as a matter of good business practice, they remain less important than efficiency and service.

(3) Co-operation places the producer in direct contact with the consumer and, by thus saving the expenses of middlemen, reduces costs.

(4) In enterprises where the workers know that they are not making profits for others' consumption, they work better. Private concerns habitually give exorbitant salaries to a handful at the top and pay most of their employees at the lowest rates they can get away with – and these ordinary workers naturally tend to respond in kind.

(5) The co-operative movement has been very successful, not only in distribution but also in production.

Con: (1) By freedom of contract, or in any case by trade unionism, the worker has already secured fair wages and equitable conditions of work. Co-operation has to face the same labour relations problems with its workers as private employers do and is no less prone to strikes. Every device by which the workers can be made contented, without destroying the system, is open as much to capitalism as to co-operation.

(2) Under capitalism, the commercial policy is regulated by a single expert individual or small group of individuals. Uniformity and continuity of policy are better secured than under co-operation, where experts have to be employed but work under harassing conditions.

(3) Middlemen perform important services (e.g. the crucial role of wholesalers in distributing goods to a wide range of retailers); nevertheless, large industrial combines and other later developments of capitalism can dispense with them very largely.

(4) Co-operation keeps all the essential features of the wage system and is therefore of no advantage to the workers; moreover, the dividend, though not of the same origin as profits, has much the same psychological effect on its recipients.

(5) Co-operation has been chiefly

It has undertaken, with great success, banking, insurance and foreign trade. There is no reason to suppose that co-operation could not be generally adopted.

successful on the distributive side. Even then, private stores are just as successful in this field. On the productive side, co-operation has been a failure; the Co-operative Wholesale Society is really nothing but a capitalist concern with shares held by unusual holders.

(See also the next article; *Collectivism*; *Co-partnership in Industry*.)

Co-operation:
Compared with Socialism

Pro: (1) Voluntary co-operation, as opposed to State socialism or collectivism, makes self-help the basis of social reform. By banding men together for a common end, it teaches self-reliance and gives independence.

(2) While collectivism would depose the capitalist only to exalt the bureaucrat, thus leaving the worker as dependent as before, co-operation would make him his own master and render impossible such abuses as sweat-shop labour.

(3) Co-operation, unlike collectivism, does not aim at the expropriation of vested interests. It defrauds no man; neither does it cripple the nation with any scheme of wholesale compensation.

(4) The main departments of human effort require special organisations to develop them properly. In the Civil Service, seniority counts for more than special merit; enterprise is stifled; responsibility is insufficiently devolved and immediate decisions cannot be given; and the ordinary citizen is rarely able to obtain reasonable consideration of his complaints or to influence the provision of the services he needs. If things go wrong in a co-operative society, the members can set them

Con: (1) Co-operation benefits only a small portion of the working class, and that the part that needs assistance least. The most optimistic and reliable estimate of the ultimate success of co-operation does not suggest that it could ever take over more than one-fifth of the national production.

(2) Co-operation simply substitutes competing societies for competing firms. The only other choice would be local monopoly coupled with absolute dependence on the central, quasi-capitalist producing organisation. Sweating and wage disputes are quite common in the co-operative movement.

(3) Co-operation based on the savings of the poorer part of the community has no chance of competing very seriously with capitalism based on profits and credit manipulation. It does not touch evils like the land monopoly.

(4) State enterprises are at least as successful as co-operative ones. The weakness of co-operation is shown by the way it is seeking help in trying to overcome its difficulties from people who are committed to collectivism.

right, withdraw, or let them continue, as they please; but in State trading, citizens have to put up with what is offered.

(See also the preceding and next articles; *Collectivism*.)

Co-partnership in Industry

Pro: (1) By giving the workers a concrete interest in the total efficiency and remunerative operation of industry, much discontent and friction can be avoided and a better spirit be developed, to the great advantage of all parties and of the community at large.

(2) It was very successful in the gas companies which started it, in the enormous concern of Lever Brothers, and in many other firms drawn from every section of industry, but chiefly engineering, shipbuilding, chemicals, pottery, and glass. Where co-partnership is in practice, strikes have been almost extinguished and the prosperity of the workers as a whole has increased.

(3) Shareholding gives the workpeople a sense of security, a sense of dignity, and a wider outlook on life and industry. They are thereby raised from the status of mere 'hands' to that of responsible members of a community.

(4) The moral and economic necessity of supplementing wages and salaries by another mode of income is met by these schemes. Workers who are called and treated as 'partners' (e.g. the John Lewis department store) not only feel that they have a personal stake in their company's welfare but habitually demonstrate this by above-average standards of service to the firm's customers.

(5) Large concerns, which are unrivalled as exponents of modern commercialism, have adopted the

Con: (1) Co-partnership is an endeavour to mask the fundamental defects of capitalism by bribing its victims. It makes no attempt to put an end to the vicious principle of production for profit alone. Consequently, it must be condemned as a deceptive and degrading palliative.

(2) It assumes the continuance of good trade and cannot guarantee an income when trade is poor. By increasing overhead charges through the issuing of preference shares, it may actually help to depress trade. The gas companies where it was most successful were quasi-monopolies enjoying peculiar advantages. The Lever concern was a trust, and was consequently enabled to avoid many of the influences which affect other firms. Co-partnership did not save engineering and shipbuilding firms from prolonged depression or their workers from unemployment. The financing of sections of the Lancashire cotton trade by loans from the operatives brought calamity on large numbers of them, even though all the alleged advantages of co-partnership were present in this practice.

(3) Workmen shareholders are kept in a strictly subordinate position and have no real say in the policy of the firms. Whatever lip-service may be paid to them as 'partners', they still have the status of wage-earning employees.

(4) Rent, interest and dividends are immoral. 'He who does not work, neither shall he eat.' It would be

principle on the grounds of commercial expediency.

disastrous if trade unionists were converted to the defence of parasitism.

(5) Co-partnership is largely the hobby of philanthropists who can afford it.

(See also the preceding articles; *Profit-Sharing*.)

Corporal Punishment

Pro: (1) Corporal punishment for certain offences is most effective, because it is prompt and feared by all. It combines the elements of the remedial, the deterrent and the day of reckoning. It teaches the schoolboy or the convict that the doing of wrong is followed by the suffering of pain.

(2) When inflicted justly and without anger, it does not brutalise the giver. In most schools where it still occurs, it is resorted to only as a final punishment. While its use against convicts should be restored, this should not be indiscriminate but reserved for appropriately serious offences – e.g. as before, for rebellion against prison discipline.

(3) It accustoms the pupil to the hardships of real life. No bitterness is left after chastisement if it has been administered for good reason.

(4) It is impossible always to 'make the punishment fit the crime'. The amount of corporal punishment can be adjusted to suit the gravity of the misdemeanour.

(5) It is better than other punishments, such as impositions, which are deadening to mind and body. Schools which dispense with corporal punishment, especially for young children, often substitute other methods which are tantamount to browbeating.

(6) Impositions and detentions are harmful because they increase the number of hours a boy is compelled

Con: (1) It is degrading and otherwise harmful to the sensitive victim, while it is no deterrent to the hardened culprit, who often boasts about it to his cronies as though it were a battle honour.

(2) Its brutalising effect is seen when we reflect that those ages when parents and teachers resorted to it most were the most brutal in other respects. It appeals to the strain of cruelty that exists somewhere in everyone.

(3) Children resent injustice coupled with indignity. Were it true that corporal punishment accustoms them to life's hardships, then every boy – but especially the good boys – ought to receive its benefits daily.

(4) It is an excuse for laziness and inefficiency in teachers. By using terror instead of discipline, a bad teacher can continue his work when otherwise the impatience of the pupils would force a change in either the methods or the staff.

(5) Impositions and detentions are more effective because they encroach on the leisure time of the miscreant and may even give an opportunity for reflection.

(6) In modern schools, there is plenty of opportunity for physical exercise, and it is nonsense to imply that depriving a boy of this for a few hours is physically harmful. Impositions and detentions in girls' schools are not considered to have any bad effect on health. Letting off

to spend indoors in physical in-activity. His natural restlessness is increased by the enforced restraint, so leading to further offences against discipline.

(7) Corporal punishment should be used for criminals convicted of violence. It brings home to them the effect of their crimes on their victims and, since bullies are generally the greatest cowards, is of the utmost value as a deterrent from such crimes in future. British prison records from earlier this century show that hardly any convicts who received corporal punishment ever repeated the offence which incurred it.

steam immediately afterwards will always be tempered by a desire to avoid repetition of the punishment.

(7) The infliction of corporal punishment on an already anti-social person who regards violence as a legitimate means of achieving his ends is not likely to have any corrective action; on the contrary, past experience indicates that it will more probably lead to a deeper feeling of enmity towards authority and society.

Degeneracy of Modern Civilisation

Pro: (1) The degeneracy of Europe and of European civilisation has been noticeable for more than a century. Literature, journalism and art have more and more laid stress on the morbid and the abnormal. Britain is not exempt, as is proved by the crazes in different classes of society for such importations as lascivious music and dances, and the violence and crude, puerile senti-mentalism of many American films.

(2) A loathsome industrialism has subjected men to machines. Working populations are marked by a mania for gambling, for watching other people, especially professionals, play-ing games which they themselves do not play, and by an insatiable desire for something new, which shows itself in the endless buying of unnecessary but much-advertised products and the incessant pursuit of machine-made pleasures.

(3) Moral laxness and crimes have been increasing, fed by weak senti-mentalism and the flood of pernicious literature and films. The most outrageous forms of immorality are

Con: (1) Britain and other European countries can be accused of de-generacy only by people who are ignorant of social history or those who idealise the fancied memories of their youth. We often confuse what we do not like with what is evil. Morbidity and sensuality are found in the literatures and art of every country and every age.

(2) Industrial progress is steadily improving both physique and in-telligence in the areas where it flourishes. The state of mind which made possible the horrors of the industrial revolution was a product of the pre-industrial period. Such evils would hardly be accepted nowadays even by the most reaction-ary. Gambling and the pursuit of new things are as old as society, and the age which watches football matches and television is perhaps less to be condemned than that where bull- and bear-baiting, cock-fighting and the murder of gladiators flourished.

(3) Immorality is no greater than in previous ages; the reason for its apparent increase is that there is less

now spreading openly in most countries and are being cynically tolerated.

(4) Mental diseases and neurotic symptoms are on the increase. Faith healers and psycho-analysts flourish; so do astrologers. The persistent demand for more leisure-time and longer holidays shows that we are less fitted to stand the strain of life than our ancestors were. Drugs of all sorts are being used extensively. Tranquillisers have taken the place of religious consolation. Venereal diseases are widespread, especially in the large towns.

(5) Divorce rates have risen steadily and the institution of marriage is becoming 'unfashionable' among an increasingly large sector of the population. The phrase 'close friend', in newspapers, has acquired a dubious new meaning – such affairs now being publicised blatantly and without criticism. More married women than ever are taking office or factory jobs; while this may be a good trend, in principle, it should not be at the expense of their children or the proper running of their homes, as is increasingly the case.

(6) Commercial interests are allowed to pander to the young, who have lost all respect for older people and their standards, while parents have ceased to exercise their duties of correction and guidance.

(7) The growing discontent and peevish attitude to the difficulties of life show lack of stamina. Higher standards of comfort bring demands for still more. Suicide as a method of avoiding reality is becoming commoner, as are insanity and nervous breakdowns.

(8) The outbreak of two world-wide wars in one generation proves that Europe has lost its moral standards. The ferocity and stupidity with which war is waged, and the epidemics of frenzy, revolution and

hypocrisy – and less 'sweeping it under the carpet'. Cruelty and barbarism such as now occasion widespread horror, when a sporadic case occurs, were characteristics of daily life that were hardly noticed some generations back.

(4) Accurate statistics of insanity were not kept in the past and there is thus no real basis for comparison with the present day. But it is certain that new medical treatments have done away with much of the mental and physical invalidism which existed in the last century without being understood. The increased, illicit use of narcotics is admittedly a serious problem (though there are signs that it is already on the wane); on the other hand, drunkenness is far less common and addiction to laudanum has died out. Venereal diseases are being attacked by the only possible method – medical treatment – and the hypocritical silence which veiled the whole subject has given way to a franker attitude.

(5) The increase in divorce has been due latterly to the considerable easing of the restrictive laws which previously governed it and may be measured against the suffering, without hope of release, which was the lot of so many people in the old days. Women are just escaping from the serfdom of centuries and are no longer content with the restricted life which was formerly their lot.

(6) Young people have always revolted against their elders' standards. Most parents continue to exercise their duties, but in a less arbitrary and despotic manner.

(7) Our ancestors bore hardships only because they could not circumvent them. For most of our population, higher standards of comfort mean progress, and discontent is a first symptom of moral and cultural advance. In relation to the size of population, it is probable that the

braggadocio which accompany it, reveal our degeneracy.

(9) Our political systems are outworn and our statesmen, particularly in the international issues, prove much inferior to men like Pitt, Canning, Castlereagh, Palmerston and Disraeli, who wrestled successfully with the problems of earlier days.

(10) Our decadence is due to a variety of causes, of which the decline of religion and the older virtues is the chief. Owing to the premature democratisation of our social institutions, power rests with half-educated crowds who are too often directed by experts in deceit and cajolery, whether journalists, politicians or advertising agents; a spirit of small-minded egoism prevails, and loyalty to State and society is replaced by general discontent and skirmishing for greater personal advantages. Children absorb these pernicious doctrines at home; at the same time, they are deprived of the stabilising influence of religion, and even the most reasonable standards of discipline and obedience are derided.

incidence of suicide, etc., is actually less than amid the hideous conditions of poverty during, say, the late Victorian era.

(8) War is the result of a complexity of causes, which have little or nothing to do with the moral standards of ordinary people. Never has opposition to war and all its attendant stupidities been more universally pronounced than in our own generation.

(9) Modern problems, owing to the interdependence of modern communities, are much more complicated than those which faced former statesmen. The widespread desire and effort to improve our political and economic systems shows that the ability to make new departures and new ventures is inherent in Europeans today.

(10) If the 'older virtues' are at a discount today, it is because their exponents, the churches, no longer expound a doctrine which corresponds with modern spiritual needs. The newer virtues of co-operation and personal initiative are being inculcated in all modern schools. Universal education and the influence of the better newspapers and the radio have raised the general standard of culture and ended the power which the leaders of society formerly possessed over ignorant populations. The supposed degeneracy of life in other countries, and the inadequacy of democracy in general, was always among the principal propaganda assertions of totalitarian regimes like the Nazis – but it is those regimes' policies which have been thoroughly discredited.

Delegation v. Representation

Pro: (1) The representative system has broken down in all today's supposedly representative assem-

Con: (1) A man is elected to Parliament on broad issues, with the necessary understanding that he

blies. Most members no longer represent the general views of their constituents – it may be questioned whether such a thing is even possible – but rather party and other interests. The general feeling that, when once an election is over, the successful candidate is free from all effective control by his constituents, has weakened the popular reverence for and faith in political democracy of the old type. The remedy is the principle of delegation.

(2) Theoretically, every elector ought to vote by proxy on every question of government; the nearer the approach to this ideal, the more perfect government is likely to be. A Member, therefore, ought to represent his constituents in each vote he gives, and should consult them on every occasion where a vote on key policies is involved. The principle of the Recall of MPS (*q.v.*) is a necessary adjunct to electoral machinery.

(3) Constant appeals to constituencies would not be derogatory to the dignity of a Member; consequently, equally good men would offer themselves as candidates. They would, in fact, be protected in a measure from the pressure and influence of parties and sectional interests.

(4) The nemesis of representation is that it allows governments to put through the most controversial measures, such as the abolition of capital punishment, without consultation. Delegates whose limits of action were determined beforehand would not have been able to condone the flouting of the League of Nations' authority after securing election on a contrary policy, as happened in 1935.

shall consider and decide on details for himself. His constituents cannot take such decisions for him. The failings found in representative institutions are due to other and various causes.

(2) Delegation is unworkable. It means either complete submission to an elaborate but inelastic party programme, or else futility. In practice, representation is inevitable unless the assembly is purely temporary and deliberative. The mechanical difficulties in the way of getting constituents to express themselves on half-a-dozen main questions are enormous; to get decisions on proposals running to dozens of clauses is impossible. Even to answer a single question, the necessary national organisation entails vast expense – as in Britain's 1975 referendum on Common Market membership. Moreover, experience in other countries (e.g. France) shows that electors soon get bored if called to the polls at frequent intervals. The Initiative, Referendum and Recall (*qq.v.*) are all compromise and faulty solutions.

(3) Delegates will always tend to be inferior to representatives in character and ability, for no self-respecting man will act as an automaton without even theoretical responsibility. Under the Delegation system, party domination continues, corruption is not eradicated, and the executive steadily encroaches on the sovereign body.

(4) Representation enables many important matters to be dealt with which cannot come within the scope of delegation, e.g. foreign policy.

Direct Action
(The Use of Industrial Strikes to Affect Political Issues)

Pro: (1) The present system of government reduces the masses of the population to a state of helplessness between elections. As events and situations change rapidly, this means the practical despotism of the government that has a parliamentary majority. Trade unions comprise the largest organised part of the citizens of the country, and trade union action is the only effective way they have of intervening to show their opinions on critical occasions. A satisfactory government would not be threatened.

(2) Industry is becoming as important as citizenship. Direct action is the beginning of the development of the industrial state which will supplement, if not supplant, the political state.

(3) Direct action can be applied only occasionally and only when the vast mass of the workers approve. The pressure put on Parliament by financial, industrial and newspaper interests is the work of a smaller minority and is more pervasive, more constant and, in many cases, no less unconstitutional.

(4) Direct action is especially to be recommended for securing the ordinary and recognised civil and industrial liberties of the subject. It is then purely in the nature of a demonstration.

(5) Politics are properly the object of such action, since one political development may spell more ruin to trade unionists than half a dozen unsuccessful industrial strikes. Industrial power cannot be gained for any purpose unless there are constant attempts to exercise it.

(6) The ballot box gives a

Con: (1) Parliament, elected on a very wide franchise, reflects and represents the will of the people as a whole. The Government of the day depends on Parliament, and its policy follows the greatest common measure of the wills of the community. It is, therefore, both the constitutional instrument of public policy and the only qualified judge of policy. To attempt to influence its action by extra-constitutional means is wrong and will end in anarchy. Opponents of the trade unions' political demands will inevitably organise their forces to resist direct action and possibly to press demands of their own. Movements have already sprung up in Britain for this purpose.

(2) Citizenship is the supreme privilege. It is impossible to separate political interests from industrial interests in the State. The former include the latter.

(3) Direct action, if persisted in, would lead to anarchy. The moral stability of the workers would disappear. It would be resorted to more and more on the most trivial occasions, sometimes by a few unions, sometimes by many, but always by a minority of the community.

(4) Parliament, the law, and the many different organs of public opinion are quite adequate to defend the liberty either of groups of people or of individuals.

(5) It is absurd for trade unions to devote their energy and power to strikes on political issues when they need to settle so many other problems more closely relating to themselves and are too divided to

fallacious result. The constitution, the party system, the machinery of government, the confusion of issues and proposals at election times, prevent the electorate from giving an informed and effective vote.

(7) The 1926 General Strike failed in its objectives through incompetent leaders. As a strike, though, it was amazingly complete.

carry through their own modest industrial programmes.

(6) All grievances can be remedied more certainly and much more easily through the ballot box.

(7) Only general strikes are likely to be fully effective and they are in fact a revolutionary weapon. The General Strike of 1926 failed largely because of its leaders' tardy recognition of this fact and their recoil from it. .

(See also *Trade Unions: Should Their Powers Be Restricted?*)

Direction of Labour

Pro: (1) The balance of Britain's foreign trade has always been delicate, owing to her large need for imports. Since the last world war, the dislocation of our economy has made it more important than ever for British industry to expand those essential trades which have the power to earn foreign currency. Canalisation of available manpower into these channels, to the extent needed, can only be achieved by direction of labour.

(2) It is undesirable for the State to have to enter into competition with private employers for available labour. The coal mining industry, even since its 'rationalisation' and the closing of uneconomic pits, has continued to be beset by manpower problems, though it is essential to national prosperity.

(3) Workers are traditionally unwilling to leave occupations and places to which they are accustomed, even in those areas where local industry has declined. Even when workers do move, the majority tend to ignore inducements to find new work in the depressed regions and still gravitate to the south-east and other already congested industrial areas.

Con: (1) If the balancing of Britain's international trade and the stepping-up of national production can be achieved only by coercion of labour, any advantages which may result from it would be nullified by the evils such a method would bring in its train. The national economy should function for the benefit of the nation's citizens and not for some overall concept which overrides the individual interests of large numbers of them. Higher wages, good conditions of work and other incentives have always been sufficient to attract labour into individual industries.

(2) The worker has the right to sell his labour where it will be of most profit to him. The coal mining industry's manpower problems stem almost solely from the discomfort and danger of the work, and it is only recently that pay increases have begun to compensate adequately for these conditions.

(3) The success of industrial development schemes in hard-hit regions like the north-east shows that it is possible to restore prosperity to areas where the older industries have decayed, without uprooting workers from their homes.

(4) During the last world war, workers accepted direction without complaint, not only for patriotic reasons but also because it was necessarily accompanied by adequate working conditions and security of employment. Both these reasons are still cogent.

(5) A great deal of the waste and disorganisation which are a natural feature of modern private enterprise systems would disappear if labour were withdrawn from unessential industries and anti-social occupations. Direction of industry and capital expenditure is not a feasible alternative, since the goodwill of the industrialist and financier is essential to the smooth working of the national economy; indeed, its absence can wreck any national plan.

(4) Measures which are accepted in wartime are not necessarily valid in time of peace. Direction of labour interferes with the freedom of the individual and operates, moreover, unfairly. Inducements to employers – such as tax reliefs for new factories established in depressed areas – are more effective and give rise to fewer problems.

(5) The efficiency of industry is seriously hampered if workers are made resentful by encroachments on their rights. Direction tends to operate mainly against the most essential types of workers. Their resentment is further increased if they are conscious that capital is allowed to operate unhindered. Any attempt to operate a scheme which is appropriate only to a Socialist economy is doomed to failure inside the framework of capitalism.

Disestablishment of the Church of England

Pro: (1) The union between Church and State is undesirable, as they are essentially different in aim. The State deals with the individual as a member of society in his relations with the world, while the Church looks on him as an individual with a soul to save and from the point of view of his relations with God.

(2) In the past, the State knew of but one religion and looked upon those who professed another as scarcely to be counted as citizens. But in Britain this was finally ended when Charles Bradlaugh (Radical MP for Northampton and a professed atheist) was admitted to the House of Commons, in the latter part of the nineteenth century, without taking the normal oath of allegiance.

(3) It may be admitted that Church and State have certain common functions, but it is never-

Con: (1) While many people in the present day have turned away from the Church, they are not in the majority – whatever the newspapers say – and religion is still one of the chief elements in national and social life. It remains a prime duty of the State to countenance religion officially and not be indifferent whether the people hold religious principles or not.

(2) Although the State no longer claims to be the exclusive arbiter of what is religious truth and admits to its counsels persons of many religions or of none, nevertheless the Church of England is historically and psychologically the National Church and should remain so.

(3) Both State and Church exist to improve society and to promote a better life for all. For centuries, no man dreamed that these two

theless not a wise policy to connect the two, as their spheres and methods differ. Such a union tends to diminish the efficiency of both.

(4) Established Churches create false ideals of religion. Many people who are lukewarm about religion seem to think that religious duties can be done for them by proxy, that the worship of God need make no demand on their life, and that the State, in maintaining an official Church, satisfies the requirements of religious duty and social morality.

(5) The State drags the Church down to its lower level, encouraging worldly prudence and an unreligious tendency towards diplomacy and discretion. Bishops and clergy, for example, through this connection with the Throne, are restrained from denouncing evils which the interests of society make it unwise to pass over.

(6) Establishment hampers the Church's efforts to reform itself. Parliament alone can sanction important changes in its rites and ceremonies. The 39 Articles show how this worked in Tudor times; the Gorham judgment and other cases show how it has operated since. Parliament, being composed of people of all types of belief, is manifestly unfit to be the authority in matters of religion. It does not even represent the feeling of the nation on the subject, for members are elected for completely different purposes.

(7) The State's role may oblige it to sanction conduct and pass laws, for civil purposes, which are not in accord with the forward teachings of the Church (e.g. the law allowing the remarriage of divorced persons). Dependence on the State thus exposes the Church to the potential weakening of its own standpoints.

(8) The Church of England can only maintain its present relationship

institutions for securing such ends were other than two aspects of the same unity. This philosophical principle should still be recognised, and the best form of recognition is by means of an official Church – which no longer entails the condemnation of other non-official Churches.

(4) An established Church, with its social prestige, attracts to itself many who otherwise would have no religion at all. Religious zeal may be stronger in the non-established Churches, but this is because an established Church, while not excluding such enthusiasts, tends naturally to lay less stress on rigid dogmatic beliefs but to combine several elements within it.

(5) The duty of the Church is to import a moral element into our political life. Its ministers are secure from pressure by the Government because they practically hold office for life and are in no sense of the term either bureaucrats or place-seekers. In recent years, the bishops and leading clergy have not been backward in denouncing social injustice and scandalous conditions of life.

(6) Parliament cannot alter either the Creeds or a single doctrine. The Prayer Book was drawn up by the Church, not the State, and was then accepted by the latter. For almost all practical purposes, the Church today is effectively self-governing.

(7) No clergyman with scruples need marry a divorced person. The connection of Church and State ensures a broad tolerance in the former, which thus attracts men of widely different individual convictions.

(8) Upon substantial matters of doctrine, the State does not claim to dictate to the Church; but where the internal conduct of the Church is a matter of national importance, it is quite fitting that the State should

with the State on one condition – that the Crown and Parliament should abstain from any interference in its internal concerns. The Royal Commission on Ecclesiastical Discipline, appointed in 1905, took upon itself the duties of a spiritual court and determined what was or was not consistent with the teaching of the Church. The theory that the State or the King should manage the Church was one of the errors associated with the Reformation and Lutheran Protestantism.

(9) The Enabling Act was a recognition that the time had come when Churchmen should manage their own affairs. Though it touched only a few points, it was a step in the right direction, and all the steps required to give the Church 'life and liberty' should now be taken.

(10) It is improper that the Government, which may contain a number of atheists, should appoint the chief officers of the Church, i.e. the bishops and archbishops, and that such political dignitaries as the Lord Chancellor, whose only necessary qualification is that he shall not be a Roman Catholic, should have a large number of livings in his gift. Parliament also creates bishoprics at its entire discretion. All religious sects should be treated as equal by the State, though that does not mean that they can be made equal.

(11) Because of its present position *vis-à-vis* the State, the Church cannot insist on its clergy adhering rigidly to its formularies.

(12) Reform has a different meaning in the mouth of each party in the Church, and there are few points on which they can agree.

(13) Some parish clergy neglect their poorer parishioners altogether – and in the big towns, indeed, are not numerous enough to attend to them, or even to all those who require it.

take a part. State participation has always helped to raise the Church in the estimation of the people. Patristic authority, furthermore, is clearly on the side of kingly authority, even when it comes to a reform in the status of the Church, so that State Churches are not simply an idea from Lutheran politics.

(9) By the Enabling Act, the Church now has sufficient scope to express its desires without separation from the nation as organised in the State. Complete freedom even to define doctrine need not mean the surrender of the position as National Church. The Church of Scotland is still national, though granted autonomy in matters of doctrine.

(10) The Sovereign does not make bishops but (on the Prime Minister's recommendation) merely allocates them to particular posts; they are 'made' by consecration. They are quite as likely to be the most suitable for the dignity as those who would be chosen, after inevitable intrigues and jockeying for influence among possible candidates, within an autonomous Church. Parliament merely sanctions the creation of sees; it neither initiates the demand for new ones nor frustrates that demand when well-founded.

(11) The Church has long been noted for allowing its clergy freedom to teach what they think is right, so long as they keep the main doctrines of Christianity as laid down in the Prayer Book. Heresy-hunting is rarer than among the Dissenting communities, with the happy result that schism is also rarer.

(12) Now that the laity have a recognised position in the organisation and government of the Church, necessary reforms can be carried through with less acrimony and less delay.

(13) If the Church were disestablished, there would be no one

(14) The traditional connection of the established clergy with the land-owning class and the well-to-do sections of the community prejudices them in the eyes of large numbers of the working population. Disestablishment would at once tone up the Church and help to remove this feeling against it.

(15) The Church has notoriously misused its very large income. Many clergymen are still living on a bare subsistence; churches of architectural value have been allowed to go to ruin or have been sold off. Much of its income was derived from ownership of slum property which the Church did little or nothing to improve.

(16) Too many of the clergy are now out of touch with the needs and requirements of their congregations.

(Some) An independent priesthood, standing on its own dignity and governing itself without any reference to an external authority, is a first necessity for healthy religion.

(17) The bishops are among the most bigoted, obstructive and useless members of the House of Lords and should be removed from it without delay. (See *Bishops*.)

(18) No Church is stronger for carrying with it a multitude of the religiously indifferent, for these only act as dead weights against true religious life and activity.

(19) The Church of England has undergone vast changes during the last century. These changes have taken it further from both Erastianism and Nonconformity. To a great extent, it has become sacramental and sacerdotal, and even those who repudiate such principles the most strongly have fallen under their influence to some degree. The conditions suitable for its establishment in England have therefore ceased to exist, both as far as its own character is concerned and because

in the parish upon whom the poor would have a *right* to call to perform services such as visiting the sick, praying with the dying, or celebrating marriages. For it is in the crises of life that they need and look to the Church most.

(14) Disestablishment would reduce the prestige of the Church, and in consequence the cause of religion would suffer. It would diminish the self-respect of many of the clergy and result in future recruits to their ranks being of inferior quality.

(15) The great inequalities of former days have disappeared and no clergyman is starving today. The Church has either sold much of its former slum property or spent large sums on replacing it with modern dwellings.

(16) The clergy would be reduced to much greater dependence on the whims and fancies of their congregations, and of the richer members in particular. It would be an evil day for religion if the Church came to be governed by those with the deepest purses, which has often happened in Nonconformist Churches.

(17) The bishops are among the peers who sit by merit and not by the accident of birth. When they intervene in debates, they invariably do so with responsibility.

(18) If disestablishment were effected, large numbers of wavering Anglicans would join the Church of Rome, while others would drift into vague theisms or ultimately into atheism.

(19) Establishment saves the Church from becoming merely the battleground of warring factions. The relationship with the State is a brake on hasty action, giving ample opportunities for reflection and compromise, because action is impossible until the assent of the State is secured. In the Roman

the mass of the people are no longer true Church members.

Catholic Church, the appeal to Rome is a similarly effective instrument of delay.

(See also *The Churches: Should They Take Part in Politics?*)

Divorce

Pro: (1) Though, in the Roman Catholic Church, marriage in theory is held to be indissoluble, in practice this has never held good and some device has been found to circumvent the difficulty, e.g. the Pope has always had the power to dissolve marriage, provided it has not been consummated, a plea which has been visibly strained in many instances. In the theology of the Western Church, the doctrine that marriage is indissoluble stands in the closest association with the 'Roman doctrine of intention' – if the intentions of the bride and bridegroom have, in any way, come short of being a genuine 'consent unto matrimony', the marriage is regarded as null and void. A theory of marriage which ignores consent can be defended neither by reason nor by authority. In England before the Divorce Act, as in Ireland now, a long process had to be gone through in each case. Only the rich could afford divorce, therefore; the poor had no hope of escaping from unhappy marriage by legal means.

(2) Marriage is a purely civil contract and should be so treated in law and opinion.

(3) It has always been held that adultery (and, above all, adultery by a wife) is cause for dissolving a marriage.

(4) Divorce for adultery was allowed by Christ; there is no difference between the Greek word *apoluo* (I put away) and divorce. This doctrine was taught by a great

Con: (1) In the marriage ceremony, no mention is made of possible divorce. Each party swears solemnly to take the other 'for better, for worse, till death do us part'. Though State and Church have erred, they should not continue in error. The indissolubility of Christian marriage is a plain and simple principle, resting on the authority of the whole Western Church.

(2) Marriage has been regarded by nearly every nation as a rite and condition of mystical significance. Its extreme importance for the continuance of the human race makes it imperative to surround it with all possible responsibility and dignity. If we looked upon it as irrevocable, we should enter upon it with more care and solemnity.

(3) When adultery is considered automatically as a ground for divorce, marriage loses its seriousness in popular estimation and opportunity is given for relative promiscuity by a succession of remarriages.

(4) Even if Christ allowed divorce for adultery, he never gave sanction to remarriage, which was expressly forbidden by the Church at the Council of Arles.

(5) The knowledge that they are not allowed to separate and remarry will always tend to induce husbands and wives to minimise differences which they might otherwise magnify into occasions for separation. The risk of their agreeing on full licence for each other in sexual relations is

many of the Fathers. The Council of Arles has been reported in two diametrically opposite senses.

(5) The denial of divorce never served to deter people from adultery. It merely contributed to increasing laxness, in both public opinion and private conduct, as regards adultery, concubinage and prostitution, and its chief effect was always to victimise the woman through the laws of property.

(6) The worst thing that can happen to children is for them to live with estranged and quarrelling parents or to be brought up in contact with one parent, whichever it may be, who is depraved and worthless.

(7) As the monarch is head of Church and State, the State clergy have no right to debar people who are not breaking the law from being married in church.

not one of which the law can take account, but one against which public opinion should express itself strongly.

(6) Nothing can be worse for children than the legal separation of their parents. A true home cannot exist in the absence of either of the parents, while both are still alive.

(7) The State must not expect the clergy to lend their churches for sacrilegious purposes, such as the marriage of divorced persons. Those who wish to defy the Church's laws can marry in a Registrar's Office.

(See also the next article.)

Divorce, Easier:
Has It Gone Too Far?

Pro: (1) Although present-day social attitudes regard it as in the interest of both the public and the individual to allow divorce, when a marriage appears to have become irretrievably unhappy, the plain fact remains that the couples concerned are breaking a solemn pledge to each other (and to their children). That Christian marriage should be indissoluble has already been demonstrated in the previous article. However, even if one now has to accept the existence of divorce as an institution, in the prevailing social climate, the massive and alarming increase in the number of broken marriages nevertheless makes it abundantly clear that relaxation of

Con: (1) It is injurious both to the State and to the individual that married couples should be obliged to remain together when their relationship has developed such fundamental antagonisms that it has become intolerable to both of them. The atmosphere in such a household inevitably brings out the worst in the characters of those concerned. Previously, when a couple agreed mutually that they wished to divorce, almost the only way they could obtain it was for one party to produce evidence of the other's adultery; this often led to the staging of a fictitious overnight 'affair', for the benefit of a private detective hired for the occasion,

the divorce laws has gone much too far.

(2) The figures speak for themselves. In 1867, there were 119 divorces in Britain. By the beginning of the Edwardian era in the 1900s, there were still fewer than 500. The Matrimonial Causes Act of 1937, extending the grounds for divorce to desertion for three years, cruelty, incurable insanity and presumed death, saw a jump of 60 per cent in the number of petitions in the first year of its operation. Between 1951 and 1970, the proportion of divorced people in the population *doubled* (with more than 70,000 petitions in the last year). Then in 1971, when the new Act came into operation (enabling couples to divorce by mutual consent after two years' separation and unilaterally after five years), divorce applications rose by more than half to a record of 110,895 ... and another 109,822 in 1972. The authorities had expected that the rate would even out after the first upsurge, but it hasn't happened. In 1974, figures for London alone showed an 8 per cent increase in petitions over the previous year.

(3) When couples knew that their marriage could not be dissolved without some difficulty, they often reconciled themselves to the situation, reached the best *modus vivendi* they could with each other and, through it, quite frequently ended after a while by recapturing their mutual affection and respect.

(4) If men and women feel that their marriage can be ended easily, should it prove unsuccessful, they will tend to enter into marriage much too light-heartedly and without the deep consideration necessary before embarking on a union that is supposed to last for the rest of their lives. Hence the ever-increasing number of young people who marry in their teens, enjoy a year or two of

which made a farce of the law. Today, the law provides for divorce by consent, with no need to specify any grounds other than the couple's mutual agreement that their marriage has broken down irretrievably. But care is still taken to ensure a wife's continued maintenance, if need be, and there are particularly strict safeguards for the welfare of any young children of the marriage. This law will be regarded historically as one of the most enlightened steps forward in our social development.

(2) Those figures merely demonstrate the extent of human misery which existed before the progressive relaxations of the divorce laws. Previously, unhappy couples were condemned to stay together, against their wills – or, perhaps, to live separate existences while remaining inexorably bound to each other by law. Such widespread frustration and suffering wreaked untold harm on the community.

(3) It is doubtful if such complete reconciliations were effected much more often than the instances (even today) of couples getting divorced, deciding later that it was a mistake and subsequently marrying each other again. It happens – but pretty rarely.

(4) 'Marry in haste, repent at leisure' still has plenty of force for most people. Since the financial provisions which a man may have to make for his wife's continued upkeep are sometimes even heavier now than under the previous legislation, he has no temptation to seek divorce without good reason. The increase in the number of teenage marriages is due mainly to the earlier maturing of young people nowadays and the greater affluence they enjoy, compared with previous generations who simply couldn't afford to get married at that age.

(5) Religion, and the morality

passionate love, then get divorced in their early twenties.

(5) Christ's teaching is unequivocal. Our moral and legal codes should be as nearly identical as possible. To claim that the law has been changed merely in response to public demand cannot justify the excessive relaxation that has been allowed. Our social and political institutions have a responsibility to give a lead – and they should at least aim at ideal morality.

that is supposedly derived from it, should be kept out of politics. The majority of people are not practising Christians; those who are can keep Christ's law in their own lives, without trying to impose it on everyone else.

(Some) Christ strove always to help individuals; it is the spirit of what he taught, not the artificial taboos with which it was overlaid later by biased humans, that we should follow.

(See also the preceding article.)

Eighteen-Year-Old MPs

Pro: (1) The present minimum age of 21, for an MP, equated with the former minimum for universal suffrage. Now that the voting age has been lowered to 18, there is no logical reason why that for parliamentary candidates should not keep step likewise. That MPs themselves are aware of the illogicality is shown by the fact that a Private Member's Bill to reduce the age for candidates has already been introduced and had its first reading in the summer of 1975. Its fate is unknown at the time of writing – but such a measure is bound to be accepted eventually.

(2) Pitt the Younger became Prime Minister – and one of the greatest in British history – when he was only 24.

(3) Britain lost America over the principle of 'no taxation without representation'. Equally, why should there be no parliamentary representation from within their own age group for those who are nevertheless still old enough to be called up into the armed forces, if need be, in time of war? There are not likely to be many 18-year-old MPs, any more than there are MPs still in their 20s, in the present Parliament; a young

Con: (1) The idea of youth in Parliament doubtless has its attractions, but it is reasonable to maintain age limits aimed at ensuring that candidates can make a practical contribution, based on their own experience. Many professional qualifications cannot be gained below a certain minimum age (often higher than 21, even), for similar reasons; the voting age is irrelevant, therefore. Eighteen-year-olds are unlikely to have much experience or knowledge other than from school education; by 21, many young people will at least have gained wider experience and knowledge in passing through university.

(2) Apart from the question of earlier maturity in those days, Pitt was the son of a famous statesman, the Earl of Chatham, and had been brought up in an atmosphere of politics and affairs of state since early childhood.

(3) Representation is, indeed, the crux of the problem. An 18-year-old could not be representative of more than a very small minority of the electors in his or her constituency. As MPs, holding 'surgeries' in their constituencies most weekends, they

parliamentary candidate has to be quite outstanding if he is to win enough votes from the mass of electors. But at least the opportunity should be there – ensuring that we do not lose the contribution that could be made by the few 18-year-olds who *are* exceptional.

would be called on to give advice and help to constituents of far greater experience than themselves. Few of the older electors would have much confidence in them. The necessary educational preparation is also sadly lacking in this country; very few schools give in-depth teaching about British political institutions (let alone about those of other countries), and nearly all 18-year-olds are inevitably still ignorant on the subject.

Euthanasia:
Should It Be Legalised?

Pro: (1) We put animals 'out of their misery', rather than let them suffer intolerable pain; yet we refuse the same merciful release to our fellow men. In spite of all that modern medicine and surgery can do to prevent disease, or abate it, many human beings still end their days by a slow and often agonising illness. Provided that strict legal precautions were observed (particularly as regards the crucial question of consent), a doctor should have the right to give an overdose of morphine to a patient who would otherwise die a lingering and painful death.

(2) Although it may not be possible to draw up a list of diseases that are always incurable, a point comes in each individual case when a doctor knows whether a patient is beyond hope or not. The patient himself should be the best judge of whether life has become, for him, intolerable. If he wishes for release from suffering, it should not be denied.

(3) If the patient is unaware of the hopelessness of his condition, the decision should be taken out of his hands. The family doctor would know best; but to avoid any risk or error of judgment on his part,

Con: (1) A doctor cannot draw up a list of diseases which are invariably fatal. A steadily increasing proportion of cancer sufferers, until recently doomed, can now be cured. People with heart disease may live long and useful lives. It is impossible to make hard and fast rules when medical science is in a state of continual change and progress. The doctor's duty is to maintain life as long as possible by every means in his power.

(2) This argument is tantamount to a plea for the legalisation of suicide. If physical suffering is a valid excuse for cutting life short, then why not other forms of suffering? Unless a patient were aware of his condition and deliberately asked for euthanasia, it would be an act of intolerable cruelty to let him know that such a measure was being considered. A request for euthanasia might easily be due to temporary despondency; a person in great pain is not always responsible for his utterances.

(3) Doctors do not always correctly estimate a patient's recuperative powers and should not be saddled with the responsibility of making what is, in effect, a

there should be consultations with a specially qualified medical assessor. If the doctors were in agreement that euthanasia was desirable, the final decision might then rest with the patient's relatives.

(4) If we are to call it murder to take man's life with his own consent, then we must call it theft to take his property with his consent, which is absurd. As for pain, no doubt it has its uses, if only as a danger signal. But not many of us would go on enduring a pain we could avoid. And none but a fanatic would advocate the cessation of human effort to alleviate or abolish pain.

(5) In practice, 'mercy killings' by relatives have usually been treated with understanding and a measure of lenience in the courts; even in the past, few of the culprits were sentenced to death, and the sentence was almost never carried out. Many unfortunate people are born who have no hope of ever leading a normal life or of being anything but a tragic liability to their families. Such people should not be forced to enter on a travesty of life, much less to continue it.

decision to murder. It could also be an impossibly heavy burden for relatives to have to be the final arbiters in cutting short the life of one linked to them by ties of blood or affection. On the other hand, legalised euthanasia would be a ready-made weapon for unscrupulous relatives which no amount of legal precautions could entirely guard against.

(4) (Some) The Christian religion teaches that it is wrong to take away human life. 'Thou shalt not kill' is an unequivocal command. Moreover, it is possible that pain itself has a significant place in the scheme of evolution and serves some mysterious moral purpose.

A civilisation based on a high conception of the value of human life cannot countenance the deliberate taking of life where no crime has been committed by the sufferer. A large number of people supported the abolition of capital punishment, even for murder cases, and there was a far better case for it than for euthanasia.

(5) The danger of such cheapening of the respect for human life was seen under the Nazis, who had millions of people put to death for imaginary 'racial defects'. It is better that a few should suffer unwanted life than that the door should be opened, even to the slightest extent, to such ruthless practices.

(See also *Suicide: Is It a Crime?*)

Examinations:
Should They Be Abolished?

Pro: (1) Examinations, as at present organised, test only a certain kind of skill. Some people have a good memory and a special facility which enables them to pass exami-

Con: (1) The ability to pass an examination is currently decried, but it is in reality a valuable quality. It shows a capacity for coping with new problems without the protection

nations and achieve brilliant results, while completely lacking any capacity for original thought or imagination. Yet such people will continue to be unduly favoured by employers and academic authorities while examinations remain in their present form and are still taken as a criterion of worth.

(2) Examinations are the bane of a pupil's life. They involve cramming, depress the pupil, and often rob him of mental vitality at an early age. Subservience to the examination curriculum necessarily frustrates any initiative on the part of the teacher and deadens the atmosphere of school life. Some of the subjects set in examinations, particularly by the older universities, bear no relation to the intended course of study and merely involve an irritating detour.

(3) Examinations are set as if all schoolchildren have reached the same mental level at the same age. Medical and educational investigators are agreed that this is not so. Nor does the mental development of boys and girls follow the same course. School records are much more reliable than examinations for the assessment of these differences and adjustments to correspond with them.

(4) Educationists are biased in favour of competition and the brilliantly clever pupil. In consequence, the less gifted pupils who need most teaching are neglected and a specialised curriculum that frustrates the true purpose of education is maintained.

(5) A test of the examination system showed that the same papers, when marked by different examiners, were placed in an entirely different order of merit and that the same papers, marked by the same examiners after an interval of some months, then received widely differing marks. Surely this proves that, at any rate

of the accustomed environment and for expressing thought in a manner intelligible to others. A *viva voce* examination will elicit any special qualities which the written examination may have passed over, or, equally well, reveal the lack of them.

(2) The mental effect of preparation for examinations is excellent, since even the dullest exert themselves, while no discoverable harm is done either physically or mentally, except to a handful of unbalanced persons. The curriculum exercises a wholesome restraint on teachers and discourages too fanciful schemes of education. Pupils of schools not subject to examinations sometimes show startling gaps in their knowledge.

(3) The principle of unequal development by age has been recognised at the primary school level by the institution of the exam for 'late developers'. At later ages, the inequality has considerably decreased. Experienced examiners can rapidly assess the general standard of papers they are marking. In national exams like the O-levels, examining boards can adjust the markings if the general standard indicates that the papers were set at a too difficult level.

(4) Teachers are no more to be trusted to give an impartial judgment on a pupil than other people. Examiners have the advantage of being impartial as between pupils. It is a flaw in our educational system that the clever and the stupid have to be taught together, but this should be remedied by better organisation of classes and the provision of more teachers. The difficulty would exist if there were no examinations. It would be equally harmful to the cleverer students to be neglected and have their desire for advancement frustrated.

(5) Modern examiners judge general intelligence as well as book

as a valid basis of judgment, examinations are useless.

knowledge. An intelligence test forms an integral part of many examinations nowadays. Where intelligence and character are both of importance in a candidate, an examination, supplemented by an interview, remains the best method of selection.

Fascism:
Should It Be Outlawed in Britain?

Pro: (1) Whatever the divergence of opinions on the cause and nature of Fascist theories, there is no denying that they have in practice caused unexampled devastation and suffering in the modern world and have set back the economic and cultural life of Europe by decades, if not centuries. (In this context, the popular equation of Fascist with Nazi, although they are not actually identical, may be accepted for practical purposes.) As the international courts officially outlawed Nazi ideas during the post-war trials of war criminals, it is anomalous that British offshoots of them should not be declared illegal and similarly outlawed.

(2) Fascism and Nazism, as movements, preach subversion and the use of violence to attain their ends. A peaceful population has no protection against them, and the fate of Austria in 1938 and of the Spanish Republican government in 1936 shows the folly of trying to deal with them without the aid of special legislative measures.

(3) Fascists seek to divide the community against itself by the provocation of racial and sectional hatred. The inflammatory nature of their doctrines has already led to disturbances and has brought suffering and fear to peaceful members of the community. Among those not directly affected, they create an

Con: (1) Many aggressive wars have been fought in the past in the name of movements and ideologies, but their causes have always been a complex of interwoven economic and political factors. The outlawing of Fascism would give no guarantee against the recurrence of war. The increasing horror and devastation of war is due more to the development of new means of killing than to the influence of any ideology. It would be no more logical to outlaw Fascism than to ban Communism (confrontations with which have in fact been responsible for most of the local wars since 1945).

(2) The only certain cure for Fascism is a contented population. Given this, or at the least a government determined to secure it, Fascist ideas would fail to secure anything more than a tiny audience, of no importance or threat – especially in Britain, where the system of government is fundamentally stable, as it was not in Spain or Austria. Violence breeds violence, and coercion in peace-time is undesirable. More harm is done by the publicity given to Fascist movements by their opponents than by any influence that Fascist ideas might have of themselves.

(3) The airing of racial questions in public enables the listener to clear his mind of prejudice and provides a

atmosphere of unrest and instability which leads eventually to disbelief in the stability of government. The influx of Asian and African people since the early 1960s has made it all the more important to prevent the kind of tensions that the Fascists strive to foment. If Fascist-style and neo-Fascist movements were outlawed, they would soon cease to trouble the peace of the community, for underground movements do not prosper in this country.

safety valve for the upholders of racial doctrines. Prejudices are not the monopoly of Fascists; if everybody holding them were to be outlawed, the liberty of a number of respectable citizens would be endangered. The penalising of people who have not yet committed any crime would, of itself, savour of authoritarian methods and be repugnant to the spirit of English law. The lack of Press publicity received by neo-Fascist movements, in recent years, has been the most effective weapon against them. To drive them underground would not only be more dangerous than allowing them to operate openly but would be an infallible means of ensuring their survival.

Full Employment

Pro: (1) Every member of a community has a right to employment. There will always be a certain minimum of unemployed persons – married women leaving work but remaining temporarily in benefit, seasonal workers, and a small hardcore of unemployables. But any talk of maintaining a permanent 'pool' of unemployed is heartless and immoral, treating the worker as a mere unit and ignoring his moral and material needs as a member of the community.

(2) Unemployment itself, by reducing general purchasing power, restricts production and breeds more unemployment. It is an integral part of the 'trade cycle' which was a feature of the old system of unrestricted competition. This unregulated and chaotic working of the economy is now condemned not only by socialists but also by intelligent supporters of capitalism. The modern trend is towards the proper planning and zoning of

Con: (1) Full employment, in the last analysis, is against the interests of the working classes. It makes for a lack of flexibility between industries and industrial areas. The growth of new industries and the decline of others, due to changes in standards and technological advances, must be taken into account. Failure to provide the available labour for the development of new industries adversely affects production and, in the long run, harms the interests of the workers, since it inevitably means a decline in the world market.

(2) The planning of industry to match available manpower cannot be achieved on a national scale. Such planning does not take into account the constantly changing relations of the different countries in the world markets and their financial interdependence. It could only exist on a basis of complete self-sufficiency, which is difficult for most countries and impossible for Britain. The alternative is for the State to finance

industry to correspond with the country's needs, and full employment is quite possible, and is indeed an integral feature, under such a system.

(3) An adequate degree of State control, together with the growth of combination among employers, should curb the anarchic practices of individuals which are the ultimate cause of international crises. The advocates of a large pool of unemployed persons are mainly right-wing politicians who see it as a way to combat inflation or those big producers who stand to gain by competition between workers in the labour market; in either case, the only way of restricting employment is to keep production at an artificially low level.

(4) No justification whatever can be made for subjecting anyone to the demoralisation and semi-starvation which was such a blot on our national life between the wars, when mass unemployment was rife. If individual employers are unable or unwilling to cope with the manpower problem by technical advances and improved organisation of production and distribution, then the State must step in and perform its duty to the citizens as a whole.

(5) We have learned enough in the last century or so to insure against the effect of sweeping economic changes caused by new inventions (e.g. automation). Compensation for redundancy is only a stop-gap. A truly effective government could see that new industry keeps pace with invention.

unproductive public works in times of crisis in order to provide employment, a practice which would lead to still further distortion of the industrial situation.

(3) Full employment means in practice a shortage of labour, and resultant competition between employers to obtain manpower. This leads to over-high wages and excessive demands from the workers, which constitute an unbearable charge on industry. The problem would inevitably be solved by the importation of foreign labour which would accept the lower standards needed for the maintenance of industry and the export markets.

(4) The demand for full employment is a Utopian socialist doctrine which has the effect of robbing the employer of the fruits of his industry. In the long run, it leads to the export of industry and the ruin of the home economy. It is to be noted that Labour governments which have upheld it in theory have never put it fully into practice.

(5) The development of automation was causing redundancies which had already negated the doctrine of full employment, long before the effects of the latest international economic crises would have made this inevitable in any case. Insistence on the employment of unnecessary workers is as reactionary as the attitude of the machine wreckers in the industrial revolution.

(See also *Unemployment, State Remedy for.*)

Gambling, Morality of

Pro: (1) Gambling is a natural human trait and is only to be condemned if carried to excess. Its

Con: (1) An evil that is old is not therefore to be condoned. Gambling may be a legacy from the animism of

suppression would lead to the emergence of something worse, just as the suppression of alcoholic drinks is followed by graver evils.

(2) Love of sport is an important national characteristic and is inevitably accompanied by some degree of gambling, because both rest on the same psychological basis. It is part of the average man's make-up to enjoy taking risks, and the taking of risks is the essence of gambling.

(3) When a man can afford to gamble, no harm whatever is done. If he gambles when he cannot afford to do so, the fault is personal to him and does not imply that the same actions by other people are a fault in them.

(4) Gambling adds an element of excitement to people's lives, which in the conditions of modern civilisation tend to be dull and uninteresting. By keeping alive the hope of personal improvement, which is difficult of attainment nowadays by more austere methods, it helps to prevent discontent and recourse to more harmful activities.

(5) In commerce, an element of gambling is essential and beneficial.

(6) Parliament has already recognised that it would be impossible to suppress gambling and, instead, has formulated plans to make practical use of this universal human instinct by establishing lotteries (following the success of the Premium Bond draw). Gamblers would thus be contributing to the public finances instead of supporting bookmakers and football pool promoters.

primitive man, but civilisation's task is to raise man above the primitive.

(2) True sport is damaged by gambling. The essence of gambling is to get something for nothing. Gamblers actually endeavour to avoid risks (though usually quite in vain) by relying on 'tips', 'exclusive information', 'systems', and other specious devices.

(3) Gambling is mere waste of effort, producing no addition to the community's wealth but increasing its inefficiency, misery and degradation. Its spread among women has had a pernicious effect on home life.

(4) The evil of gambling is that it distorts clearness of thought and helps people to avoid facing the more unpleasant realities of life.

They would be far better employed in making personal efforts to improve their condition of life than in relying on illusory hopes of unearned wealth to achieve it for them.

(5) Trade which aims at getting a benefit for oneself by doing service to others is quite dissimilar from gambling. Speculation, which is true gambling, should be suppressed.

(6) In countenancing such immoral practices, the Government is abdicating from its proper function, which is the leadership of the people. It has been officially estimated that, in 1974, betting on horses, dogs, gaming machines, bingo and football pools, in Britain, amounted to the huge sum of £2,437 million – or nearly half the total budget for education throughout the UK that year. One can readily imagine the benefits that money wasted on gambling would bring if devoted to more productive purposes.

(See also *Lotteries*.)

Homosexuals, Social Recognition of

Pro: (1) Recent legislation, with its acceptance of homosexual relations between 'consenting adults', while maintaining strong measures against suborning of the young, has freed homosexuals from the previous excessive social stigma and from the dangers of blackmail and other evils. But more needs to be done if they are to have true equality in law. The necessary social recognition can be achieved by educating the public to realise that homosexuality itself is not a perversion but as natural to its subjects as is heterosexuality to the majority.

(2) Probably the greatest step forward in securing social recognition, though it would obviously take time to condition the British public to accept it, is to permit marriages between homosexuals – on the same terms as marriages between consenting heterosexual couples. Such ceremonies have already taken place between homosexual males in the Netherlands and, after the initial indignation from some sections of the population had subsided, no consequent harm has been apparent to that nation's social structure.

(3) All humans have some of the genes of the opposite sex, to greater or lesser extent. The more these genes are out of balance, the more the likelihood of homosexuality. The individual can in no way be blamed for this situation. In extreme cases, there is the problem of 'transsexuals' – people wrongly classified at birth. Another important reform required is for such victims to be able to obtain the necessary remedial treatment, free, under the NHS. This should include surgical rectification, hormone treatment and, above all, social rectification (i.e. teaching them the habits and attitudes of the other sex to which they should

Con: (1) As so often happens with the problems of minorities, the fuss made over them has assumed far larger proportions than the concern expressed over many other, more serious issues. Since practising homosexuals were freed from the threat of criminal proceedings (provided their relationships were conducted in private and did not imperil young people), there has been ever-increasing publicity about them, with 'gay' comedians on television, the publication of 'gay' newspapers, and the rest of it. All this is surely social recognition enough – if not too much.

(2) One of the prime purposes of marriage is procreation – which obviously cannot apply among homosexuals. There is no longer any legal bar on them living together, if they wish, and many of them do so throughout most of their adult lives and are regarded by friends as though they were in fact married. But to consecrate the relationship with a formal marriage ceremony would be a hideous travesty.

(3) Psychiatric and other treatment is already available through the NHS for those deemed to need it and willing to have it. As for the so-called 'sex change' operations, it is highly doubtful whether any of them are more than partially successful, at best. In the vast majority of these cases, to judge by the appearance and demeanour of subjects who have gone out of their way to vaunt their new identities in public, the changes wrought seem relatively superficial – sometimes distasteful, often pathetic.

(4) To cite the practices of former civilisations is entirely irrelevant. Otherwise, if we were to accept them as precedents for our own standards of social behaviour, it would be

properly belong). At present, few can afford the high cost of such treatment from private doctors.

(4) In some ancient civilisations, bi-sexuality was regarded as the norm; relations between opposite sexes were necessary for procreation, but those between the same sex were held to be the source of true love. Most of such civilisations were renowned for their prowess in the arts, literature and philosophy. Today, too, homosexuals continue to make outstanding contributions in these and many other fields, and it is accepted that they have as much talent to offer as any 'normal' person – and often more.

hard to argue against the merits of chastity belts or the *droit de seigneur*! It is understandable that the feminine traits in male homosexuals should give them particular interest and fulfilment in such work as dress design, interior decorating and other artistic fields; but there are many more 'normal' people working in these fields who are just as talented – though they may not make such a fuss about it.

Immigration:
Should The Present Restrictions Be Lifted?

Pro: (1) Britain always prided herself in the past on holding her doors open to the needy and to victims of oppression from other countries. Protestants from France, Jews from most European countries, refugees from Poland, Hungary and other parts of Eastern Europe, and workers from every Commonwealth country . . . all these have already enriched our economy and our social and cultural life. Since the early 1960s, successive restrictions have been imposed to stop the big post-war increase in the influx of immigrants. But experience has proved that most of the fears which led to these restrictions were ill-founded, and we should now return to a more liberal policy again.

(2) Beginning with Malaysia and Singapore in the 1950s, Tory administrations offered British passports to minorities which might be discriminated against when former colonies became independent. (The practice continued right up to the independence of Aden in 1967.)

Con: (1) The welcoming of immigrants was reasonable when the population was relatively small and industrial opportunities were increasing rapidly. Britain has now reached a stage when the population is already too large for comfort. Even before the economic recession of the mid-1970s, industry had ceased to expand at anything like its previous rate; and, in the pressure for jobs, it is inevitable that recently arrived immigrants find it difficult to get work or are among the first to be laid off, swelling the unemployment burden. The net rate of (non-white) Commonwealth immigration soared from 60,000 in 1960 to 130,000 in 1961 and 170,000 in 1962. Clearly, this was more than the country could easily absorb; hence the 1962 Act, which resulted in the rate dropping to 50,000 the following year. This was still generous enough, while causing fewer problems for all concerned.

(2) The chief motive for the 1962 Act was not so much to ease the

By 1968, as a result, there were 400,000 Asians throughout the world who had the right of entry to Britain as full British citizens. Through our ensuing legislation, however, we have reneged on our promise to many of these people. We have a moral obligation – and should keep our word to them.

(3) The 1968 Bill, which came into force on 1 March of that year as the Commonwealth Immigrants Act, was pushed through Parliament in less than a week. Two years later, in a case before the European Commission of Human Rights, the British Government admitted that this Act was racially discriminatory in 'intention and effect'.

(4) Recent history shows that Britain is perfectly able to take a higher rate of Commonwealth immigration, if the political will is there. The general trend in the rate is still downwards: 38,219 in 1971; 25,633 in 1973. But in the intervening year, 1972, the total shot up to 62,506, because that was the year we accepted some 25,000 Asians expelled from Uganda. Although emergency arrangements had to be made initially, the great majority of the Ugandan Asians settled in very quickly. In terms of any extra strain on jobs, accommodation, schools, etc., the higher intake caused far fewer difficulties than had been anticipated – proving that we *could* successfully absorb a bigger total each year, on a regular basis, than the numbers allowed in at present.

(5) It took years to persuade the British Government to remove such anomalies as the double standard for male and female immigrants, whereby husbands allowed entry were entitled to bring in their wives with them but, previously, wives were not entitled to bring in their husbands. However, several injustices remain. For instance, in India, Pakistan and Bangladesh, dependants seeking to

pressure on space and resources, caused by the huge increase in immigration in the preceding 2–3 years, but more because the uncontrolled influx presented too great a risk of straining race relations. Subsequent legislation against race discrimination, as well as the work of the Race Relations Board and the efforts of local community officers, will serve as proof that the original concern about the size of the problem to be tackled was well founded.

(3) This particular Act was introduced to reduce the sudden huge increase in the flow of East African Asians – particularly from Kenya, which had just embarked on 'Africanisation', thus depriving many of the Asian inhabitants of their former means of livelihood. As with all other British legislation on the subject, however, the purpose was not to bar the door completely to immigrants – merely to cut the rate to a level we could cope with. That precaution remains necessary to this day.

(4) The Ugandan Asians were a special case. Victims of political blackmail, they faced danger not only to their property but possibly even to their lives (which had not been the case in Kenya, for instance). But their reception, on humanitarian grounds, necessitated the establishment of special camps and many other costly and difficult arrangements which could certainly not become a regular feature of our immigration procedure. Even though there was a specific campaign on the Ugandan Asians' behalf, the task of resettling such a big additional influx took a good while longer than had been hoped.

(5) Steps have now been taken to hasten immigration procedures in these countries (and to revise the list of questions asked). One cause of the delay is the need to sort out fake applications from the genuine. Many

join heads of families already settled in Britain are having to wait up to four years for a first interview with British officials. Even then, the red tape of documentary proof and checking can mean a wait of another 2–3 years before would-be immigrants receive their entry permits. There have also been complaints that some of the questions asked by immigration officers are misleading or irrelevant – even dealing with such unlikely topics as chickens, oxen and string beds.

(6) The contribution made to the British economy by Commonwealth immigrants in recent years has been invaluable. They have filled the least popular jobs in public transport, industry, public health services and many other fields. A large proportion of doctors and nurses in our hospitals are of Commonwealth origin – and without them, many hospitals would have had to close. Transport authorities often claim that they are obliged to run fewer bus or underground services than in former years because they cannot get enough staff. That is just one example of Britain's national needs which a sensible easing of the immigration restrictions would help us to fulfil.

supposed 'dependants' turn out to be no relation of the person concerned (i.e. the immigrant already in Britain). There have also been many cases of couples arranging to become engaged, at long distance, to permit one to join the other over here; then, once the formalities have thus been circumvented, the engagement is broken off. ... The plain fact remains that the Government has undertaken to admit all genuine dependants as soon as possible and, over the next few years, the number admitted from India, Pakistan and Bangladesh is likely to rise to more than 20,000 annually – double the present rate.

(6) The answer to staff shortages in the hospital service should be to make its conditions and incentives more attractive to our own people, not to rely on those from abroad who are more willing to accept its low pay and other drawbacks. Without dwelling on the aggravation of the housing problem, the creation of bad feeling in communities where it was previously almost unknown, and the allegations of immigrants' contribution to the rise in crime (which have probably been exaggerated), one fact is salient: in 1970, the last year for which authoritative figures are available at present, the United Kingdom's coloured population was about 1,300,000. Even at that level – and it has certainly grown appreciably since then – the figure represented well over 2 per cent of the total population. In other European countries which have been praised for their enlightenment in accepting large-scale immigration from their former colonial territories – notably, France and the Netherlands – the equivalent percentage is nothing like as high as ours.

(See also *The 'Brain Drain'*; *British Commonwealth: Is It a Reality?*)

Indeterminate Sentences for Professional Criminals

Pro: (1) There is a small class of prisoners, the professional criminals, who consist of formidable offenders, men who are physically fit, who take to crime by preference, decline all normal work and, unlike the habitual criminal whose offences are of less gravity, are not amenable to reform. They should be sentenced to an indeterminate period of imprisonment (i.e. without a specified date for its conclusion, within the criminal's probable lifespan).

(2) These offenders should not be released until they have given satisfactory proofs of such an improvement in character as would make it safe to the community for them to be at large again. They can be observed by competent experts, who could arrive at accurate decisions. There is no need to detain them in prisons proper; penal colonies would be suitable for the purpose.

(3) Whether the aim of punishment is the protection of society or the reformation of the criminal, there is no justification for keeping a man in prison after he could safely be released. The indeterminate nature of the sentence would be maintained only as long as it were not safe to free the man.

(4) To prevent abuses, a maximum period can be fixed. This is probably desirable while the system is in the experimental stage. Preventive detention gives greater scope for education and remedial training than penal servitude or hard labour, which it replaces.

(5) The criminal of this type should be treated exactly as persons suffering from epidemic disease, who are isolated to prevent them from injuring society.

(6) Where tried, as in some parts

Con: (1) Except, perhaps, in the degree of their offences, there is no real difference between the habitual and the professional criminal. Provision is already made for incorrigible offenders to receive long sentences (8–10 years) after a certain number of convictions, even if their ultimate crime was relatively minor, and this has been undeniably successful as a deterrent. The cry for indeterminate sentences is mainly an endeavour to avoid thoroughgoing social and prison reform.

(2) Conduct in prisons affords no proof of reform; most professional criminals show exemplary behaviour while in jail. Indeterminate sentences would give an impetus to religious hypocrisy. Jail conditions render psychological examination difficult; freedom is the only condition under which we can accurately judge of character.

(3) The indeterminate sentence would, in practice, always become a long-period sentence, thus robbing the criminal of hope, if he does reform, and lessening the chances of him being willing to reform.

(4) Such sentences infringe the liberty of society and good government. Men serving indeterminate sentences would be put entirely at the mercy of a few officials, without check or criticism from the community.

(5) There is no analogy between disease and criminal acts; disease is not punished. Society must be just even in protecting itself.

(6) The indeterminate sentence in the USA is imposed, more often than not, on the less professional of criminals, who are still thought to have a chance of redeeming themselves.

of the USA, it has worked well. One advantage is that it prevents criminals from making plans with fellow prisoners to participate in the commission of new crimes on the expiry of sentence.

(7) Prisoners under indeterminate sentence could still be released provisionally, on parole. A system of after-care should be developed to deal with these, as other cases.

(7) This would be an unfair risk for the community. There are already Discharged Prisoners' Aid Societies.

(See also *Prison Reform*.)

Individualism

Pro: (1) Government exists for the sole purpose of defending the lives and property of citizens. All other duties, e.g. control of education and the country's economic services, should be left to individuals.

(2) By their very nature, Government offices and State undertakings are never, even in the simplest matters, so well or so economically managed as a private business run for profit; they are inevitably more governed by routine and red tape.

(3) As Government has to rely on taxation, it follows that the more duties it undertakes, the more heavily they weigh on taxation, thus depressing industry while restricting private enterprise. Whereas the capitalist pays for his own mistakes, the cost of Government mistakes is borne by the taxpayers.

(4) In trying to run enterprises for profit, the Government lays an indirect tax on industry, raising money by indirect means.

(5) History is one standing protest against the folly of overlegislation, even though most of such legislation was undertaken with the most excellent motives. The best legislative work of this country is that which

Con: (1) If Government confines itself to protection against robbery, violence and petty dishonesty, citizens are still exposed to robbery and maltreatment by the growth of economic forces which remain within the strict letter of the law.

(2) While many anti-individualists would agree that the State has committed mistakes in the running of enterprises, most State organisations never reveal such scandals of mismanagement, inefficiency, not to say corruption, as are found in big private concerns. This is proved, for instance, by the latter-day failure of private enterprise to cope satisfactorily with railway traffic and the coal and cotton industries. Big private undertakings are equally notorious for red tape, often to an even greater extent. If State enterprise is so badly managed, why did its private competitors complain about its menace to them?

(3) Governments should be concerned with service, not with profits. If the capitalist fails, the people who pay for his mistakes are his creditors and shareholders.

(4) Would not the profits of a private company cost as much to industry, while the Government

has freed us from the legislative enactments of previous centuries.

(6) The more we increase the number of indictable offences, the more criminals we create (often needlessly) and the more corruption we render possible.

(7) The more Government undertakes, the more it checks that wholesome spirit of self-help which once carried the English-speaking races to the foremost position in the world. The British Empire was won for us entirely by the energy of individuals, despite the blunders of various governments.

(8) Government interference tends to preserve the less fit members of society against the workings of natural selection and thus to lower the standard of society. Overdependence on Government is a sign of weakening fibre. It was a potent factor in bringing about the decline of Roman civilisation. Every tendency for people to initiate enterprises for themselves should be encouraged.

(9) The rule of the majority is not any less a restriction on the freedom of individuals than that of kings, aristocrats or plutocrats.

(10) The strength of Britain in the past was due to the triumphs of private enterprise. If the country is to remain strong, it must free itself from the recent additions to Government control. However necessary such control may appear as a temporary measure, its evils are shown by the muddles and contradictions into which the various government departments get themselves.

would have to take just as much in taxation?

(5) History is a record of the sacrifice of the economically weak to the economically strong and of the ruin of industry and resources in the interests of immediate profits for a small section of the community.

(6) Even when laws are not completely successful, the conditions after they come into operation are infinitely to be preferred to those existing before; the Factory Acts are an example.

(7) Good legislation adds to the freedom of the subject. Association, of which the State is one form, is a more potent force than individualism or self-help. The natural trend of industry is towards association; the trade union has rescued its members from the miseries that resulted from freedom of contract.

(8) The most 'fit' are not necessarily the best; the 'less fit' secure their survival by association, and collectively are just as successful as the powerful individual. The power of association is one more weapon in the struggle for existence.

(9) In a democracy, the rights of all get a place; as it is not a homogeneous group, it tends to accommodation and elasticity. No one should have the right to cause suffering to his fellow men, either directly through the infliction of violence or indirectly through economic and moral coercion.

(10) The inadequacy of individualism was proved in the Second World War, when many firms were taken over by the government to ensure efficient running, industry and labour had to be inspected and directed, and the Food Ministry assumed most of the functions of private distribution. The nationalised railways and coal mines needed many years to clear up the muddle and inefficiency of unrestricted private enterprise.

Industrial Expansion

Pro: (1) A steady increase (overall) in industrial output, and thus in trade between the nations, is necessary for the world's economic survival and for raising the living standards of all the world's peoples. Cyclical ups-and-downs are inevitable, but the general trend must always be towards expansion. The economic crises caused in the Western world by the actions of the Arab oil-producing nations, after the Middle East war of October, 1973, demonstrate the chaos which can result when this trend is thrown out of balance by abnormal factors. Nevertheless, it was only a matter of time before industry began to adapt itself to the new conditions and resume its former progress.

(2) At the present rate of increase, the world's population is expected to double, to 8,000 million, within the next 35 years. (See *Birth Control*.) Only by expanding the production of industry – notably, for example, in such fields as housing, transport, textiles, and all the farm machinery, chemicals, and so on, for the necessary growth in agricultural output, as well as future undersea farming – can we hope to meet the essential requirements for this huge populace. The process of industrial expansion will also be crucial, in itself, for providing the extra inhabitants with enough jobs.

(3) To husband the world's natural mineral deposits, scientists have long been investigating alternative materials in place of various metals, etc., and new methods of creating energy, which, similarly, will not use up existing resources. Without industrial expansion, in its broadest sense, such alternatives cannot be developed adequately to fulfil even our present needs. Moreover, it is the only way to

Con: (1) Ever since the Industrial Revolution, expansion has been pursued for its own sake and there has been wide acceptance of the erroneous belief that industry and national economies alike would collapse unless they continued to grow. But there is clear evidence that, in many cases, the need is for contraction rather than expansion. As a result of the oil crisis, for example, it is doubtful if the motor manufacturing industry will ever be the same again, either in its total volume of production or in the nature of the vehicles it turns out, which will have to become generally more economic in fuel consumption than hitherto. Far from being undesirable, such a rationalisation of the industry heightens the possibilities of reducing pollution, reversing the continual worsening of traffic congestion, making better use of existing resources, and forcing the introduction of a proper, comprehensive transport policy.

(2) The real problems to be tackled are over-population and the stark fact that the world's natural resources are *finite*. If the present extravagant increase in consumption continues unabated, all known oil deposits will be exhausted within the first half of the 21st century, as may important metals like copper. Instead of the spendthrift industrial expansion now encouraged, we should be seeking new ways to lessen the scale of demand, as a deliberate policy – before the pressures of over-population bring it about in any case. With increasing automation certain to reduce the overall proportion of jobs, in the long run, one of the big tasks for the future will be to educate people into using the greater leisure made available to them.

ensure that the benefits are shared among all peoples. If the level of world industry remained comparatively static – not merely in manufacturing but in related fields like energy supply and communications – the inevitable consequence would be simply to widen still more the existing gap between the rich and poor nations.

(4) Increased trade among nations with otherwise deeply opposed political and social systems is always conducive to the maintenance of peace between them. It was crucial in helping to end the East–West 'cold war'. Any industrial expansion which permits a growth in this trade, thereby facilitating the improvement of relations between the power blocs, is surely to be welcomed – it's to everyone's advantage.

(5) In modern conditions, 'biggest is best' – greater efficiency, a wider range of products made available to more people, and cheaper prices.

(6) (Some) The biggest drive for the creation and building up of industry nowadays is in the Third World – the developing nations striving to achieve economic self-sufficiency and to start remedying the pernicious imbalance between themselves and the major industrialised powers. Are we to deny them that right?

(3) The search for alternatives is all too often along the wrong lines. In Britain, for instance, the rivalry for custom between the two nationalised energy suppliers, gas and electricity, is illogical and wasteful. It is a prime illustration that – quite apart from the future possibilities of harnessing inexpensive new sources like solar energy – the expansion of these particular industries, to meet anticipated consumption levels, could not only be avoided (by a coherent joint energy policy) but is actually unnecessary. The heedless acceptance of supposed 'progress', for its own sake, bedevils fields like transport, too. Instead of hideously expensive jet planes, it would be much cheaper and less pollutive to use airships for international freight-carrying purposes; internally, we could make far greater use of our inland waterways for transport between industrial centres, rather than continue to despoil the dwindling countryside with new motorways for the benefit of the juggernauts. If the pace of industrial production becomes somewhat slower and we have to make do with less as a result, then that is – quite simply – the price we must pay for mankind's survival.

(4) When a nation exports some of its skills, products or raw materials (exchanging them, in effect, for others it lacks), these are usually surplus to its domestic requirements and do not necessitate any expansion of its existing industry for the purpose. In some cases, notably in 'planned economy' countries, emphasis on foreign trade is at the expense of consumers at home; certain governments would do better to concentrate first on making fuller use of their *present* resources to meet unfulfilled demands within their own countries.

(5) On the contrary, many big industrial concerns are now recog-

nising that a return to smaller units produces greater efficiency and is often the best way to satisfy local needs.

(6) (Some) It is only natural that developing countries should wish to end the economic dominance of their former colonisers. But attempts to make an immediate, massive increase in their own manufacturing industries are not necessary to achieve this. Usually, the principal wealth of such countries lies in their raw materials – which, in colonial times, were acquired by the capitalist nations at the cheapest possible prices. The first priority should be for the developing countries to receive a fair return for the resources they do possess. Through multi-lateral international agreements – and not by such unilateral decisions as were imposed by the Arab oil-producing nations, which threw everything out of gear – they should be guaranteed higher (and stable) prices for their raw materials in world markets.

Industrial Psychology, Applied

Pro: (1) The essential idea of Scientific Management – that the processes and conditions of production (including salesmanship) are capable of being improved by systematic study – is a sound one. Industrial psychologists have realised the shortcomings of the generality of Efficiency Experts and the great advantage of their work is that they look upon the problems chiefly from the human point of view.

(2) Industrial psychologists aim first and foremost at improving the conditions under which workers operate, so that unnecessary strains, whether due to physical fatigue, mental boredom or emotional antagonisms, e.g. between foremen and

Con: (1) Industrial psychologists are merely Scientific Managers and Efficiency Experts under another name. They are aiming almost exclusively at making the worker more efficient within the capitalist system. They expect to increase 'productivity', i.e. more output per man. In the long term, though, the net result will be a reduction of working staffs and more unemployment.

(2) One of the most important factors in industry is the question of incentives. The supporters of this movement rely on it to save the industrial system from the consequences of its imperfections. Industrial psychologists necessarily

workers, may be eliminated. They take no side in disputes between employer and employed; all they are concerned with is that the knowledge at the disposal of the community which relates to these problems shall be applied and extended. In doing this, they have achieved excellent results, though the study is still incompletely developed. Even in a Communist State, industrial psychology would be needed.

have to work under the conditions imposed by these flaws, heightening the suspicion with which they are regarded by most of the employees for whom they prescribe. The beneficial results are therefore likely to be small, but industrial psychology's semblance of concern for the welfare of the workers no doubt consoles those who believe that, with trifling adjustments, the present system is satisfactory and likely to be permanent.

(See also *Scientific Management*.)

The Initiative

Pro: (1) The Initiative, under which on the demand of a given number of the electorate, a government must examine a certain question and make proposals for dealing with it, is the nearest approach yet made to the ideal State in which the whole body of the people makes its own laws. (It is usually combined with the Referendum.)

(2) The Initiative is necessary to save a country from the stagnation caused by party quarrels and the possibility of a government's deliberately shirking vital problems. It affords the opportunity of getting important questions discussed without forcing any political party to commit itself to any particular solution.

(3) In Switzerland, the Initiative has had a remarkable success, as is proved by its adoption for both federal and cantonal purposes. The Initiative, coupled with the Referendum and the Recall, has also achieved success and popularity in more than a score of States in the USA.

Con: (1) The theory on which the Initiative is based is bad. The State should depend on intelligent conceptions of progress steadily applied, not on bursts of public enthusiasm which may well be ill-informed or whipped up spuriously.

(2) The Initiative lowers the responsibility of legislators, who feel that, if anything goes wrong, it is not their fault. The tyranny of party government is not restricted when the Initiative is not combined with a Referendum, because the government can then pass whatever legislation on the subject it wishes. Even if the two are combined, the government will usually get its way, since the Referendum tends to be conservative in outcome.

(3) The practical effect of the Initiative is small. It may work in the special conditions of a small, multi-lingual country like Switzerland, but not in those of bigger States. In the USA, the application of direct popular sovereignty has not resulted either in great social advance or in the reinforcement of liberty.

(See also *The Referendum, More Use of*; *Recall of Representatives*; *Delegation v. Representation*.)

Intelligence Tests

Pro: (1) Tests of the capacities of children and adults, where used, and decisions as to the kind of work for which they are most fitted, formerly depended entirely on unscientific and stereotyped examinations. It is now widely conceded that such examinations are inadequate, and intelligence tests are generally used to supplement them. There is a strong argument for abolishing written examinations altogether, at some stages, and for using intelligence tests in their place. They are already used at all stages of primary education to provide an index of the child's potentialities.

(2) In adult life, manual dexterity, memory, reasoning powers, swift reaction to sensations, etc., are required to varying degrees in many different occupations. The crude guesswork on which employers have had to rely in the past for information about their work-people has put many square pegs in round holes, with unfortunate results to both employer and employed. Intelligence tests have been used with great success in the armed forces to determine the kind of jobs for which men are best suited.

(3) Intelligence tests do not claim to be character tests, but the fact that they do not deal with every side of life is no reason to ignore their application to the sides they do test.

(4) There are so many different versions of these tests that the danger of students 'boning up' all the answers beforehand is negligible.

(5) That intelligence tests are remarkably accurate is proved, for example, by the fact that the results of the tests applied to the American Army by Columbia University examiners gave a grading of the soldiers almost identical with that

Con: (1) The use of written examinations is admittedly limited, but no adequate case has been made out for their abolition, especially in the higher levels of education. They are the only method of testing the acquisition of knowledge, the possession of which is even more important than the capacity to react quickly to situations where experts are required. Many intelligence tests have no conceivable relationship to the problems of school or of life.

(2) Trial and error, and experience, are the soundest tests for vocational suitability. Putting square pegs in round holes is almost always due to the rigidity of our economic system and labour market, whereby a young person entering one occupation is too often obliged to remain in it for the rest of his life. The result of an intelligence test may be rendered futile by the lack of jobs considered suitable for the examinees. Since production can never be correlated with the capacities of potential workers, promotion on the basis of the employer's judgment is the only satisfactory method of exploiting intelligence.

(3) These tests have the great shortcoming that they cannot test character – the qualities of initiative, hard work, determination, honesty, etc., which are more important in life and business than mere cleverness. Neither can they provide a fully reliable test of the all-important quality of power to grasp new ideas.

(4) Intelligence tests are limited in number and scope and can thus be made the subject of cramming.

(5) They frequently break down in practice, because, for a start, they set questions to which the examinee must answer yes or no, though the

given by the officers who had had the same men under them for many months.

(6) There is a strong case for their being included in entrance tests for all universities. This would eliminate the wastage arising from the admission of students who are capable only of cramming.

only intelligent answer is often long and qualified with all sorts of reservations. The testers often encounter resistance in adult examinees because of the apparent absurdity of the questions. Intelligence testing of soldiers ignores the qualities of endurance and courage which may be their most important assets.

(6) The wastage of university students is usually due to much more complex social or psychological causes.

International Auxiliary Languages

Pro: (1) In areas like the Mediterranean and India, common languages for communication between people speaking different tongues became widely accepted in the past to satisfy an obvious need. Latin was the international language of Europe for many centuries (and, within the Roman Catholic Church, is still used freely as a means of communication between church-people from different parts of the world). Commercial, political and social relations would be made easier by the adoption of an international auxiliary language.

(2) Esperanto and Ido are scientifically constructed languages, with flexible structure and the simplest grammar. They can be learned with ease by nearly everybody, arouse no national jealousies, and are not without literary possibilities.

(3) Basic English (consisting of a vocabulary of about 800 essential words with which any ideas can be expressed) is eminently suited to become an international language. It has obvious advantages over an artificial language and can be learnt in a very short time even by those ignorant of English.

(4) That Basic English should replace good normal English is not suggested. But there is no gainsaying

Con: (1) Enough people are able to learn the one or two other languages besides their own which enable the business of the world to be carried on successfully. The newspapers and news agencies already spread, through translation, more information about the world than can be properly assimilated. It is erroneous to argue that the ability to communicate with people of other lands will promote international understanding. For example, many French people are well acquainted with English, and many English with French, but they have rarely been able to comprehend the psychology of each other's country.

(2) For many purposes, English and French are international languages already. They have acquired qualities, in the course of centuries of growth, far superior to those which any artificial language could have.

(3) If only its absurd spelling were rationalised, English would rapidly become accepted as the world's prime international language, even by those nations which do not regard it as such already. Its grammar is less complicated than that of most other languages. In its excessive simplification, Basic English has lost

its value where a good working knowledge of English is required, without a great expenditure of time. Basic English has been used in schools in Denmark, Poland, Rumania, and Czechoslovakia, and is making headway in the East.

(5) In international affairs, the use of an international language would save an enormous waste of time and expense involved in the use of interpreters and translators. It would also tend to avoid many of the disagreements and irritating misunderstandings between statesmen and diplomats, a good proportion of which are certainly due to their insufficient knowledge of one another's languages. Now that diplomacy has become world-wide in its scope, and so highly publicised, the old-fashioned closed corporation of diplomatic exchange is out of date. Accordingly, a language in which all speakers have the same standing, thereby ensuring that none can suspect collusion between others speaking an alien language, is more than ever necessary.

most of the vigour of the true English tongue.

(4) Basic English can no doubt be learnt with ease. But language has a dual function. It should enable us not only to express our own thoughts but also to understand those of others. Students of Basic English may express themselves adequately in English but would be lost in trying to understand an Englishman who used a vocabulary going well beyond the 800 or so essential words of Basic English.

(5) The value of an interpreter is that he understands the idioms and turns of speech of a language as well as its more academic conceptions. Misunderstandings between statesmen would continue even if a common language were used, since they arise more from fundamental antagonisms in philosophy and interpretations of the meaning of words – and at times also from a clash of temperaments – than from any mechanical language difficulty. Many words are capable of different interpretations: for example, 'democracy', 'freedom', 'honour' – all words which occur frequently in international discussion. An artificial language would be equally unable to establish a definitive meaning for such words.

Internationalism

Pro: (1) Despite the upsurge of nationalism that marked the period between the wars of 1914 and 1939, it is clear that the struggle of the future will be between classes and ideologies and not between nations. Nationalism has become obsolete as a basis of political organisation, since the development of communications has begun to render the whole world an economic unit.

(2) The nation is not eternal. It

Con: (1) National rivalries and nationalism are more accentuated than ever. They transcend the class war, just as they destroy international agreements.

(2) The nation is a fundamental fact, and national patriotism is a persistent virtue. Nations may well form associations for their mutual economic benefit (for instance, the EEC), but each insists on retaining its individual identity.

has existed for only a few hundreds of years, originating in response to the economic needs and development of the time. It will probably remain always as a reflection of differences in culture and custom, though these are tending to lessen with the increase in international communication, but its part in the world will sink to that which the province, the county or the clan now plays in relation to the nation.

(3) The economic problems of most nations are similar. Hence, trade unionists and capitalists alike have been led to establish their own international organisations. The UN is a public recognition that isolation is an anachronism.

(4) A beginning has already been made in Europe with the EEC. Its first fruit, and probably the most important, was the abandonment of former national antagonisms between France and Germany.

(5) One example of the inevitability of internationalism is provided by the new African nations. They were mostly formed from territories arbitrarily thrown together by the economic needs of their conquerors, and their alignments are bound to be fluid.

(6) The advent of Socialism in some form or other, if only because all alternatives break down, will see the triumph of internationalism. General prosperity and culture will overcome the narrowness of nationalism.

(7) Internationalism is a noble creed to which all religions pay at least lip service. It must be the basis of world organisation if civilisation is to be saved from destruction by war and human folly. National differences are in reality no greater than those which often cause regional antagonisms within a country, and mutual tolerance can smooth them out.

(8) Internationalism is compatible

(3) The international organisations mentioned, especially those of labour and political groups, cannot become of really major importance until their members control all the nations to which they belong, which is impossible. International combines often operate by making agreements to respect national frontiers. The UN is an organisation of sovereign States and could not exist otherwise.

(4) The history of the EEC provides all too many examples of its member-nations fighting principally for their own economic interests. Their attitude to nations outside their own organisation has often tended to be restrictive and mistrustful; it is only very recently that they have evinced the least sign of anything approaching true internationalism (and even then, the professed intentions have yet to be borne out).

(5) That separatism and not association is fundamental is proved by the new African countries, several of which were split by separatist demands within a short time of gaining independence.

(6) It is by no means certain that Socialism will triumph. Nevertheless, if it does, the national divisions and national peculiarities will survive. This is recognised even by the Communists, whose gospel is internationalism. A series of Socialist or Communist societies might not even be so closely allied as to form a federation.

(7) Internationalism postulates an unprecedented change in human nature. Most religious sects are limited by national frontiers, and their adherents, while they might aspire to internationalism, do not generally attempt to practise it.

(Some) Internationalism is bad because it implies the continuance of national divisions. Cosmopolitanism – a single World State – is a preferable objective.

with true patriotism. It is only objected to by the 'my country, right or wrong' type of person.

(8) Internationalism in practice means anti-patriotism, and propaganda in its favour should be stopped.

(See also *United Nations Organisation*.)

Ireland:
Should Ulster Join Eire?

Pro: (1) Despite the sectarian violence and near-civil war in Ulster since the late 1960s – stemming from the Protestant majority's fears and the Roman Catholic minority's grievances – it is almost inevitable, historically, that the whole of Ireland will eventually be reunited. Recent events have set back progress towards this, obviously; whatever time it takes for passions to cool, though, some form of agreed reunion will be the only commonsense solution in the long run.

(2) The north-eastern part of Ulster was responsible in large measure for the disastrous history of the Irish nation after 1913. The Covenanters committed treason before the Nationalists and set an example for unconstitutional proceedings. Today, clearly, reunion would be impossible until law and order has been restored in the North; but this does not preclude measures aimed at progress towards it – with power-sharing as the first step, until mutual suspicions have been proved groundless.

(3) The existence of two governments in such a small island is absurd. Partition cannot be a permanent solution.

(4) If Ulster is as superior in wealth as its protagonists claim, it would naturally have the dominant economic role in a united Ireland rather than be despoiled and dominated.

Con: (1) The rest of Ireland is different in religion and race from the majority of Ulstermen. Northern Ireland's Protestants are implacably hostile to the dominating role played by the Catholic Church in Eire. Their belief that persecution, due to religious and political bigotry, would be their lot if they joined the Republic is reinforced by Eire's refusal to grant such elementary rights as facilities for divorce and its often absurd but rigid censorship of literature and culture generally.

(2) Ulster has deserved well of England, which it supported throughout two world wars with Germany – while Eire, by its neutrality in the last war, provided a home for enemy activities. Notwithstanding the fearful strains of recent times, the great majority of Ulster's people remain deeply loyal to the United Kingdom – and the strength of this emotional attachment must not be under-estimated as a factor in their opposition to joining Eire.

(3) Hard facts dictated partition in the early 1920s. They have not really changed.

(4) Ulster would remain in a minority, unable to resist the extirpation of the things it cherishes. It would also be looked on as the milch cow for reviving the decrepit finances of Eire.

(5) The nature of its industries differentiates Ulster from the rest of Ireland, connecting it more directly

(5) All Ireland was an economic unit before political exigencies of the time led to what was then intended as a temporary official separation; neither side can be assured of future prosperity until they form such a unit again. The thousands of workers who now leave Eire to work abroad in England could be retained to build up the country's industry if the economy of Ireland as a whole were reintegrated.

(6) The Unionist question kept Ulster's industrial workers years behind the industrial workers of Great Britain, in conditions and ideas, and imposed a near-authoritarian rule on the country. With a united Ireland, Ulster's workers would soon be in the van of reform and playing a key part in the maintenance of political democracy.

with Glasgow, with the textile and engineering districts of England, and with England's international trade. The agricultural South has nothing to offer which would compensate for the cutting of this connection.

(6) Ulster's comparative prosperity was due to the steadiness and efficiency of its workers and traders – legacies of their Protestantism and Scottish extraction. Union with Eire would mean the levelling-down of Ulster, not the levelling-up of all Ireland. Allegedly undemocratic forms of government in the province, before the outbreak of the present troubles, were Ulster's only protection against subversive propaganda from Eire and the terrorist means used to secure its ends. This is borne out by the fact that, even though measures had already been agreed to iron out inequities of which the Catholic minority complained, the extremists gave them no chance to take effect before resorting to armed violence.

Jury System

Pro: (1) A man has a right to be tried by his peers, and twelve ordinary men are more likely to arrive at the truth than a single judge, however capable.

(2) Misdirection of the jury by the judge is dealt with by the appeal courts and any errors can be corrected there.

(3) In all cases where the credit of either party to a suit is at issue, the jury is the best tribunal, for it estimates better the effect on public opinion.

(4) The system has always worked well. It was established to abolish flagrant abuses, and jurymen have time and again enforced justice despite powerful pressure on them. The system should not be abolished

Con: (1) An innocent man would, in nine cases out of ten, prefer to be tried by a judge than by a jury, because he would be appealing to a higher order of intelligence – and, more especially, to a trained intelligence.

(2) In all cases that are not straightforward, juries are at the mercy of the judges and are therefore useless.

(3) Whatever the merits of the jury system in criminal proceedings, these do not apply to civil proceedings. Certain verdicts delivered by juries in civil cases in recent years were notoriously unjust and stemmed from sheer prejudice and ignorance.

(4) As a rule, the jury is influenced by one dominant personality. It is

as it is the chief bulwark of the common man against legal sharp dealing.

(5) The jury system, at times when legislation lags behind the social conscience, enables juries to force the hand of the legislature by refusing to find a verdict in accordance with unjust laws. In this way, the abolition of the death penalty for stealing was obtained.

(6) A jury is often better able to form a correct opinion upon facts connected with the daily life of the working classes than a judge, who has only academic knowledge. The judge, who is usually of advanced years, is likely to be more prejudiced than a jury of a dozen different persons.

(7) The process of explaining a case fully to a jury often elucidates facts which would otherwise be overlooked. Knowledge is rarely complete until it has been expressed.

(8) A judge has too much to do, e.g. he cannot take notes and at the same time carefully watch witnesses. He is more likely to be impressed by documentary than by oral evidence.

(9) Trial by a single judge or by a small group of selected experts, instead of by a jury, can never give ordinary people the same guarantees of justice as trial by their peers. It is certain, too, that experts from different fields, serving on a panel of this kind, would frequently disagree.

also well known that a judge's summing up, however impartial in appearance or intention, will often indicate his own views between the lines – and few juries ever take a contrary view.

(5) Though the object of criminal proceedings is not to ventilate grievances but to administer the law, it is to be noticed that juries failed to check the multiplication of death sentences on frivolous grounds during the eighteenth century, and that judges, too, have contributed to social progress by their rulings.

(6) Juries are apt to be prejudiced, especially if they are susceptible to public opinion, which is often wrong. People serving on a jury are not required to have a wide knowledge of the subtleties of character, with the result that their verdict often depends less on the facts than on the unfavourable or favourable appearances given by those in the case.

(7) Appeals to emotion constitute part of the stock-in-trade of lawyers, who are well aware of the susceptibilities of jurymen. Judges are harder to move and pay more regard to facts.

(8) Juries are quite incompetent to weigh evidence. That is a laborious and technical process. They are more taken in by superficialities and by oral testimony, which makes a greater impression than documentary evidence and is easier to follow.

(9) The alternative to a jury system is not necessarily trial by a single judge. A group of experts in law and psychology, with, perhaps, one or two ordinary citizens, would be more satisfactory than either.

(See also the next article; *Indeterminate Sentences for Professional Criminals.*)

Justices of the Peace:
Should They Be Replaced By Stipendiary Magistrates?

Pro: (1) Our courts of summary jurisdiction are entirely inadequate for the business with which they have to deal. Most crimes committed in this country are tried before them. Every year, Justices of the Peace, sitting in about a thousand courts, deal with about more than half a million non-indictable offences. They also deal with a small residue of more serious crimes in proceedings for committal for trial. A body of men dealing with work of such importance should be above suspicion of prejudice or incompetence. Stipendiary magistrates properly qualified for the task (already employed in London and some of the larger towns) should everywhere replace the voluntary JPs.

(2) Many of the voluntary magistrates have scant knowledge of law or legal procedure, and most of them make little attempt to acquire such knowledge.

(3) Many magistrates – perhaps a third of the total number – never attend the courts at all; and of those who do attend, many are old and deaf, careless of fact, and warped by prejudice.

(4) Many voluntary magistrates are far too ready to accept police evidence against the man in the dock.

(5) Another serious objection to the present system is the extraordinary diversity and inconsistency shown in the decisions and sentences of the various courts.

(6) The present system has been tolerated so long only because the people coming before the courts of summary jurisdiction were, on the whole, without influence or social standing. Now that motoring

Con: (1) It is not necessary to appoint stipendiary magistrates for all police courts. Our voluntary Justices of the Peace are perfectly capable of dealing with the type of case that comes before them. Proceedings for committal for trial are merely formal. The voluntary magistrates are on the whole both conscientious and respected, and the British public is satisfied that it gets justice, even if legal technicalities are sometimes waived in favour of common sense.

(2) There is always a Clerk of the Court – usually a trained solicitor – who can be consulted on any legal points which are too technical for a magistrate himself to deal with. The judicial authorities have also instituted training courses for magistrates and provide other guidance to help them in their task.

(3) A good number of Benches are already too large for efficiency and a reduction in the number of magistrates attending is, in fact, desirable. A Bench of from three to five magistrates is quite enough.

(4) Naturally, magistrates vary in competence, but the best of them are fair-minded and painstaking, and quite able to secure fair play.

(5) It would be possible to raise the standard of efficiency, without departing from the voluntary system, by a different method of appointment. Justices of the Peace should not be selected, as still too often happens, for their political views and services, but for judicial qualities and suitability for office. Efforts to achieve reasonable consistency of sentencing feature promi-

offences form the bulk of the work dealt with, the position has altered and dissatisfaction is widely expressed.

(7) Appeals have been relatively rare, not because justice is done but because appeals involve expense which few can afford and would usually cost very much more than the fine imposed.

nently in the official guidance magistrates already receive.

(6) If the voluntary magistrates have been able to deal out justice to the poorer classes, the same treatment should be good enough for motorists, who are in any case now drawn from all sections of the community.

(7) That the smaller courts do their work satisfactorily is shown by the relative rarity of appeals against their decisions.

Land, Nationalisation of

Pro: (1) Land differs totally in kind from all other kinds of property, inasmuch as its value is not the result of human labour, which alone constitutes a valid claim to property of any sort.

(2) Land is limited in quantity but is essential to all.

(3) Land is still concentrated in the hands of a relatively small proportion of the population who constitute a near-monopolistic body, having undue economic, political and social power. They exact ever-higher prices for use of their land but spend as little as possible on behalf of their tenants.

(4) The private ownership of land (other than owner-occupied land, of reasonable size) is a menace to the health, comfort and prosperity of the community. There is no such thing as an indefeasible right in property.

(5) Most of the country's largest landowners today have done nothing to earn the land for themselves. Often, their ancestors stole it from the common people and previous owners.

(6) The present land system is the ruin of agriculture. It motivates against the most efficient large-scale farming and equally against peasant proprietorship. The agricultural

Con: (1) Land has no value unless human labour has brought it into cultivation or built on it or exploited it.

(2) Land is no more limited or essential than capital or food. All commodities are limited. Land plays a less important part in the country's economy than it did a century ago.

(3) The landlord monopoly is not so complete as is imagined. There are many small owners, especially since the practice of buying houses and land on mortgage from building societies has become general. (It is estimated that some 50 per cent of British families now live in their 'own' homes, in this sense.) The large estate is more generously managed than the small one, and tenants are treated better.

(4) Land nationalisation is a gross interference with the natural right of private property.

(5) The enclosure movement laid the foundation of England's prosperity. The origin of the property is irrelevant. Where an institution is well established, those who benefit from it do so without incurring blame and should not be made to suffer unjustly on account of alleged historic injustices.

(6) Merely to transfer land from private owners to the State would not

worker is without hope and the farmer without independence.

(7) The countryside has been depopulated because of the inadequate pay and living conditions imposed on agricultural workers.

(8) Rural depopulation leads to overpopulation in the towns. But the chief cause of urban overcrowding is the extortionate cost of privately-owned land for housing schemes, and the consequent soaring prices of both freehold and rented property. It has been estimated that, in the 'boom' years of the early 1970s, the huge profits made by property speculators far exceeded those of such crucial industries as ship-building and aircraft.

(9) Under the Community Land Bill published by the Labour Government in March 1975, unbridled property speculation will be ended by giving local authorities not merely the right but, after a transitional period, the statutory duty to acquire all land needed for private development. The proposals will ensure ultimately that virtually all development takes place on land that is in, or has passed through, community ownership.

(10) The change to the new system will be gradual – it could take ten years to become fully effective. While it will bring land much needed for community development into local authority ownership at reasonable price levels, the Government has stressed that owner-occupiers are excluded.

(11) A further advantage of the plans is that they will not place a heavy financial burden on local authorities or the Exchequer. On the contrary, the Government has estimated that, eventually, the local authorities could save £350 million a year on the land they need for development, plus an annual profit of £500 million from sales of other land for private development.

increase the farmer's or the labourer's interest in the land. Post-war legislation has helped to ensure a certain security to the tenant farmer.

(7) The countryside has always been undergoing depopulation. The chief cause nowadays is a distaste by the younger generation for the supposed dullness of rural life and a desire for the (equally supposed) excitements of town life.

(8) Urban overcrowding is due to overpopulation. Far less than the price of land, it is the soaring cost of labour and raw materials, in the present inflationary period, which has aggravated housing shortages by slowing down the rate of new building and redevelopment. Earlier legislation showed that it is quite possible to prevent large-scale property speculation without nationalising land.

(9) The Bill, as initially proposed, is unworkable. Despite Government assertions that all relevant expert bodies were consulted beforehand, the private specialists in property development (who have carried out more new building than anyone else) appear to have been ignored. Worse still, some of the proposals are contrary to elementary principles of justice – for instance, the suggestion that people could have their land taken under a compulsory purchase order without being told why and without the right to either a public inquiry or a private hearing.

(10) The land nationalisation proposals were introduced mainly to satisfy the dogmatic tenets of the Labour Party's left-wingers. They will lead to fewer and dearer houses, with less choice in design and location. Few local authorities have the drive or efficiency for satisfactory performance of their proposed new triple role as monopoly planners-developers-landlords.

(11) Local authorities, already one-third understaffed, will need

(12) Mainly because of onerous taxation, many large landowners in recent years have been driven to split up their estates among a number of purchasers or to sell them outright to companies, which are concerned solely with profit-making. Land nationalisation, as now mooted, is the only way to retain what was good in the old system while ensuring a more equitable distribution of wealth and power.

nearly 13,000 new staff to operate the scheme. Even if new staff could be found, their added cost would take years to recoup.

(12) Public interest would be served best by a fair system of taxation which allowed the landowner enough incentive to develop his land and left the developer with sufficient freedom to carry out the tasks at which he is more expert than anyone in either central or local government.

Liberal Party:
Is It Unnecessary?

Pro: (1) The electorate is now confirmed in its habit of supporting, in steady proportions, the Conservative and Labour parties. The Labour Party stands for increasing State control of the main national industries and equalisation of the present differences in wealth, while the Conservative Party advocates the principle of private enterprise. One wing of the Liberals inclines to the former view, the other to the latter. It would simplify matters and benefit the country if each wing joined its affinity and these two conflicting ideas were made a clean-cut issue.

(2) Individual liberty is already a slogan of the Conservatives, and the Labour Party lays equal stress on it, in certain fields (e.g. its insistence on a voluntary 'social contract' and its reluctance to re-impose a statutory prices and incomes policy).

(3) The Liberal Party served a useful purpose when it was supporting Free Trade, the fiscal policy suited to the needs of the nation, against a Tory policy of protection. The balance of world trade and industry has changed so much that no overall policy of either Free Trade or protection is possible; in any case, through our membership

Con: (1) Liberalism represents the 'middle way' and is therefore more often likely to be in the right than either of the major parties which stand to right and left of it. There is probably less disunity among Liberals, overall, than among various sections of the Tory and Labour parties which are habitually at loggerheads with other sections of their own party. The Liberal Party has tended to be a power-house of ideas and many of its proposals have been adopted as their own by one or other of the two bigger parties.

(2) The stress laid in the past by Liberals on the necessity of individual liberty is just as urgent today. For neither of the two other parties, whatever they may say, is concerned with the rights and privileges of the private citizen so much as with the rights and privileges of a series of organised vested interests. Thus, in the matter of political liberty and the most efficient ordering of our political institutions, Liberalism has a crucial task to fulfil.

(3) Though Free Trade was temporarily abandoned, the tendency today throughout the world is towards the lowering of tariff barriers and the abolition of restrictions. It is now generally recognised

of the EEC, the Liberals' European ideal has now been achieved.

(4) The Liberals lost the support of the working-class voters, who now tend to vote Labour, and of large sections of the middle classes, who turned to the Conservatives, originally, out of fear of the alternative. The tendency of the younger 'intelligentsia' to turn Liberal is ephemeral and has more to do with dissatisfaction with the main parties on particular issues than with any genuine change of outlook. Liberalism is now like a general staff without an army.

that tariffs, quotas, exclusive bilateral agreements and the restrictions involved in Commonwealth Preference have done more to worsen than to improve the condition of world trade.

(4) The votes won by Liberals in recent elections give ground for supposing that the party has regained supporters of all classes up and down the country. It may hope to retain these and gain more, as the inadequacy of the other parties' programmes becomes increasingly apparent to the electorate as a whole. The six million Liberal votes in the first 1974 general election, and the 5,300,000-plus retained in the second poll that year, proved that the party's support was far from ephemeral. On the basis of overall votes, their share of the poll (compared with the Labour and Tory totals) would not have given Liberals the 13 seats actually gained; under a more equitable system, they should have had more than 80 seats.

(See also *Proportional Representation*.)

Liquor Laws:
Should They Be Relaxed?

Pro: (1) The restrictions imposed by Britain's liquor laws, notably as regards the permitted opening hours for public houses, are a legacy of undesirable social conditions in earlier ages – accentuated by the puritanism of that Nonconformist conscience which has long had undue influence on British affairs. The present laws no longer reflect the prevailing social conditions of the day.

(2) It is well known among travellers that abuse of alcohol is in inverse proportion to the strictness of a country's liquor laws. France,

Con: (1) As the law stands, public houses can serve alcoholic liquor for at least nine hours a day, in most areas. Drink can still be consumed with meals at other hours, in restaurants and clubs, and it can be bought from 8.30 a.m. on normal weekdays in the wine departments of supermarkets, etc., for consumption in one's own home whenever one wishes. Surely that is more than adequate provision for all normal needs? Do we really want to return to the days of Hogarth's Gin Lane?

(2) The appearance belies the facts. Drunkenness may be less

which has the most liberal laws in this respect, probably has the least amount of visible drunkenness in public (except, perhaps, among some tourists!). The very tough restrictions in parts of Australia, on the other hand, gave rise to the notorious 'six o'clock swill', in which many men drank a vast amount in a very short space of time, because the bars were closed at the early hour of 6 p.m. It became so bad that the restriction has now had to be eased, by extending the hours to more reasonable limits. Opening hours in Britain, though slightly less restricted than they were, still present a similar problem – of people trying to consume a few more drinks quickly before 'time' is called.

(3) When pubs or bars have longer permitted hours than are now the rule here, the result is if anything a tendency towards lower rather than higher consumption, overall. Because people are not under the pressure of time, they are more inclined to make a drink last over a longer period and thus often end by drinking less than they would have done if their hours were restricted.

(4) When something is forbidden or unobtainable, human beings always tend to want it much more than they would have done if it were readily available. Prohibition in the USA, for instance, certainly led many people to become regular drinkers who, but for the restriction, would probably have remained only infrequent drinkers. Station buffets, small café-restaurants and so on, which are in any case open for very long hours, would have no objection to serving liquor throughout that time, and there is no logical reason why they should be barred from doing so.

visible in France, but the overall problem there is actually far more acute than in Britain. According to the latest official statistics published in Paris, an average of 21,955 French people die from alcoholism every year and France has more cases of cirrhosis of the liver than any other country. Britain's latest liquor laws, by allowing an extra ten minutes' 'drinking up time' after the official hour of closure, have largely ended the indecent haste exhibited by some drinkers previously in the last minutes before closing time.

(3) Even if longer hours had the paradoxical effect of leading some individuals to drink less (though it's to be doubted if they'd do any such thing), the tendency would be more than outweighed by the availability factor. As a parallel, look at gambling; many people have always liked to bet, but the number has grown out of all recognition since betting shops were legalised. In terms of total consumption, it would inevitably be the same with drinking.

(4) Nothing exceeds like excess. ... Over-strict measures will always produce a backlash, human nature being what it is. But Britain's liquor laws are not unduly strict; within the framework of the State's responsibility to protect people from themselves to a certain degree, the present laws are if anything fairly generous. Moreover, one purely practical objection to any further relaxation is that publicans themselves would be very largely opposed to it. Apart from the burden of even longer hours than they have to work already – with all the daily re-stocking, cellar work and documentation, etc., from 10 a.m. to past midnight is quite usual – they would face great difficulty (and expense) in finding the necessary extra staff.

(See also *Prohibition*.)

Lords, Reform of the House of

Pro: (1) As an institution, the House of Lords is an anachronism and out of sympathy with the modern democratic spirit. It is the only institution of its kind persisting in the modern world.

(2) While the House of Commons has been made representative of the whole nation, the House of Lords has stood still. Its members – even those translated from the Commons as Life Peers – represent no one.

(3) The attendance of peers is notoriously small; in fact, a great many attend only to vote on party measures or those affecting their private interests. It is desirable to relieve peers from parliamentary duties when such work has come to them solely by inheritance but they are ill-suited for it or find it irksome.

(4) The majority of the peers are, inevitably, Conservative and largely opposed to the programmes of both the Liberal and Labour parties. When enlightened legislation is needed urgently to meet serious situations, the Lords often tend to oppose it. Even the reducing of their veto period to one year has not curbed the power of the Lords, since they can still hold up nearly every measure brought forward in the final year of a Government's term of office, in the hope that electoral changes will prevent them from being brought forward again. The only solution is for the function of the Lords to become purely consultative.

(5) If the Upper House is to function as a body of elder statesmen and act as a bulwark against over-hastiness on the part of the Commons, it should be reconstituted on an elective basis. We do not object to the son's inheriting his father's title, but we object to his making or unmaking *our* laws.

Con: (1) The House of Lords has grown up with, and forms an integral portion of, the British Constitution and, consequently, is much more adapted for its purpose than any new Second Chamber could be.

(2) It thoroughly represents the material and intellectual wealth and culture of the nation and expresses those aspects of national life more fully than the Commons. The House of Lords has already undergone one of the most important reforms in its history: the policy of creating only Life Peers – of all parties, or independent – from men and women who have shown exceptional ability in their professions. These new peers, experts in their fields, have brought added authority to the Lords' parliamentary contribution – and they are much less subject to the powerful party machines which have helped to lessen public regard for the House of Commons.

(3) The House of Commons also gives examples of small attendances and of voting in obedience to party orders without necessarily hearing a word of the debate. The peers who do attend are at any rate keenly interested in the topics discussed, and important subjects draw a large attendance.

(4) The Lords have always had very good reasons for their opposition. If their policy is conservative, it is not without advantages, for from 1914 onwards it is the House of Lords which has championed the traditional liberties of the subject and resisted the growing power of the Executive. The period during which the Lords can exercise their veto is now dangerously short.

(5) If the House of Lords is put on an elective basis, it will either be subject to the operations of the party

(6) The House of Lords is an irresponsible body. It should, like other Second Chambers, be a body responsible to the people in whose interests it is supposed to exist. Accordingly, it should be elected by them, or at least by their representatives.

(7) It is possible to have a reformed Second Chamber which, while consisting entirely of men qualified to deal with a nation's affairs and responsible for its acts, will yet be free from party ties.

(8) There is no scheme of reform which, while adding greatly to the moral strength of the Second Chamber, would reduce its value as a predominantly conservative body. This has been the universal experience in other countries, where the Second Chamber is always to the political right of the Lower House.

machines and lose its independent character, or, if its party majorities are markedly different from those of the Commons, be in a continuous state of conflict and rivalry with the Commons.

(6) The House of Lords is responsible because it is independent. All Second Chambers should be removed as far as possible from the transient gusts of popular control. It is noteworthy that several of the most progressive laws enacted in recent years were initiated in the Lords.

(7) It is difficult to see on what basis such men would be selected. If they are to be chosen by the Government, endless opportunities for packing the House with their protégés would arise; if various sectional interests are to be represented, there would be no concession made to democratic practice. Election by popular suffrage would certainly not bring forward the most suitable people, as experience in the Commons has shown.

(8) Reforms which strengthened the role of the House of Lords would incur the risk of placing the forces of reaction in a stronger position than at present.

(See also *Single-Chamber Government*; *Bishops : Should They Be Excluded from the House of Lords?*)

Lotteries

Pro: (1) By the legislation passed in 1975, which now permits local authorities to run relatively small lotteries for their own benefit, Parliament at last recognised that there is a definite public demand for lotteries and that it was unfair for the puritanism of the few to hinder the harmless enjoyment of the many.

(2) A lottery in itself is a quite innocuous amusement and provides a modicum of excitement in many otherwise dreary lives. It involves no

Con: (1) The public already have only too much opportunity for gambling, which is a national evil, involving loss of time and money and creating misery for the families of those who waste their substance on it.

(2) A lottery, like all gambling, is an immoral attempt to gain something for nothing and can never be entirely harmless. It encourages idleness and waste of time. Moreover, a sudden change of fortune

destruction of wealth but merely transfers money from one pocket to another, with the consent of both parties to the transaction. The new legislation will restrict the prices of lottery tickets to levels which will not encourage excessive gambling. Even if it didn't, and a few gambling addicts were to stake more than they could afford to lose, that is no reason why the moderate gambler, any more than the moderate drinker, should be penalised.

(3) A law which cannot be enforced and which is systematically evaded should be removed from the statute book. That has been the case with lotteries for years. Many local charities and sports clubs have long depended on small lotteries for survival. Despite legal technicalities about the use of skill, football pools are also lotteries, in effect – and the Government has recognised this by imposing a tax on winnings.

(4) A well-organised lottery is an excellent way of raising money. The Irish hospitals are now wealthy and well equipped on money raised by this method, and most foreign countries find lotteries a useful adjunct to taxation. One of the leaders of the Greater London Council has said that a London lottery alone could provide a £5 million profit annually, which could be devoted to the arts and other amenities now of low financial priority.

(5) The Government's proposed new lotteries do not, in fact, go far enough. At present, the top prizes permitted are £1,000 for weekly lotteries and £2,000 for larger quarterly lotteries. But earlier experience with Premium Bonds soon showed that, to retain public interest and ensure no drop in revenue, the prize levels had to be raised.

through sheer luck rather than merit, such as is occasioned by the winning of a big prize, often brings unhappiness by placing the winner on a different social level, where he tends to lose his former friends but is not accepted by his new financial equals.

(3) The law in this connection admittedly needed revision, but it should have been tightened up, not relaxed. The tax on gambling profits effectively sanctions immorality; since it was imposed, the gambling 'industry' has expanded out of all recognition.

(4) State lotteries may be useful in countries where the citizens habitually resist direct taxation and the bulk of revenue has to be raised through indirect taxes; but this does not apply to the British public. Even if one accepts official lotteries as the least harmful form of gambling, the gain in revenue will be a drop in the ocean against the volume of official expenditure; the Government has stressed that they will not be a substitute for the rates or an alternative method of financing local government.

(5) Even in this betting-mad country, there is a limit to the money available for gambling. Seven of Britain's biggest voluntary organisations have warned that the official lotteries, despite their relatively restricted size, will compete 'disastrously' for cash which now goes to local charities and sports clubs.

(See also *Gambling, Morality of.*)

Luxury Taxes

Pro: (1) Some luxuries are harmful in themselves and should be discouraged. Luxury enjoyments absorb productive powers which could otherwise be usefully employed in satisfying the more urgent wants of other people. Luxury taxes supplement income tax and level up its inequalities.

(2) They would bring in a considerable revenue, especially if directed to objects susceptible of gradual taxation. The operation of VAT (and previously of Selective Employment Tax) proves that luxury taxes *per se* could be applied successfully. Evasion can be checked and administration economised by using existing machinery as much as possible, as was done with entertainments tax and, formerly, with purchase tax.

(3) The people taxed would be those whose way of life indicates that they can well afford to bear additional taxation.

(4) The imposition of luxury taxes would tend to diminish working people's resentment against ostentatious wealth. On the other hand, the imposition of VAT on goods bought by all classes, as happened previously with purchase tax, recognises the rise in the standards of living of the poorer classes, so that the rich need have no cause to complain that they alone are bearing the brunt of taxation.

Con: (1) Luxury cannot be defined, and Puritanism is not a proper object of State action. The price of luxurious commodities does not necessarily depend on the amount of labour involved, and the labour itself can be controlled by purposive direction. There is no point in taxing a man for buying antique furniture in order to induce him to buy cheaper, newly made stuff.

(2) Separate luxury taxation is useless for revenue because, if the taxes are high, the yield diminishes quickly – and evasion is still easy for the unscrupulous. The results in France were disappointing. In any case, a more effective form of luxury taxation already exists – and has already been applied to many goods – through the Government's ability to vary the rates of VAT on different products. Hence, for instance, the 25 per cent VAT imposed for a while on luxury electrical goods like freezers, compared with the standard rate of 8 per cent.

(3) The taxes would inevitably prejudice the buying of commodities if imposed on possession of them, and tradesmen with stocks in hand would suffer. Luxury articles are not generally those which are most frequently the subject of exchange and renewal.

(4) Luxury taxes would merely serve to entrench the popular superstition that the salvation of the poor lies in the persecution of the rich. The poorer classes are already favoured by differential taxation.

Military Training, Compulsory:
Should It Be Restored?

Pro: (1) Nations should rely on their whole manhood for defence purposes and not on a limited pro-

Con: (1) The moral argument is misleading: the real national service that we owe is the fulfilment of

fessional class. It is the moral duty of everyone to take part in the service and defence of his country and to be trained so that he can do this effectively. In Britain, the only answer is the restoration of National Service – and this time, perhaps, with young single women also conscripted, for training in non-combatant jobs.

(2) After every war in the past, British governments have neglected the national defences, only to find themselves unprepared when the next crisis arose. Witness the frantic haste with which preparations had to be speeded up after the Munich fiasco in 1938. This danger would be greatly reduced if every citizen received basic military training.

(3) The training and discipline received by young National Service-men makes them better citizens. Physically and morally, the benefit is enormous. The voluntary associations can still be used for refresher courses and for the training of older men.

(4) The mingling of young people from many different backgrounds, during National Service, promotes respect and comradeship between them and inculcates a spirit of team-work and mutual toleration which has a beneficial effect later on their return to civilian life.

(5) Modern warfare demands intensive weapon training, which can be given to large numbers only through the method of conscription for peace-time service. Unless a large number of combatants is available at once, an aggressor might well overwhelm his victims before they can be mobilised for defence. Brief annual periods of reserve training, after National Service, will help to keep the ex-conscripts reasonably abreast of new weapons and methods.

(6) In times of peace, a citizen army is much the cheapest form of the duties of everyday life. This is the most effective way to strengthen the nation's moral power and financial resources. Conscription in peace-time is in any case not really efficient, militarily, because of the lack of continuity and the difficulty of training conscripts adequately in today's complex weapons before their period of service ends.

(2) Immediate conscription in wartime, as carried out after 1939, is adequate. For peace-time purposes, especially now that Britain's overseas commitments have been reduced, the regular army can meet all normal needs. Britain's main problems in 1940 arose from short-age of materials, not men. Even in the First World War, a time came when Britain had more conscripts than the armed forces could usefully absorb.

(3) To take young men away at a crucial moment in their civilian training is unfair and, for those studying for professional qualifica-tions, might actually unfit them for their future work. Military training in peace-time necessarily involves long periods of demoralising idleness or futile occupation.

(4) Despite recent reforms, the preservation of class distinction is probably still stronger in the armed forces than in almost any other sphere of life today.

(5) Weapons are continually changing and only those who have recently been under arms will be up-to-date in their training. The main things to be learnt in peace-time military service are discipline, team-work and smartness, and these could be learned just as well from other, non-military forms of service. Reserve training after National Service, even if for only a couple of weeks annually, would involve in-creasingly large numbers – and in-dustry simply could not afford to lose so many workers, however briefly.

military establishment, and any extra expenditure on it should be regarded as insurance.

(7) A citizen army is a valuable check on the policy of a government, as it must be persuaded of the rightness of acts it is asked to carry out.

(8) Compulsory training enables the responsibilities of citizenship to be realised by all. Those less fit physically are assigned to light duties, while conscientious objectors can do hospital or other useful work for the same period of service.

(9) Whatever air and sea successes a country's forces may achieve, no war can ever be won decisively without a large army to follow them up on land.

(10) Strength and numbers of military personnel remain the fundamental basis of military effectiveness. This was proved conclusively in the Second World War.

(6) The expense of maintaining a huge conscript army was prohibitive for a small country like Britain. It is all the more unnecessary now that we have abandoned the large military presence 'East of Suez' which was a legacy of our imperialist past.

(7) The existence of a large army encourages a government to be reckless in diplomacy and to take on commitments which increase the risk of war.

(8) Compulsory military training, as formerly operated in Britain, left a large part of the population without this reminder of their civic responsibilities. Moreover, it actually had a demoralising effect, since many young men decided to avoid conscription by emigrating and were thus lost to the country.

(9) In these days of nuclear arms and missiles, our only hope of defence lies in highly trained regular forces, enlisting voluntarily for long terms.

(10) Military effectiveness depends less than ever before on the mere weight of numbers of armed men. The building up of aircraft and munitions industries to war strength is a much lengthier and more complicated business than the elementary training of recruits, and it is on this that a country should concentrate for preparedness against war.

(See also *Social Service Conscription*.)

Minorities, Rights of

Pro: (1) Ever since the remaking of Europe after the First World War, it has been recognised that national minorities have a right to a certain autonomy. Such oppression as took place under the Austro-Hungarian and Tsarist Russian regimes is dis-

Con: (1) People who settle in a foreign country have no right to remain in it as an organised separate community. They should assimilate themselves with the community which has received them; otherwise they are liable to become nurseries

PC—E

credited today, but not all national minorities have been liberated, while some of the new countries which arose as a result of such liberation have been guilty of oppression in their turn. The attempt to solve the problem quickly by the summary ejection of foreign communities, such as that of the Asians from Uganda, offends against the principles of justice.

(2) The fact that some members of national minorities have abused their privileges is not an argument for depriving others of them. Subversive elements in a foreign country are not necessarily organised in compact national communities; indeed, they may prefer to permeate the indigenous population. The only logical consequence of this argument is the expulsion of all foreigners, which is repugnant to civilised countries.

(3) Not all minorities are formed by immigration. Some of them are communities and nations which have been forcibly annexed in the past to suit the economic needs of conquerors, as in the former Belgian Congo; others were summarily attached to another country, as in the creation of Czechoslovakia. Justice demands that they should be given full rights; failure to do this always leads to conflict and, in the end, the offending governments are usually forced to concede what they would not grant willingly.

(4) Separation by proper agreement would involve provision for possible economic problems. International bodies have usually concerned themselves with minorities only in so far as these affect the interests of the Great Powers. The cause of justice would be immeasurably strengthened by some provision which was incapable of misinterpretation and by United Nations action to implement it.

of unrest and can be used by unscrupulous aggressors as outposts, just as the Sudeten Germans in Czechoslovakia were used by Nazi Germany.

(2) The whole idea of artificially fostering separatist feelings in a community abroad is absurd and unreal. Left to itself, the second generation normally becomes part of the indigenous population, as seen notably in the USA. The preservation of national festivals is harmless and may enrich the cultural life of the foreign minority's host country, but that does not give minorities the right to try to elevate such national expressions into the political sphere.

(3) The linking of different communities together into nations was usually inspired in the past by considerations of economics; the agriculture of Slovakia complements the industry of Bohemia. In the same way, Zaire would probably be bankrupt without the mineral wealth of Katanga. In modern economic conditions, the creation of small units amounts to economic suicide; the whole trend is towards ever larger units. The political and economic *rapprochements* of the Western European countries are examples of this tendency. For small minorities today, the only possibility is a form of independence which is politically meaningless.

(4) Separation by agreement, while it might be desirable, is not feasible in the case of the few minorities which are left. A better solution, and one more likely to allow for economic difficulties, would be a painless transition – perhaps via 'Dominion status' – for such minorities as are recognised as having a right to independent existence, with the option of eventual federation.

Motor Traffic:
Should It Be Restricted?

Pro: (1) The first car appeared on British roads in 1888. By 1914, there were 140,000 vehicles on the road. In an island the size of Britain, there is hardly enough room for the more than 17 million vehicles we now have – yet, before the economic situation began to cause a temporary slow-down in 1974, statisticians were predicting an increase to 29 million vehicles by the year 2000. Motor cars have already become a menace to amenities of town and country, through noise, air pollution and the disfigurement of towns with a chaotic collection of signs and bollards. Parked cars fill every available space. It is high time to call a halt to this erosion of our amenities by restricting either the ownership or the circulation of cars.

(2) Since it would be impracticable to forbid car ownership, taxation could be used to restrict it. In any case, private motor traffic costs the country far more than it yields in revenue.

(3) All towns and cities, even large villages, have had to impose parking restrictions, and a system of tolls to restrict entry into central London has been proposed. Commuters, in particular, should be discouraged from bringing cars into city centres. Public transport should be improved, and subsidised out of taxation if necessary, with free or cheap parking at the termini for long-distance commuters. It has been estimated that traffic congestion in cities costs, in various ways, more than £1,000 million per year. It is absurd that a machine capable of high speeds should be used for journeys which, because of traffic congestion, average barely 11 m.p.h., as in London.

Con: (1) Attempts to limit the ownership of cars are as absurd as the so-called Red Flag rule which tried to curb their speed in the early days of motoring. The motor car is valued because it has enriched leisure, performs a public service and increased the pace of economic advance. It is regarded almost as an extension of the personality, and any further attempts to restrict it would certainly arouse fierce resistance. Damage to amenities arises only because the development of the motor car has outstripped the development of towns and town life.

(2) Motorists are already heavily taxed, and wholesale evasion would be the immediate result of excessive taxation. This kind of restriction is a form of rationing by the purse, and as such is undesirable.

(3) No sound scheme for taxing circulation in cities has yet been found, for the expense of enforcement and possibilities of evasion are formidable. Similarly, the problem of discrimination between users, in the granting of exemptions, cannot be solved on a basis that all would accept as fair. Bye-laws to ensure the provision of parking space with new buildings and a more imaginative approach to the parking problem generally would enable us to take advantage of the door-to-door service which is an essential part of town life. Many people are forced to use cars precisely because of the inadequacies of public transport, but it would take many years (and vast sums) to improve the latter sufficiently to overcome the problem.

(4) While railways performed a great public service in their time, they are unsuited to the increased mobility of modern populations, owing to their natural inflexibility

(4) The railways, which have been allowed to run down owing to our shortsightedness, are much more suitable for traffic between cities, being both faster and safer than motor transport. Failure to develop rail freight facilities adequately is largely to blame for the continual, unwanted increase in the use of 'juggernauts', those huge lorries which aggravate traffic congestion and wear out road surfaces.

(5) There is a limit to the building of new roads in an island the size of Britain. Not only is all available land needed for housing, agriculture, and open spaces for recreation, but motor roads are themselves unbeautiful, and too much road-building would destroy the countryside, the enjoyment of which is the main ambition of many car owners. A system of junctions and fly-overs at the edge of towns can create a nightmare landscape as bad as anything produced by the Industrial Revolution.

(6) The accident figures have reached appalling levels. During 1974, nearly 7,800 people died on the roads, and total casualties (serious and minor injuries) were more than 750,000. These figures alone should be an unanswerable argument for restriction of motor traffic.

(7) In the attempt to ease congestion, towns have built – at great expense – by-passes and ring roads of doubtful value. Re-routing of traffic is destroying the amenities – and roads – of once-quiet suburbs. Pedestrian precincts in town centres are of limited size and application. Ambitious schemes for new towns ban pedestrians from ground level altogether, as if motor cars had the prior claim to existence. The planners seem to have lost all sense of proper priorities.

(8) It took only a short time for society to curb individual enterprise on the railways a century ago.

and the inevitable delays involved in the transfer of freight. Passengers have made clear their preference for door-to-door transport.

(5) The building of motorways and the improvement of the older trunk roads have concentrated a great deal of the increased traffic of recent years. A well-made and landscaped motorway, or an imaginatively conceived junction system, can be architecturally beautiful and even give interest to some kinds of landscape.

(6) The fact that the USA, with more motor cars than any other country, has an accident rate per car less than half that of many European countries shows that the cause of accidents must be sought elsewhere. Better roads, better training in the driving and maintenance of vehicles, and perhaps more frequent replacement, could do much to improve accident figures. It took many years of invention and legislation for railways to reach their present level of safety. In relation to the population increase, the ratio of accident figures in Britain is actually being lowered. The present emphasis in car design is above all on new safety features.

(7) Road improvements in and around cities have been tackled piecemeal and too cheaply in the past. Bolder planning could remake our older city centres on more dignified lines and remove many of the worst atrocities of nineteenth-century building. Many new towns have shown the way, by incorporating pedestrian precincts and environmental areas, with distributive roads away from the main arteries. Travelators, chair-lifts and monorails are among other ideas suggested. Either old or new city centres could be completely re-planned on split-level lines, with through traffic, parking and pedestrians completely isolated from one another.

Motorists permit themselves to deface beauty spots with their vehicles, to break speed limits, to carry dangerous loads in inadequate vehicles, or to drive while unfitted by drunkenness, physical incapacity or lack of judgment and knowledge, powerful machines of whose internal workings they often have only the vaguest idea. The permissive attitude to motoring is out of step with more urgent present-day needs, and some rules should be laid down which would do for motoring what the Factory Acts and Public Health Acts have done for other aspects of community life.

(8) It is unconstructive to draw inferences about the behaviour of motorists from the actions of a comparative few. For every delinquent car owner, there are a thousand or more law-abiding ones. In one form or another, private transport has come to stay, and our best plan is to accommodate our lives to it.

(See also *Public Transport, Free.*)

Multi-National Firms

Pro: (1) The growth of multi-national firms has arisen naturally from the economic structure of the free world as it has developed in the past century, coupled with the tremendous improvement in communications and transport facilities between all parts of the globe which has occurred during that period. Often from small beginnings, the firms concerned have become very large corporations with branch companies or subsidiaries in dozens of places abroad, far from their own home bases. It has been fashionable in some quarters to criticise these companies and to suggest that their power and influence is undesirable. But whatever their faults may have been in earlier days, these have long since been outweighed by the benefits which the firms now bring to the economies of their own and other countries – for instance, through creating new industries in under-developed countries and providing the local inhabitants with more jobs, and through bringing a

Con: (1) The growth of multi-national firms stems basically from the misconception that 'biggest is best' – a traditional belief of the capitalist economies which more and more experts are now beginning to question (see *Industrial Expansion*). By their very nature, these huge corporations tend to be monopolistic and to squeeze out competition wherever they operate, thus enabling them to fix arbitrary price levels for their goods and services. With their world-wide networks, they are able to employ artificial transfer prices between various subsidiaries as a means of reducing their tax payments. Because of the size of their operations, they are able to indulge in very large-scale currency manipulation, which has undoubtedly harmed the economic interests of the countries concerned. Many of them have also been guilty of political interference, particularly in developing countries.

(2) The extent of their invasion of rival industrialised countries, quite

vast number of products and services within reach of peoples who could not otherwise have hoped to enjoy them.

(2) Their supposed influence has been exaggerated. A United Nations report listed only 650 firms which it classed as multi-national corporations (divided mainly, in origin, between the USA, Japan and Europe). Big though the companies are, that total cannot be enough to give them complete or undue dominance. Nor are they restricted to industry and manufacture, as many people suppose; companies of this scale are also found in commerce, mining, transport, banking and other services – which, again, shows that their role is a long way short of monopolistic.

(3) An official French report recognised that foreign investment in the country has been beneficial because the companies concerned have improved the employment situation in regional industry, because they offset economic recession and 'because foreign companies behave like good citizens'. In one region alone, Alsace, 49 per cent of the work force, in the last twenty years, obtained their jobs through foreign companies. The establishment of a large multi-national firm in a provincial locality has also brought indirect benefits to the area, by helping to encourage the regional development of various services needed by the company itself, such as communications, tourism, banking and insurance.

(4) In many of the world's under-developed countries, multi-national firms can take much of the credit for the discovery and subsequent development of natural resources (e.g. oil, minerals and other raw materials) which are now the principal elements of wealth in those countries' economies. Usually, the existence of such resources was

apart from the under-developed nations, is shown by the fact that about 400 multi-national companies (mainly Japanese and American) now have bases in Europe. Today, some 30,000 Americans work in Brussels alone, where more than a third of the 400 companies have their European headquarters. France has 50 such companies on her soil. The American General Electric company's takeover of the French firm Machine Bull in 1966 effectively deprived France of her own computer industry, obliging the Paris Government to set up a new French data processing and computer concern, in association with German and Dutch firms. The wide range of activities carried out by the various business giants ranked as multi-nationals merely serves to emphasise just how all-pervasive the spread of these companies has become.

(3) When a multi-national firm installs a new factory in another country, creating more jobs locally, the government of that country may well welcome it. All too often, though, these big corporations merely buy up an existing local company. This not only makes little or no extra contribution to the economy of the host-nation but may actually have a negative effect. To combat the practice, France now insists that any foreign investment of 20 per cent or more in a French company must first be approved by the Finance Ministry. Among other measures to keep a firm hand on the multi-nationals, the French Government has imposed rigid control over the prices charged by foreign oil companies in the country.

(4) The production techniques of most multi-national companies are determined first in the industrial countries and then transferred to the developing countries. But the techniques are not always appropriate for the purpose. They tend to be

previously unknown to the local inhabitants, who in any case had neither the technological nor financial means to exploit them. Besides introducing the necessary production techniques to these countries, the multi-nationals have also added immeasurably to the local wealth through the scale of the export earnings they have facilitated (by virtue of the world-wide marketing and distribution techniques they employ).

(5) Of the 650 multi-national corporations in the United Nations list, 74 are Japanese. Internally, Japan's early post-war domination by American multi-nationals has led to a policy whereby foreign companies are now allowed to operate in the country only if they do not disturb the development of local industries. Externally, the Japanese have learned from this domestic experience that their factories abroad cannot prosper if they ignore the public interest – for instance, by causing pollution or by failing to make a social as well as an economic contribution to the communities where they are located. In short, Japan is keenly aware that the behaviour of the multi-nationals can make or break the development of a harmonious world economy, and the 'good neighbour' policy of its own big corporations reflects the present-day attitude of the great majority of multi-national firms in general.

(6) Whatever may have been the position in the past, no single multi-national company is powerful enough to bring about radical political changes for its own ends nowadays, even in the most newly independent of the developing countries. Alleged instances in the past attracted such adverse publicity later that it is doubtful whether a multi-national firm would so much as contemplate any attempt of this nature today. While there is some

capital intensive and labour saving, whereas nearly all developing countries have a shortage of capital and a surplus of labour. Many of the companies ignore this and continue to operate in ways contrary to the local people's best interests – particularly in some African and Asian countries where the governments are still too weak, inexperienced or too much in need of foreign investment to be able effectively to control and channel the activities of the multi-nationals on their soil.

(5) The normally aggressive attitudes of these huge enterprises have been tempered mainly by the awareness that Japan is vitally dependent for its very survival on the goodwill of other countries, both for its markets and for its raw materials (a lesson brought home particularly by the oil crisis of 1973–4). In short, the behaviour of the Japanese multi-nationals remains motivated by self-interest and not by the altruistic paternalism which seems to be implied opposite. Indeed, Japan's *internal* policy on the issue has set a pattern for other nations to follow in protecting their own interests against the multi-nationals – and the policy is already being copied by some of the developing countries, such as Indonesia and South Korea. While it is true that Japanese multi-nationals have helped to develop the economic resources of other Asian countries, there have been undesirable side-effects socially. The gap between rich and poor has grown larger, and the increased urbanisation resulting from industrialisation has disrupted traditional values and ways of life.

(6) To suggest that multi-national corporations would no longer try to interfere politically in countries where they operate, if they thought they could get away with it, is regrettably naïve – and disproved by events. The notorious case of ITT,

truth in allegations that foreign companies have made gifts to politicians in various countries with a view to gaining favoured treatment, it should be borne in mind that such practices are part of the local way of life in many Asian and African countries, and they cannot be classed at the level of attempted interference in government policy.

(7) The top managements of most multi-nationals are not merely among the most skilful in the world but also among the most far-seeing, particularly in anticipating the responses necessary to long-term trends. Accordingly, the nature and philosophy of many of these companies have already changed greatly. They recognise that, rather than merely exporting their own goods to foreign markets, the main impetus in future will have to be, increasingly, on providing the means for local manufacture in other countries. At the same time, as management from the centre becomes ever more complex, there are the first signs of a trend towards the devolution of authority and eventually it is likely that, while the skeleton of a multi-national may remain, the individual parts of it abroad will be much more autonomous than at present.

the giant American conglomerate, and its role in helping to engineer the downfall of the late President Allende of Chile, is now a matter of public record. Even more recently, major US oil firms have had to admit publicly that their local companies in two different countries (one Latin American, the other European) had made sizeable 'political contributions' to parties in the areas where they were based. Though not stated explicitly, it was clear that the level of these 'contributions' was a good deal higher than any routine form of business insurance in such countries.

(7) Because of their sheer size, multi-national companies are able, if they so decide, to eliminate virtually all competition in any of the smaller countries they care to enter. Indeed, this has even happened in some of the larger industrialised countries. The danger is particularly acute when multi-nationals are overwhelmingly dominant in areas of high technology. Just how extensive such dominance can be is instanced by IBM, which now holds about three-quarters of the world market for high technology computers. It is often claimed in defence of these industrial giants that size is necessary for economic efficiency, in present-day conditions; but this is readily disproved by the example of China, which, with about 25 per cent of the world's population, has managed very well without the assistance of the multi-national companies in its determined progress towards becoming an advanced industrial power.

Newspapers:
Should They Be Reformed?

Pro: (1) The Press in Britain has travelled very far from the days when periodicals were read by the cultured

Con: (1) The influence of the Press on the general public has been greatly exaggerated. The election of

few and broadsheets contained the only comment on the events of the day for the unlettered many. In these days of almost universal literacy, the Press has become a great power that can make or break governments and systems of government and change the fortunes of a country, and it is time that some control was exercised in the interests of the public.

(2) As newspapers have grown in size, they have fallen in number. Through amalgamation and the buying up of bankrupt competitors, a situation has been reached where a handful of national daily newspapers are read by almost the whole population. The fortunes made from the sale of popular newspapers created a class of 'Press barons', some of whom had no real interest in any but the purely financial aspects of the newspapers they controlled. The true function of a newspaper, the dissemination of information, was distorted by the pressure of financial interest. Today, apart from the few 'quality' papers, most newspapers resort too readily to sensationalism and superficial entertainment to bolster their circulations – and their presentation of news can still be subject to the personal predilections of the proprietor or the interests which he openly or otherwise represents.

(3) Because of the predominance of advertising as a source of revenue, the interests of advertisers influence the policy of a newspaper – not in suppressing news items, perhaps, but certainly in the nature of its efforts to achieve a bigger circulation (when higher rates can be charged for advertising space). A newspaper which is prepared to risk the loss of advertising custom can scarcely hope to survive, or even to be started.

(4) The popular press is guilty of gross errors of taste, both in the kind of news it prints and in the methods used to obtain it. Unwarranted in-

a Labour Government in 1945, and that of President Roosevelt for his second and third terms of office in the USA, took place despite opposition beforehand from an overwhelming majority of the newspapers – thus proving readers' ability to form their own judgments. People are, in fact, far less credulous now than in the days before compulsory education and national newspapers existed.

(2) The amalgamation of newspapers and the tendency towards monopoly are merely examples of the general trend of world economy today. The days of small newspapers are gone, except as local papers in the provinces and suburbs, where they still have a viable role. Under the system of private enterprise, there are enough newspapers of different political views to cater for all main interests, and the effect of a proprietor's influence is no more undesirable than would be that of a Government monopoly. In the past, the reading of newspapers was confined to a leisured minority; the presentation of news in easier-to-read form and the inclusion of items of general interest are the very reasons why newspaper reading is now indulged in by the whole population.

(3) Advertising is a legitimate occupation which has naturally grown in extent with the growth of industry and trade generally. Advertisers do not influence the policy of newspapers directly in the pushing of their products, and there has been no evidence for many years (except, possibly, on some of the very smallest local papers) of advertisers trying to get specific news items modified or suppressed.

(4) While some reporters err through excess of zeal or lack of scruples, the Press generally does its duty of informing the public without unwarrantable intrusions. Far fewer people than might be supposed

trusions on privacy have had to be condemned by the Press Council in all too many cases.

(5) Journalists themselves have complained of their servitude to financial interests. The power wielded by the great editors of the past, who built up the reputations of our best known national newspapers, is virtually unknown today. It is a traditional dictum that 'news is sacred but comment is free'. However, many papers today 'angle' their news so that it supports their own views.

object to the publicity they are given, and many even find that they have benefited from it.

(5) Journalists have the remedy in their own hands to a large extent. No journalist who objects to the policy of a newspaper need work for it. Comment on and interpretation of news do not necessarily amount to falsification, and most facts can be interpreted in more than one way. The existence of rival newspapers, and of the radio and television news services, gives the public adequate protection – and the Press Council has proved an effective deterrent against any really serious excesses.

Nuclear Weapons:
Should They Be Banned Completely?

Pro: (1) Nuclear weapons are not merely more deadly weapons than any before but are of a completely new nature, in that they interfere with the very structure of the Earth and its atmosphere. Apart from the horrific destruction caused by their explosions, they can contaminate whole areas of the Earth by radioactivity which may last for hundreds, even thousands of years.

(2) Nations become more cautious about the use of weapons only if both sides in a dispute possess them. That was why neither side used poison gas in the Second World War – but Mussolini's Italy was prepared to do so in 1936 against the Abyssinians, who could not retaliate. Hence, the greatest danger from nuclear weapons lies in the possible temptation of a nation possessing them to employ them against another which does not – a danger accentuated by the fact that more and more countries already have or are in sight of nuclear capability.

(3) The belief that wars can be

Con: (1) The invention of new weapons has been a consistent feature of mankind's history, from the sling and the club onwards. The first use of gunpowder was probably met with similar protests. There is a good case for reducing the existing stocks of nuclear weapons, both to save the crippling cost and as an insurance against any of the present prolific stocks falling into the wrong hands. But there is an even better case for retaining an agreed minimum of such weapons, as a mutual deterrent.

(2) The very horror aroused by nuclear weapons has made the superpowers determined not to go to war with each other and to abstain from using them in a war already begun. Hence, the USA refrained from the use of even 'tactical' nuclear weapons in the Korean war and Indo-China. It was the world-wide fear that nuclear weapons might be used which brought the Cuban crisis to a speedy end in 1962. The natural course of history is thus more

won by these weapons alone is a fallacy. The Japanese had already been effectively defeated before Hiroshima and Nagasaki in 1945; the bombs merely hastened their surrender. No war will be won without the occupation of territory by troops on land. But the perils of radio-activity could postpone large-scale occupation indefinitely, while the scale of destruction on both sides in a nuclear war would render any normal political or governmental control virtually impossible. The super-powers' present weapons systems have long since out-moded the 'first strike' idea, whereby one nation would hope to get in first with such a lethal blow that its enemy could not retaliate in kind. Accordingly, the only hope of mankind's survival is to abandon all these utterly destructive weapons, for all time.

(4) Because previous attempts at prohibiting weapons have failed, it must not be assumed that they always will. Clearly, while the major power blocs still mistrust each other, it can only be achieved step by step. But progress *has* already been made: the partial test ban treaty of 1963; the nuclear non-proliferation treaty (1970); the first strategic arms limitation pact between the US and the USSR (1972), and their 1974 agreement to restrict their anti-ballistic missile systems and the size of underground nuclear tests. Following the successful conclusion of the European security conference in 1975, the big powers all expressed the hope that this would give a new impetus to the Vienna negotiations on the mutual and balanced reduction of armed forces, previously almost deadlocked. Vast difficulties and suspicions remain to be overcome; but, essentially, the will is now there.

(5) So far from benefiting by the discovery of nuclear weapons, the

effective, of itself, than any attempts to impose a formal ban.

(3) The use of nuclear weapons would tend to shorten war and thus, in the long run, to save life – as, indeed, happened through their employment against Japan. While it may seem callous to make a balance-sheet of human lives, particularly those of civilians, the dictates of overall strategy nevertheless require it; and the plain fact is that, because nuclear weapons are delivered by air, from missiles or bombs, the loss of combatant lives would be minimised. The knowledge that armies would still be in existence to fight each other, despite the use of nuclear weapons, is thus another deterrent factor. That being said, no government would willingly countenance the huge potential loss of civilian life; so a nuclear balance between the powers is the best guarantee against any use of such weapons.

(4) Apart from the argument over whether it would actually be wise to ban all nuclear weapons, were that possible, it is unrealistic to imagine that the latest gradual disarmament moves will be any more successful than previous such attempts, for the necessary degree of mutual trust is still sadly lacking – and likely to remain so for the foreseeable future. Since the SALT I agreement, for instance, various American authorities have privately alleged that the Russians, if not actually violating the terms of the pact, have pushed close to the limits (on such matters as jamming and the use of silo covers to impede the agreed satellite surveillance of strategic systems). And how can agreements like the non-proliferation treaty succeed when, even now, more than thirty important nations have not signed it? Those countries, moreover, include the two other nuclear powers, France and China, as well as India (which has exploded a nuclear device 'for

development of the civilian, industrial use of atomic power has been crippled by the priority given to war research. No way has so far been perfected for using the thermonuclear process for peaceful purposes. A situation has arisen where only those countries which cannot afford the bombs are able to pursue civilian research satisfactorily.

(Some) Whatever their potential side-benefits, research and discoveries which might end in destroying the earth or the human race could very well be dispensed with.

peaceful purposes') and other near-nuclear nations like Argentina, Brazil, Egypt, Israel and South Africa.

(5) Research for purposes of war usually has a beneficial effect on civilian progress, and so it has been with the atomic bomb. Radio-active by-products are used in hospital work; much progress has been made in the production of electricity in Britain from nuclear power stations. Civilian and military research projects have proceeded side by side, to their mutual benefit. Without the incentive which produced nuclear weapons, this would not have been possible.

(See also *Armaments, Limitation of Conventional*; *War: Is It Desirable?*; *War: Is It Inevitable?*)

Nudism on Beaches
(*and Other Allotted Public Places*)

Pro: (1) Before arguing the case for permitting nudism in public places, it is essential to establish the case for nudism itself. Clothing is unnatural and unhealthy. It is one of the artificial conditions which civilised man has created for himself, to his own harm. Exposure of the skin to light and air is one of the natural conditions of health. Essential vitamins are manufactured in the body by the aid of sunlight. By covering the skin, man loses the normal reactions to changes of temperature and renders himself more subject to colds and disease. The more clothing one wears, the more one's body loses its natural resistances and the more one is susceptible to cold. A man who is accustomed to going heavily clad feels no warmer than one who is used to wearing little or nothing.

(2) Clothing encourages prudery by habitually hiding the body and so indirectly suggesting that it ought to

Con: (1) For the white races, clothing is necessary in most parts of the world as a protection against cold and damp or against strong sunlight. It is one of the means by which man extends his conquest over nature. Suitably equipped, men may go to the Poles, up into the stratosphere or down to the bottom of the sea. Even primitive man wore skins and sought the shelter of caves. Nature provides the lower animals with fur or feathers; man must use his intelligence to provide his own protective covering.

(2) Few people's bodies are beautiful enough to be pleasant to look upon. A certain degree of exposure to sun and air is acceptable nowadays, but nudism in public is neither necessary nor desirable, and all races except the most primitive stop short of it. Although the disappearance of previous hypocrisy on the subject may be welcomed, the 'pin-ups' and

be hidden. A healthy human body, hardy and bronzed everywhere and not just in patches, should be beautiful and strong and a pleasure to the eye. The photos of lovely nude bodies now regularly published in popular newspapers, while possibly harmful for a prurient minority, prove that nudism has become generally accepted and is no longer regarded as shocking by most people.

(3) People who are shocked by the nude are of two types: those who dislike the unusual, because it puts them to the trouble of readjusting their mental habits; and those who project their own evil thoughts into the world around them.

(4) To discard clothing is courageously to take advantage of modern knowledge of the laws of health. In several European countries, there are now specific areas – beaches or off-shore islands – which are effectively reserved for nudists. They attract more and more people each year, with a consequent clear improvement in their general health standards. Such areas are not private nudist camps but are on public property, open to all. They are usually fenced off, with warning notices, merely to avoid offending people who might wander in by accident and not wish to be there. Britain ought to permit similar facilities.

(5) It is not suggested that nudism should be allowed in public at any time and any place. (The recent craze for 'streaking' among young people enjoyed only a very temporary vogue!) But there is a definite demand for local authorities to set aside stretches where it would be freely permitted. In places where nudism is practised, self-consciousness ceases to intervene – and it is the person wearing clothes who seems indecently out of place.

other nude pictures printed in mass-circulation newspapers prove merely that we are passing through an age of sexual permissiveness – which, as its advocates have always insisted, has nothing to do with the cult of nudism.

(3) It is not only the puritanical who are disgusted by nudism. All people of good taste dislike extremes, whether in dress or in undress.

(4) To discard clothing is to turn the tide of civilisation backward. To practise nudism in everyday life would be entirely unpractical. What has become acceptable on a few beaches in France, Germany or Scandinavia is not necessarily suited to the average British temperament (or climate!). If people in Britain wish to adopt the cult, they should do so in private – more than enough clubs exist, secluded from outside gaze, to cater for them. There is no call for allowing it on public beaches, which would not only risk inadvertent intrusion by other people, including children – whatever the warning notices – but would cut into seaside space that is already overcrowded.

(5) Whether regular or sporadic, nudists represent only a tiny minority of the British population. It may be conceded that the rights of minorities should be respected, within reason; but that has never meant acceding to demands which are to the detriment or undue disquiet of the majority.

Pacifism

Pro: (1) Pacifism is a belief which reflects the noblest aspirations of man. Throughout the Gospels, Christ enjoined it on his followers, and all the so-called Christian nations, however much they may backslide in practice, profess lip-service to it. The early Christians survived and flourished precisely and only through the practice of passive resistance to persecution. It is also an essential article of the Buddhist faith. After a brief period of domination, the Moslems were forced to abandon their aim of conversion by conquest, and many surviving Moslem communities exist contentedly under alien domination.

(2) That a pacifist attitude was not unpractical was shown by William Penn, who established peaceful relations with the American Indians and was enabled to build up the colony of Pennsylvania, whereas other colonists encountered bloody resistance.

(3) The charge of cowardice is made against pacifists in times of national hysteria and for propaganda purposes. Men volunteering for non-combatant service, such as driving ambulances, have saved many lives in wartime at the constant risk of their own, and absolute pacifists who refuse to take even this limited part in war have shown by their fortitude under violent persecution that they are as brave as any soldier, perhaps braver than those whose fear of the herd drives them into battle.

(4) The results of all wars prove the error of expecting progress to follow the use of force. Especially in a modern war, there are no true victors among the peoples as a whole, and the issues for which the war is fought are never settled by it.

(5) War gives rise to vice, cruelty

Con: (1) It is disputable whether Christ was as pacific in outlook as pacifists suppose. Many of his sayings can be quoted to illustrate a more militant attitude. Countries adopting Buddhism have survived in a warlike world only by mutilating their doctrine beyond recognition. A third great religion, Islam, had holy war as an integral part of its beliefs and established itself by direct military conquest. The Christian sects in general have abandoned passive resistance, recognising it to be unpractical.

(2) Penn's pacifism had no lasting influence on the Indians and was suitable only to the early stages of contact with them, before they realised the intentions of the colonists. Pennsylvania very soon abandoned its Quaker form of government and became like other colonies. Pacifist communities, from those of earliest man onward, have been short-lived and limited. The course of history is against their survival as such.

(3) Pacifism is a refuge for people who, for physical or emotional reasons, cannot adjust themselves to the rigours of life in the community. A case can be made, perhaps, for people who, out of genuine religious conviction, refuse to risk taking human life but are willing to work in helping to save it. But it is illogical in the modern world that other pacifists who refuse to fight in defence of their countries should decline even to contribute some form of humanitarian service.

(4) That professed aims are not always achieved by a war is not relevant to the argument, since these aims are not necessarily identical with the situations and stresses which are the real causes of the wars.

and meanness, and there is no one taking part in it who is not demoralised by it. The so-called warlike virtues arise simply from herd instinct. Pacifism represents those emotions which lift man from the animal level. Women, who are concerned with the propagation and nurturing of children, are particular sufferers from war and are natural pacifists.

(6) The stage which modern weapons have reached, with the invention of the H-bomb and the possibility of complete annihilation for the human race, makes pacifism more than ever the only possible creed consistent with our survival.

Thus the First World War, although not fought for that purpose, brought about the liberation of many nations and classes of people from reactionary domination.

(5) The waging of war can also bring out the best instincts in people, who often discover an idealism, brotherly love and willingness to co-operate with one another which tend to atrophy in peace-time. Even if war is a deplorable way of stimulating such virtues, it remains true that there is no inspiration in the pacifist creed for the mass of people, and this is no less true of women than of men.

(6) The existence of new weapons, however horrific, does not change the situation, and a pacifist nation would merely be tempting others to use such weapons against it.

Parliament, Reform of:
Devolution

Pro: (1) The chief cause of the present inadequacies of the parliamentary machine, with the consequent loss of its prestige throughout the country, is the enormous pressure of business. Since 1874 at least, Parliament has been overworked. Lack of time has sometimes meant that important legislation has not been passed; money has been paid away for matters the Commons could not discuss; Scotland and Wales have had insufficient attention paid to their special interests; the power of departments has increased to an alarming extent; and efficient government is possible only if the Cabinet practically ignores the Commons. Worst of all, foreign affairs have passed out of the Commons' control. The system of committees for dealing with particular questions, which can occupy up to 90 per cent of an MP's time, is too often used to

Con: (1) The internal problems of Parliament are due to more fundamental causes than physical insufficiencies. The party system has wasted enormous amounts of time. The short-sightedness of members will, eventually, ruin even sectional parliaments. It is an exaggeration to say that matters of importance have been neglected. Scotland and Wales have had all the important Bills they wanted. No reliance can be placed on statistics which purport to show that these parts of the British Isles have received inadequate attention, because one Bill for Scotland may be more important and beneficial than twenty Bills for England.

(2) The removal of all local affairs would mean the inanition of the federal body, since the electors would not be enthusiastic over foreign, economic and other business that did not appear to concern their

support party interests rather than for objectively constructive study.

(2) All the major parties now pay court to the principle that, in one form or another, local affairs should be handed over to local Parliaments. It is immaterial whether, as some wish, Scotland, Wales and England should have a Parliament each, or whether, as others wish, a less grandiose form of regional autonomy should be chosen. Such a federal system would not destroy the main principles of the United Kingdom, since the federal or central government would retain its supremacy. MPs might sit part of the year at Westminster and part in the local Parliaments.

(3) Federal devolution would provide Britain with valuable experience for her participation in the EEC's eventual progress towards European political union.

(4) Decentralisation would re-infuse life into institutions that are now being attacked. By getting rid of purely local business, Parliament would be free to undertake the task which it is elected to perform, viz. to supervise the estimates and criticise and control the Government's policy. Popular interference, if continuous, is beneficial. Devolution by function, rather than devolution by area, is tantamount to revolution and is the denial of political democracy.

own region. There would be constant bickering between the various parliaments, as no system of devolution would prevent the adoption of different policies on matters that seem local but really affect the whole country.

(3) Devolution would have little or no bearing on any moves for European political union – a dubious prospect in the foreseeable future, anyway – since in this context Great Britain would have to remain a whole unit.

(4) (Some) If a federal government means that the uninformed masses are to direct foreign policy and dictate to the executive continually, it will not promote prosperity or success.

(Some) Geographical political theories are out of date. Devolution by function, not by area, is necessary. The constitution is worn out, and federal schemes merely try to postpone radical alterations.

Parliament, Televising of

Pro: (1) The one-month experiment of live broadcasts of the House of Commons at work, in 1975, aroused great public interest and was regarded by most people as a convincing success. Subject to the final decision of MPs themselves (unknown at the time of writing), it has been agreed in principle that it

Con: (1) After the first upsurge of interest in the Commons broadcasts, listening figures fell away long before the end of the month. (The law of diminishing returns, or 'familiarity breeds contempt' – take your pick!) The regular televising of Parliament would soon bore viewers, similarly, and would merely become an expen-

should become a permanent feature. The precedent has thus been set for the next logical step – the televising of parliamentary proceedings, which many MPs have been urging for years.

(2) The House of Commons' own microphone system proved adequate for the broadcasting experiment, and the small box installed within the Chamber for the radio commentators soon became part of the scenery, barely noticed by the MPs. The latest television equipment would be similarly unobtrusive, no longer requiring the extra-bright lighting and mass of cables, etc., which formed part of the objections when the televising of Parliament was first mooted.

(3) Live broadcasts of noisy periods like Question Time were a revelation to many members of the public who had not been aware previously that Commons proceedings often resemble a bear garden rather than a polite debating society. After the first shock, however, it was not long before listeners came to realise that this was genuine democracy at work and that, notwithstanding all the interruptions and schoolboyish jibes, a great deal of useful parliamentary business was being accomplished. The visual always makes more impact than the aural; television, therefore, would be far more effective than radio in bringing home the democratic process to the public at large. Further, by giving people a greater sense of involvement and participation, albeit at second hand, it would help to restore their hitherto dwindling faith in the efficacy of Parliament.

(4) Parliament already recognises people's right to see it in action, by the provision of a Public Gallery. Television would simply be an extension of this. It would also help to ensure higher attendances by MPs than is now often the case!

sive waste of air time – except, perhaps, for really important occasions like the Budget, which are relatively infrequent.

(2) To expect television's requirements to be no more obtrusive than those of radio, within the Chamber, is quite unrealistic. Despite the advent of very small TV cameras and the enhanced ability of zoom lenses to get close-ups from considerable distances, the number of cameras and other installations required would inevitably be more visible.

(3) The rowdiness of some parliamentary proceedings shocked many members of the public to an extent that should not be underestimated, and it is naïve to suggest that this encouraged any great revival of respect for Parliament. Too many MPs were clearly 'playing to the gallery' during the Commons radio broadcasts. How much worse some of them would be if they thought TV cameras were on them! There may be a case for radio coverage, particularly when it is selective and is used to give the added interest of actuality in subsequent news bulletins. But television would have pernicious effects far outweighing any possible advantages.

(4) There would be an increased danger of voters electing a candidate because of his 'television appeal', rather than for any other merits he might have. Moreover, the televising of Parliament would still not bring home to constituents – particularly those criticising the apparent absence of their own member – the realisation that perhaps 90 per cent of an MP's work is done in committees, not in the Chamber.

Party Government

Pro: (1) Party government is desirable and beneficial, and in some form or other inevitable. Only if the government is directed by a coherent group with a settled policy can progress be made or public business be done.

(2) Coalition experiments have generally been a failure. A national coalition is particularly inefficient in peace-time, because its pace is regulated by the most conservative section. If a Government receives its mandate from a sufficient majority of electors, it has no right to abdicate from its position of supreme responsibility in attempting to share the burden with its defeated political opponents.

(3) Party government ensures a thorough discussion of all important topics. There is no possibility of collusion to rush controversial measures through without publicity.

(4) The group system has failed repeatedly on the Continent. It is a synonym for unstable Cabinets, intolerable intrigue and failure to carry out much-needed reforms.

(5) There are only two real parties in the House of Commons today – the Labour Party and the Conservative Party. These correspond with the only two real forces in the State. In the course of time, the Liberals are bound to disappear; any success they may be enjoying is ephemeral and is due only to voters' temporary dissatisfaction with the other parties on particular issues.

(6) It is impossible to prevent the growth of parties under a representative system. Any such devices as *ad hoc* coalitions, formed mainly to pass one specific reform and then dissolved, are futile (as shown by experience in Italy and pre-Gaullist France). All the disadvantages that

Con: (1) On many questions before Parliament, there is a general measure of agreement. Yet, to maintain the prestige of the party, unimportant points are frequently used for purposes of obstruction. Proposals cease to be judged on their merits but are judged on their supposed influence on the party fortunes.

(2) Coalition government was eminently successful during the Second World War, when the complexion of the government had ceased to correspond with the country's wishes in some ways but a general election was impracticable. There is no doubt that it called forth an immeasurably increased amount of devotion and hard work from the people.

(3) Debate is reduced to a farce. A party government can always use its majority to enforce its will and can stifle discussions by use of the 'guillotine' and other parliamentary devices. The net result is that the Cabinet is master of Parliament.

(4) The group system ensures a greater elasticity of policy and greater responsibility for the individual members.

(5) Three parties in the House of Commons make a group system inevitable, for the long-term trend will be for them to approach approximate equality of numbers. The Liberals were within only 5–6 per cent of a large-scale breakthrough in the last two general elections (1974). If their share of seats in the Commons represented even half their share of the poll, they would already hold the balance of power.

(6) Party systems are full of dishonesty, log-rolling, secret influences and other undesirable practices, which destroy the uprightness and

are put down to party systems are inherent in political life of any kind.

independence of the individual and bring politics into disrepute.

(See also *Coalition Government.*)

Payment by Results in Industry

Pro: (1) The workman paid by results is rewarded according to the energy, efficiency and initiative which he puts into his work. This is more just than the time-work system by which lazy and active, efficient and inefficient, get the same. Where payment by results is adopted, the morale of workmen goes up and they take greater pride in their work.

(2) Production is stimulated; machines and plant are used to the fullest extent and most economically; the workman gets higher wages and the employer higher profits; and the consumer benefits by lower prices. This is particularly so in the export industries and in building, where a high rate of production will be needed for many years to come. Fears of victimisation are groundless when a guaranteed minimum wage is also secured.

Con: (1) The important thing in industry is the general standard of the workers and not nice discrimination of merit. Indeed, the inefficient worker may be just as hard-working as the most efficient. All piece-work systems sooner or later result in the cutting of prices for work done and are more for the benefit of the employer than the worker. The logical outcome of dealing according to results is the turning of the inefficient adrift.

(2) While production may increase in quantity, it can equally prove harmful to quality, which is harder to measure. In the building trade, it is likely to lead to scamped work and the decline of honest craftsmanship. In many trades the work is non-repetitive and cannot be paid in this way. Wherever payment by results is applied, though, it has the effect of setting worker in competition with worker, to the detriment of team-spirit and morale within the factory.

Peasant Proprietorship and Small Holdings

Pro: (1) Peasant proprietorship encourages the growth of a sturdy, independent and thrifty class of men who are in every way the backbone of the nation. It satisfies the requirements of the capable and self-reliant man who, perhaps, works badly under other people's orders. Determined men are enabled to start with a minimum of capital and to rise in the world.

Con: (1) Peasant proprietors and small holders, to judge from those countries where they flourish most, are both illiberal and ultra-conservative. They survive only at the cost of great toil by themselves and their families, who are miserably overworked. The proportion of failures at starting and in bad seasons is very high, while successful peasants are only anxious to become ordinary

(2) Small holdings increase the population on the land and bring into cultivation areas now deserted. The 'magic' of ownership secures the best a man can produce from the land. Peasants pass on their qualities of hard work, etc., to their children, who escape the vices of the town-dweller. Rural depopulation is checked and the State depends less on unnatural urbanisation for its strength. The nation's foreign indebtedness is reduced and its resources are developed. Land which is tilled intensively by peasants is more productive than large farms. Britain's agricultural future lies with the development of dairying and mixed farming, for which small holdings are suitable, provided that co-operative methods of marketing are practised.

(3) The setting up of small holdings leads to more intensive cultivation, since the small holder is not content with as small a return per acre as some farmers will accept. As a result, on the Continent and also in England, the small holder has literally worked marvels. Market gardening is especially suitable for him. Most English farms, in any case, cannot enjoy expert specialised management, because they are too small.

(4) Disadvantages can be largely removed by adopting co-operation, so that the whole area of a small-holding colony becomes a single economic unit. The advantages of wholesale management are thus combined with those of individualism. Small holders have known great powers of co-operation, and the system has triumphed in Denmark, Holland and Belgium. They have carried out extensive works, bought machinery, and organised sales.

(5) Small holdings would be particularly well suited for the establishment of farm colonies for farmers. Even so, the advantages are social rather than agricultural.

(2) The trend of English agriculture has always been against the peasant. His children, at all times, have flocked into the towns, and rural depopulation is complained of in peasant communities. The best land is already occupied, and the largest part of England consists of clays and chalks only suitable for extensive cultivation. The nation's chief farming strengths come from the plough, which small holders are least likely and least fitted to use, and from its stock farming and breeding, which require large tracts of pasture land for grazing. The average small holder cannot hope to succeed as a dairy farmer.

(3) Large farms are capable of intensive cultivation and they enjoy the advantages of organisation, for small holdings are uneconomical in management, labour, and buying and selling. They cannot produce corn or cattle, nor practise crop rotation, nor manure heavily, nor drain effectively. Market gardening is hazardous, as crops cannot be stored, nor is it capable of great expansion without lowering prices. Many of the Continental peasants survive on industrial crops like grapes and tobacco, which cannot be raised extensively here.

(4) The small holder is generally averse to co-operation, which in any event is not of much use for corn-growing and cattle-raising. Machinery which is wanted in several places at the same time is thus not available. Co-operation is most suitable for buying and selling, without which small holders fall into the hands of moneylenders and middlemen.

(5) They would have to take the worst land. State farms on the corporate system would be much more likely to succeed than an individual system that would crush

the unemployed who wish to live on the land. Credit can be supplied by agricultural banks.

(6) They are a good way of raising the standard of agricultural workers' lives, since even now farm workers' wages are well below the average in other spheres. In offering an alternative to the agricultural labourer, they would cause wages to be raised under stress of competition.

out the weaker. The State's efforts to promote small holdings after the First World War were dismal failures.

(6) Profit-sharing, State-managed agriculture, or industrialised farms will do more to raise standards. Minimum wages already exist. Small holders are too much at the mercy of local dealers and conditions to reach a uniformly respectable standard.

Pollution of the Environment:
Are Tougher Laws Needed?

Pro: (1) Under the latest anti-pollution legislation, the maximum penalty for a first offence is only £400 – which is derisory compared with the enormous amount of damage which may be caused by the offender.

(2) The Control of Pollution Act 1974 (which received the Royal Assent on 31 July of that year but has not yet been fully implemented) does strengthen the previous legislation. There has been some back-sliding from it already, though, on grounds of the cost entailed in carrying out the necessary improvements. If the authorities seriously intend to combat pollution, the provision of adequate finance for the purpose is essential.

(3) The danger of well-meaning measures failing to be implemented is illustrated particularly clearly by what has happened with the new Water Resources Act. In theory, it gives Water Authorities wide powers to act; in practice, they come under the Department of the Environment – which has told them to withhold action, because of the financial problems. These cash difficulties, which apply to both industrial companies and farms, affect even more critically the Regional Water

Con: (1) Much tougher legislation has been enacted recently. What counts is to implement the existing laws properly. If that is done, stronger measures will not be necessary.

(2) This Act contains a new code regulating the deposit of waste on land and laying down conditions for the regulation of waste disposal sites. Local councils in England and Wales are constituted as waste disposal authorities and are required to carry out a survey of all the problems. The Secretary of State for the Environment is also given wide-ranging powers to make regulations to deal with dangerous or intractable waste. The new law re-enacts and reinforces, almost in their entirety, the previous Rivers (Prevention of Pollution) Acts 1951 and 1961, the Clean Rivers (Estuaries and Tidal Waters) Act 1960, and parts of the trade effluent legislation. In addition, it now applies to certain underground, tidal and coastal waters not covered before. It is, in short, extremely comprehensive.

(3) The Water Resources Act imposes much more severe penalties than before and has also expanded the number of offences (for instance, now bringing estuaries under

Authorities themselves. They, too, are now major polluters, because they have taken over the responsibilities of the various, fragmented bodies formerly in charge; that means they have become responsible for various sewage works producing effluent which is not up to standard, but they are unable to remedy the situation simply because they do not have enough money for the costly remedies entailed.

(4) The new legislation appears to have been framed on the assumption that industry is the most serious polluter – whereas, in the view of many independent experts, agriculture is potentially the chief culprit. Modern agricultural methods (e.g. the vast use of inorganic fertilisers, over enormous areas, and the concentrating of livestock for intensive rearing) are infinitely more pollutive than those of traditional agriculture. This is a further area in which much stricter measures are clearly needed. Moreover, the law now allows a new defence in cases of alleged pollution by farmers: that the act complained of was in accordance with good agricultural practice. That's the kind of loophole through which an offender could drive a coach and horses!

(5) Until recently, pollution offences were, incredibly, covered by the Official Secrets Act! That extraordinary restriction (ostensibly to protect confidentiality of industrial processes, but having the effect of protecting also the anonymous bureaucrats involved) no longer applies and full publicity may now be given to offences. Whether it will be, though, could be another matter. In view of the habitual reluctance of civil servants and local government officials to disclose any information unless they have to, great vigilance will probably be needed to ensure that they comply. Regulations should be introduced, therefore, to

protection). This in itself is a most valuable step forward. If there has been delay in implementing some provisions – though it certainly hasn't happened in all cases – this may be attributed solely to the national economic difficulties which have brought a slow-down in everything from industry's capital investment to the building of new schools and hospitals. Any such temporary hold-ups will be remedied as soon as economic conditions improve. In the interim, attempts to bring in tougher anti-pollution measures would be both ineffective and pointless.

(4) One feature of the new legislation which should not be underestimated is that the Secretary of State is now entitled to take precautions to *prevent* pollutive danger; formerly, he could do nothing until an offence had occurred. This power of prevention rather than attempted cure will be an extremely important weapon – against agricultural as well as industrial pollution. In pleading 'good agricultural practice', the burthen of proof will be on the defendant; in the present climate of opinion, he is likely to find courts less easy to convince than he may anticipate.

(5) To condemn new provisions of the law at this early stage is premature, to say the least. It is probable, in fact, that the unfavourable publicity received by polluters will have a cumulative and ever greater impact in deterring other potential offenders. Most people today are thoroughly perturbed about the pollution problem, and there is increasingly likely to be a public outcry if officials are caught trying to cover up. The force of public opinion is the all-important factor in the fight against pollution. It brought about the latest, much tougher laws against offenders; it will ensure that there is no let-up in the struggle; and it remains far more

compel them to publish regular reports on all cases of pollution (within the area for which they are responsible) and on the action taken in each instance.

effective than proposing yet more laws which would be more honoured in the breach than in the observance.

(See also *Preservation of Beauty Spots* . . . .)

Premature Burial:
Are the Safeguards Inadequate?

Pro: (1) Owing to the absence in most countries of completely foolproof laws governing the disposal of the dead, to hastiness in burying victims of epidemics, and to uncertainties arising in certain cataleptic and other morbid states which counterfeit the appearances of death, the danger of living burial is a very real one. In Britain during the last twenty-five years, several dozen cases have been officially recorded in which undertakers or mortuary keepers detected signs of life in people who had been certified as dead. If such mistakes are known to this extent, is it not probable that even more terrible mistakes have been made at a later stage, by the premature burial of still-living bodies?

(2) The first safeguard it is essential to tighten concerns the issuing of death certificates. At present, if a doctor has seen a patient within fourteen days prior to death, he can sign the certificate without examining the body. Only a few years ago, a Home Office pathologist reported that, of five bodies taken to a London mortuary, all certified by doctors as natural deaths, one was in fact due to multiple injuries, another to disinfectant poisoning and a third to gas poisoning. Clearly, the law should be changed so that doctors should not sign a death certificate

Con: (1) The present laws and regulations are sufficient. Premature burial may occur, but it must be exceedingly rare in Europe. The essential point which must be borne in mind throughout all these arguments is that, in cases where people have shown signs of life after being taken to mortuaries, the signs have been relative in the extreme and the victims were moribund to the point of no return; despite immediate treatment in intensive care units, their deaths have always been established finally within a matter of hours, or a day or so at the most.

(2) Premature burial is a very good subject for newspaper scare stories, but none has ever yet been proved true. In the vast majority of cases, it is relatively simple to establish that a person is dead, with complete certainty. When subsequent signs of life showed that mistakes had been made, special circumstances usually applied. Outside his hospital or surgery, a doctor can do little more than look for evidence of heartbeat and breathing. Both may be undetectable in a cold, unconscious patient without special tests being made. But, precisely because he is fully aware of the possibility, a doctor will normally try to delay issuing a death certificate in these circumstances until such tests have been carried out.

(3) Equipment of this nature

without having seen the dead person.

(3) Another important safeguard should be the provision of up-to-date testing equipment in mortuaries. This is needed especially for avoiding the danger of mistakes in one ever-increasing category: people in barbiturate comas. The risk is heightened in such cases because the victim's pulse and breathing may be slowed down to an extraordinary extent while in the coma.

(4) The controversy over transplants led the Department of Health to plan setting up an advisory panel – its members including a neurosurgeon and a neurologist, as well as heart, liver or kidney specialists – to decide when a brain was technically dead. The fact that such experts were considered necessary, in this special situation, suggests that there must also be room for doubt over the precautions in determining 'ordinary' deaths (when the extra care required for transplant operations is not called for).

(5) Obviously, a panel of consultants, as described in the previous paragraph, would be neither necessary nor feasible in most cases. It is not being argued that stricter safeguards should be applied other than in circumstances where it is recognised that these are clearly advisable – and there is a precedent for this. Prior to cremation, rather than burial, it is still a rule that more than one doctor must certify the cause of death. Reasonably, therefore, the two-doctor rule could be instituted for all deaths in categories where doubt is liable to arise (a very small proportion of the overall total).

(6) Among other proposals which have been made are: (a) that a doctor, even though he has already issued a death certificate, should examine the body again on the day before the funeral; and (b) that a bottle of chloroform with a loose

already exists in some mortuaries. Mainly as a precaution in drug cases, for instance, Sheffield mortuary installed an oscilloscope machine which can detect the slightest movement of the heart muscle – and its lead has been followed by others. It is admittedly desirable, perhaps, to require all municipal mortuaries to have such equipment.

(4) Transplant operations are, indeed, a special situation, involving public emotion to a very considerable degree. But it would be quite impossible to take such elaborate precautions for all deaths. There simply aren't enough specialists available; the number of bodies awaiting burial would very soon become intolerably large; and, in any case, such precautions would be absolutely unnecessary for all but a tiny handful of deaths.

(5) The rule that at least two doctors must examine a body before it is cremated was brought in at the turn of the century mainly to meet early fears that cremation might be used to conceal evidence of crime. The precaution is no longer necessary, if ever it was. The early fears have proved groundless, and the Cremation Society has long been pressing for parity with the regulations for burial. Another reason for the two-doctor rule originally was to guard against premature burial (or incineration), and this has been equally groundless.

(6) The scaremongering about premature burial is neurotic and quite unjustified. In Western countries, the possibility is so remote as to be virtually non-existent. Even if it did happen that an apparently dead body were placed in a coffin before the moribund victim was completely dead, the act of shutting the coffin would presumably ensure speedy and painless death by suffocation. So-called 'spirit messages' are not evidence, as there is no proof

stopper should be placed in each coffin, as a general practice. The depth of many people's anxiety about premature burial must not be underestimated. If we are to believe the reality of the alleged 'spirit messages' from the other world, the proportion of people prematurely interred is surprisingly high.

that they actually emanate from the dead. (See *Spiritualism.*)

Premium Bonus System

(The Premium Bonus is one variety of bonus systems. These are numerous and complicated, but depend mainly on rewarding workers on the basis of increased output. The general principle of the Premium Bonus is that, instead of fixing a piece-work price for the job, the employer fixes a 'basis time', in which the job ought to be accomplished. If it is done in less time, the workman is paid, over and above the standard time-work rate, a bonus proportionate in some way to the time saved. There are many systems, e.g., Halsey (the simplest), Rowan, Bedaux.)

Pro: (1) The Premium Bonus gives an incentive to the worker in the shape of increased wages for increased work. The employer does not pay for all the time saved on each job but only for a part of it. His overhead charges are reduced by the full employment of his machines and he is thus aided in meeting competition. Whereas under a plain piece-work system an employer's costs may not decrease very much per unit of output, under this system great economies are effected.

(2) The charges of injustice and dishonesty made by some workers against the system are met by a fair and liberal estimate of the 'basis times'. It is much better for the workers than the piece-rate system under which they are charged with losses such as waste of time in delivering materials, or waste of time due to lack of co-ordination between different departments.

(3) Bedaux Limited, the business concern responsible for the best known of these devices, claimed in 1933 that the results of their system 'in over 200 plants in different

Con: (1) The Premium Bonus has all the disadvantages that 'payment by results' entails both for the worker and for the goods made. In addition, it tries to get more from the worker for less pay than he would earn from normal piece-work. Its suspect nature is shown by the fact that often employers have introduced it first almost casually, by offering workmen extra money on pay day and letting them work the system or not, as they pleased.

(2) The underlying dishonesty of the system is not rectified by setting up a false standard as a 'basis'. Fundamentally, it is an attempt to get a lot by giving a little. In the hands of self-seeking employers, it would bear very harshly upon the workers.

(3) The figures quoted show that the workers receive only a small share of the advantages (for which, however, they have to work much harder). It is practically impossible for the average worker to check the bonus due, and the utmost secrecy surrounds the methods used in working out rest allowances. The introduction of the Bedaux system

industries during the past eleven years have been an increase of production of 44 per cent, accompanied by an average reduction of labour costs of 20 per cent, and an increase of labour earnings of 15 per cent'.

has caused many strikes in Britain and elsewhere.

(See also *Industrial Psychology, Applied*; *Payment by Results in Industry*; *Scientific Management*.)

Preservation of Beauty Spots and 'Sites of Special Scientific Interest': A Need for New Policies?

Pro: (1) The present laws give inadequate protection to recognised beauty spots and to sites declared of special scientific interest – which embrace areas of unique plant growth, of uniquely important geological formation, or harbouring rare and threatened wild life. New legislation is required which effectively inhibits forms of change in these areas incompatible with their special status.

(2) As the law stands, it is weighted in favour of the despoiler. For example, a farmer whose farm happens to be situated within a national park may apply for planning permission to erect a large new building which would be completely incongruous in the area; if his application is turned down, he has the right of continuing appeals – and, what's more, appeals conducted at the public expense. The Nature Conservancy can make an order designating a site as one of special scientific interest; but at present it has no means of reinforcing that order against an owner or occupier who wishes to make changes prejudicial to the special character of the site (e.g. farmers ploughing up the land).

(3) The present penalties for the

Con: (1) Since the National Parks Act of 1949, ten national parks have been created which cover some 5,228 square miles, or close on 9 per cent of the total area of England and Wales. The idea was not to change the character of these territories but to control their development in accordance with two main principles: (a) to preserve the characteristic beauty of the landscape within the park area; and (b) to ensure that the public has ready access to the parks and facilities for recreation and enjoyment. The Countryside Commission also has powers to designate areas in England and Wales, other than the national parks, as 'areas of outstanding natural beauty'. The existing laws cover a wide range of contingencies to reinforce the necessary protection for these places and, if properly observed, are quite adequate for the purpose.

(2) Nobody denies the value and importance of such areas as part of our national heritage, but their protagonists' enthusiasm sometimes goes too far. If they had their way, the amount of land set apart would become larger than our economy could bear. Proper protection for the sites can be provided only if they are not allowed to proliferate unduly.

destruction of 'scheduled' ancient buildings, or of trees on which a protection order has been made, are trifling in comparison with the financial gain which is usually to be made by the infringement. We need new legislation which provides for realistic penalties, reviewed at frequent intervals.

(3) A just balance has to be struck with the requirements of agricultural and urban development. It is neither desirable nor possible for a landscape – urban or rural – to be subjected arbitrarily to paralysis. A landscape is a dynamic entity, not a fossil.

(See also *Pollution of the Environment: Are Tougher Laws Needed?*)

Prison Reform

Pro: (1) The objects of imprisonment are the protection of society and the reclamation of the criminal. The prison can be made one of the chief agencies for the latter. Our present prison system still does too little to reform the criminal; hence the number of recidivists. Even the Borstal system, though an advance on previous methods, is not beyond criticism. It follows too closely the ideas of the English Public School, with its emphasis on loyalty, patriotism and *esprit de corps* – ideals so remote from the previous experiences of these boys that they tend to breed hypocrisy rather than honesty and independence.

(2) Every prisoner should be regarded as mentally sick and given the special psychological treatment adapted to his case.

(3) The present system has several serious defects. The slavish discipline enforced destroys all independence in the prisoners. Some of the work exacted is futile and the machinery used out of date. Creative activity, even for the more intelligent prisoners, is insufficiently encouraged. The net result is that the prisoners are not fitted to find work or resume a normal life in society; instead, they often develop various kinds of mental disorders

Con: (1) The duty of the State is to the public as well as to the individual. Advocates of 'pleasanter prisons' are apt to forget that a term of imprisonment *must* do more than merely reform the criminal. It is of the first importance that the sentence should act as a deterrent, not only upon the criminal himself but upon others who might be tempted to follow his example.

(Some) The prison system has, in fact, gradually been humanised and transformed by administrative measures, so that the old strictures no longer apply. The systems of Borstal, probation and suspended sentences prevent most of those whose characters are capable of reform from entering prison before they have had an excellent chance of making good.

(2) Much of the reformatory system is completely unrealistic. It leads to gross hypocrisy on the part of the prisoners, whose sole idea is to escape proper punishment and obtain release, often enough in order to commit further crimes.

(3) Such conclusions are drawn from observations made by criminologists on nervous subjects. When prisoners are allowed too much freedom from discipline, the risk of them corrupting one another is vastly increased. Many men have been

which render them a misery to themselves and a menace to others.

(4) Educational work in prisons, voluntary or otherwise, needs extension and development. Those jails which are in too remote places to make this feasible should be done away with.

(5) Most law-breakers offend through economic pressure. Others are physically degenerate and therefore fitted for occupational or education centres, or else suffer from obsessions and mental weaknesses which it is the proper function of the psychiatrist to treat. Recent advances, notably in connection with psycho-analysis, now give real hope of such treatment succeeding. A few moral degenerates who are past hope should be kept in mental hospitals. The handful who are deliberately and so to speak inexcusably, habitual criminals, ought to be sent to a penal colony. The present system deals adequately with none of these several classes. The single psychiatric prison is too limited in its scope. If each prisoner were given, on release, a fully stamped insurance card, enabling him to draw unemployment insurance until he found a job, all those unfortunates who are now driven by poverty to crime would be given a decent chance. The cost would be less than that of maintaining a man in prison.

(6) The Elmira State Reformatory in New York, Sing Sing Prison under Osborne, the Neudorf Convent Prison near Vienna, and other such places, have been successful in their humane methods of dealing with their inmates. The success of Britain's open prisons shows how much is to be hoped for from a new outlook, but experiments here are on too small a scale.

(7) Prison diet is badly balanced and inadequate for health, and most of our prisons are grossly deficient in sanitary conditions and general

taught a trade in prison, enabling them to earn a respectable living in the outside world, for the first time in their lives.

(4) Incorrigible offenders should be shut up for life, as dangerous to society. It must be recognised that there are some criminals whom no amount of educational work can reform – and that high-security jails will always be needed for them.

(5) Most of the psychological theories of crime rest on shaky foundations and have yet to be convincingly proved. The treatment suggested tends to be objectionable in itself and would be very difficult, tedious and expensive. The criminal code is concerned not with antecedents, causes and expectations, but only with the facts of crime. To allow a discharged prisoner to draw unemployment benefit is equivalent to paying a man to keep out of prison. It would be an unwarrantable charge on the public finances.

(6) Elmira was long a by-word among prisoners who had a much better life inside than outside its walls. New York State declined to support it. Sing Sing also has since been reorganised on the old lines. Many experts consider that, except possibly for the type of prisoner who is not normally a criminal and would be unlikely to repeat his offence, it has yet to be established that open prisons in Britain are any more successful than other forms of detention.

(7) Punishment must be to some extent retributive, to satisfy the sentiments of the community and of the criminal's victims. Much of the concern for the criminal is due to a perverted sympathy which forgets the suffering of those whom he has wronged.

(8) If prison is to be reformed, let it be made more unpleasant. For several classes of criminal, guilty of offences against both person and

health and cleanliness. Prison officers suffer from low pay and status, and not enough officers of the right calibre can be recruited under present conditions.

(8) In past ages, when punishment was savage, crime was more rampant than it is today – which proves, yet again, the ineffectiveness of drastic methods.

(9) At present, not only are our prisons grossly overcrowded – Britain's total prison population in 1975 was more than 40,000, of whom probably about a quarter were sleeping three to a cell – but not enough accommodation is provided for prisoners on remand, young people, and others who should be segregated from hardened criminals.

property, jail conditions are at present quite inadequate as a deterrent and bear no relation to the damage the criminal has inflicted. Many slum-dwellers have to endure harder conditions than men in prison.

(9) New remand and observation centres will solve the problem of segregation. The overcrowding of prisons is further proof that, at a time when severe measures are needed to combat the rise in crime and violence, life in jail is not sufficiently rigorous. If it were, many more men would give up a life of crime rather than risk terms which, in present conditions, they regard with some equanimity.

(See also *Indeterminate Sentences for Professional Criminals*; *Corporal Punishment*.)

Private Medicine

Pro: (1) All people should have the right to choose the doctors they prefer and, within reason, the timing most convenient to them for medical treatment, operations, etc. In theory, the National Health Service does allow people to change to another general practitioner, if they wish; but in reality, because many overworked NHS doctors already have full lists, it is often difficult to find another doctor in your home area who is willing to accept you as a Health Service patient. As for the timing aspect, the NHS allows for no freedom of choice at all.

(2) Envy of people with money is a root cause of the opposition to private medicine. It may be argued that, whether under a capitalist or a socialist economy (or a mixture of both, as in Britain), one universal reason for trying to earn higher incomes is to be able to buy things

Con: (1) It is quite wrong that the few should take precedence over the many. For all its flaws and problems, Britain's National Health Service represents an ideal which has been achieved by no other nation and which must rank as one of the greatest social advances in history. Its object is to make the best possible medical and surgical treatment available to the whole population, without favour. While it may not always achieve this, its shortcomings are due mainly to inadequate finance, in the adverse economic conditions now prevailing, and will be remedied in the fullness of time, when the economy improves. It would still be possible to get much nearer to the ideal, even now, if all members of the profession gave the NHS their whole-hearted support.

(2) The belief that opposition to the buying of privilege is raised

one could not afford before. Even if one ignores that point, as part of another, broader issue, the fact remains that it is financially possible for the great majority of people to secure the advantages of private medicine. There are several thriving medical insurance schemes, which cost appreciably less than most ordinary insurance policies and which enable subscribers to meet the charges of treatment as private patients. Subscribers still pay their normal National Health contributions, which thus benefit other people.

(3) Most of the important advances in medicine have been made by private doctors, working on their own, or by privately financed research organisations. Many consultants maintain private practices, where their earnings are high, so that they can afford to devote several days a week to working in public hospitals or free clinics.

(4) Since the NHS began in 1948, official health figures show that its hospitals have made little progress in the control of killer diseases such as strokes or cancer – whereas, in the private sector, heart disease and cancer are two fields in which marked improvements have been achieved during the same period. Waiting lists at NHS hospitals are so long that some patients are having to wait more than two years for any but emergency operations. Because of staff shortages and the pressure on hospital beds, elderly patients who might 'block' beds for a lengthy period are sometimes refused admission in favour of younger patients – a hideous dilemma for the doctors, who know that their decisions may well condemn old people to an earlier death than might otherwise have been avoidable. Lack of money for the facilities they need is fast destroying morale among NHS staff and has led increasing numbers

mainly from those who cannot afford that privilege is held, typically, by moneyed people themselves. It ignores the real cause: the present-day trend towards an increasingly egalitarian society, not by lowering standards but by enabling everyone to have access to higher standards. The commercial horrors of private medicine are illustrated by the USA, where many people are ruined financially by an unexpected spell in hospital – and where the poor, unable to afford medical insurance, may well die because they cannot pay for the treatment necessary.

(3) The latest developments in heart surgery and many other advances in surgical technique were all perfected at NHS hospitals. Only through the NHS has such expensive equipment as the kidney machine been made available to patients, even in their own homes, who could not have hoped to buy them from private sources. Similarly, NHS doctors are able to give out prescriptions for extremely expensive medicines, etc., which their patients obtain for only a nominal charge. Before the NHS was established, such medicaments would have been beyond most people's reach.

(4) The problems of the NHS are not denied, though it should be stressed that the overall picture is by no means as serious as asserted opposite; some regions are worse hit than others. The fundamental difficulty, as stated earlier, is the Government's inability to provide more finance. The Conservative Government began cutting back funds for the NHS in 1973. The following year, a delegation from the British Medical Association told the Prime Minister that £500 million was needed to get the Health Service back on its feet. No extra cash was forthcoming – and since then, inflation has rendered the shortfall even more critical. In short, governmental

of young doctors, who can ill be spared, to decide to emigrate. In these deteriorating circumstances, the public's need for the services of private medicine has become more acute than ever.

(5) An aspect of private medicine which should not be underestimated is its importance for business companies and their employees. It is recognised practice for many firms to pay for their staff to have free medical treatment – which has the further advantage of ensuring continuity of contact, through telephones in their private rooms, etc., and is thus mutually beneficial. The right of companies to pay for private medicine in this way is sound common sense. It is an attractive inducement when recruiting staff; it relieves employees of many anxieties and obviates delay before they receive treatment; thereby, in turn, it makes for greater efficiency overall. Large companies habitually provide a sick bay on their premises, which is open to all the workers without charge.

(6) It is not suggested that the NHS should be done away with and that all medicine should return to the private sector. That would be neither feasible nor desirable. But the reverse is equally true. There is room – and need – for both private and public medicine.

policy is to blame and not the essential structure of the Health Service itself. That being said, it is all the more important that the existing facilities should be shared fairly and that such anomalies as private beds in NHS hospitals should be abolished.

(5) Private firms have no more right to buy privilege than do private individuals. As long as a private sector exists, however, there is one constructive solution that they should adopt. If a company wishes to offer its staff facilities of this nature, it should get together with other firms to establish a clinic of their own, with all the companies involved paying jointly for the staff and equipment. That way, while priority could still be given to their own employees, they would at least have created a new medical facility which other people could use as well. Many of the larger trade unions have long run convalescent homes, for the benefit of their members, to supplement NHS facilities but without cutting across them.

(6) Some countries already have an entirely public medical service without any private sector, and this has not prevented them from being among the most progressive in the medical field (e.g. the Soviet Union). One of the principal objections to private medicine is that it leads to a diversion or dilution of medical skills from the public sector. When the two are still accepted side by side, as in Britain, the existence of one should not be at the expense of the other.

(See also *State Medical Service*.)

Profit-Sharing

Pro: (1) As the worker creates to a large degree the profits pocketed by the capitalist, it is only right that he

Con: (1) As long as workers have no share in losses as well as in profits, any scheme for profit-sharing

should be allowed a share in them. Though he cannot directly contribute to losses in bad years, he may do so indirectly by the establishment of a reserve fund and by forgoing bonuses in good years.

(2) Under the present system, many employees have no interest in the success of a business or in the prevention of waste or of damage to machinery. Profit-sharing improves the quality and leads to an increase in the quantity of the output.

(3) It has generally succeeded very well where it has been tried, especially when there is some provision for the workers to take up shares in the company. Failures have been due to employers' attempts to use the system as a weapon against trade unionism.

(4) Profit-sharing brings worker and capitalist together. Strikes are prevented, industrial unrest avoided, and all sides benefit. Before the gas industry was nationalised, the old South Metropolitan Gas Company introduced a scheme of this nature – and enjoyed more than a quarter of a century of industrial harmony.

(5) Profit-sharing is especially suitable for agriculture, where regulation by trade union methods is difficult owing to the variation between local conditions. It incorporates many of the advantages which are claimed for a co-operative system, but without involving any new departures in management or changes in habit.

(6) Profit-sharing could be organised nationally, with a Ministry of Profits to pool and distribute them. It would be a suitable arrangement for industries where nationalisation was not feasible, and is in general far more desirable.

amounts to charity on the part of the employer. The employee has no claim beyond the competitive value of his labour; profits depend on the wisdom and skill of the employer in using his capital.

(Some) Profit-sharing is a concealed form of paying wages and is unjust in that it is not reasonable to invite men to receive more or less remuneration for their services in consequence of causes entirely beyond their control. The details and rates are generally at the mercy of the employer, who may sometimes try to use them to depress standard wages. Trade unions, knowing that their activities bring better results, frown on profit-sharing.

(2) It is only occasionally that workers get a sufficient share to interest them. In all such schemes operating in Britain, the number of non-sharers is as great as the number of sharers. Payment by results is a much more efficient method of encouraging increased production.

(3) Its success is greatest where labour forms but a comparatively small part of the costs of production, e.g., ship-building. At least half the schemes initiated have failed, and most of them are intended to isolate the workers from trade union influences.

(4) Profit-sharing is no cure for the ills of our industrial system. It merely leagues a section of capitalists and workers together to exploit the consumers. It is often made an excuse for getting a contract of service which turns the worker into a temporary serf.

(5) Agriculture has proved in the event as susceptible of trade union organisation as other industries. Agricultural conditions can also be improved by industrialising farms. Profit-sharing is least applicable, because labour is such a large item in the cost of production, and it lacks the element of individual independ-

ence which is fundamental to a co-operative system.

(6) The difficulties are too complex for any such national scheme to work. Profits are best shared on a national scale by means of a special tax on them, whereby the revenue can be returned to the country as a whole.

(See also *Co-operation*; *Co-partnership in Industry*.)

Prohibition

Pro: (1) Where liberty in the consumption of drinks containing alcohol leads to licence, and licence to such evils as are apparent, the State should carry out its duty of protecting the public by prohibiting all intoxicating beverages.

(2) It is erroneous to suppose that the suppression of one evil leads to the creation of others to replace it. That has not been the case in history when great social advances have taken place.

(3) Prohibition has been a success time and again. It increases a country's industrial efficiency and the prosperity of the working classes. Many leaders of industry and of religion support it. In a country like Britain, with an efficient police force and a traditional respect for the law, evasion would be negligible.

(4) To impose the will of a minority on the majority of a democratic community is quite common in this and other countries, and the results are rarely serious under modern conditions. Nevertheless, the imposition of the will of the majority on the minority is the established rule in most States today, where serious issues are at stake. Prohibition, therefore, will come only with the general consent of the electorate. However desirable one may believe the measure to be, that consent will take time to secure. But it is by no

Con: (1) Prohibition is a gross attack on the liberty of the individual. The existence of a small proportion of admittedly harmful results is no excuse for victimising the bulk of the population, any more than cases of gluttony or unsound habits of diet would justify the State in saying what people shall and shall not eat.

(2) The imposition of near or total abstinence by force would suppress much good with the evil and replace one evil by others which might be worse. Prohibition is a symptom of an unsound view of sociological problems: drunkenness is less a cause than an effect of bad social conditions.

(3) Prohibition in America has been tried and abandoned (1919-33). It was the produce of a neurotic Puritanism, which attained its ends by highly dubious means. It led to an increase in the use of other drugs, encouraged defiance and mockery of the law, produced widespread corruption in the ranks of public officials, and weakened belief in other, quite separate moral issues. It removed or distorted a whole group of social habits without putting anything in their place, while its effects on the generation growing up were thoroughly bad, for they were surrounded by an atmosphere of contempt towards public authority.

means a remote or improbable prospect. As formerly in America, many more people in Britain now advocate prohibition than is usually realised.

(5) Palliative measures, which have now been adopted by anti-prohibitionists only because they fear defeat, are not adequate to deal with the colossal waste and suffering due to alcoholic indulgence.

(4) Elsewhere, too, prohibition has been put into practice only by underhand methods, which have enabled a minority to dictate to the majority.

(5) All the evils which constitute the alleged justification of this policy can be removed, and in fact are being removed, by education, by improvements in social conditions, and by the efforts of the manufacturers of alcoholic liquors, who are no more enamoured of excess than are their opponents. Often their proposals are thwarted by the fanaticism of these opponents.

(See also *Liquor Laws: Should They Be Relaxed?*)

Proportional Representation

Pro: (1) The present system of election produces unrepresentative Parliaments and may even reverse a national verdict. In 1929, for example, the Labour Party polled fewer votes than the Conservatives but obtained 32 more seats in the House of Commons. On the other hand, a majority may obtain much more than its fair share of seats, i.e., of power, so that representation in the House of Commons is dangerously one-sided. In the last 1974 election, the Labour and Conservative Parties polled just under $11\frac{1}{2}$ and $10\frac{1}{2}$ million votes and gained 319 and 277 seats respectively; the Liberals, with about half those levels (nearly 5,400,000 votes), won only 13 seats. Our present system is indeed a gamble and the swing of the pendulum acts without discrimination; it summarily dismisses from Parliament many of those most competent to serve the nation.

(2) Under proportional representation, the House of Commons would represent the nation fairly. The majority would have a majority of

Con: (1) On the whole, the present system is fair, and its shortcomings affect all parties about equally. The weight of public opinion is reasonably reflected in the Parliaments elected, and any undue predominance which the present system appears to give to one-party government is offset by the influence of other manifestations of public opinion.

(2) Under proportional representation, minorities would still be at a disadvantage in by-elections, which often have an influence on policy much greater than their immediate bearing on the state of the parties in the Commons. The difficulties of the present system might be met by adopting the less radical method of the second ballot (*q.v.*).

(Some) Present tendencies indicate that we shall eventually return to the fundamental characteristic of British opinion – that is, of being roughly divided into two parts, presumably still represented by the Conservative and Labour Parties.

seats and substantial minorities would be represented in accordance with their strength. When three parties plus minority nationalist groups have seats in Parliament, as now, the anomalies of our present system are increased; but the need for reform was apparent and reform was demanded when there were only two substantial parties.

(3) Today, if the House of Commons is not representative, if it is weak in personnel, it loses respect. The House will retain its authority only if it is truly representative of the nation. The excessive powers exercised by the party machine tend to diminish the prestige of Parliament. With proportional representation, MPs would have greater freedom from caucus control; they could, without giving up their main principles, take independent action when they deemed it in the national interest to do so, and yet secure re-election.

(4) One scheme submitted to Parliament provided for constituencies returning some five members each. Such constituencies would overcome the limitations of the present system and permit a broader scope of representation. Those returned would be the ablest of the party politicians, plus other candidates known and approved by virtue of their personality or previous public service.

(5) Under proportional representation, MPs would to a great extent continue to be associated with parties, and parties would in general form the basis of government. Governments would, where necessary, be formed by a frank co-operation of parties in respect of policies held in common. That is, they would be less partisan and more national in character. The Scandinavian countries use proportional representation in all their elections, with the result that, while their governments can be,

(3) The House of Commons has lost prestige in recent years for quite different reasons – the parties' internal squabbles being among them – and its position is not to be restored by any mechanical devices such as proportional representation. It is significant that, in the debate on the Representation of the People Bill in 1948, the Conservative Opposition did not speak in favour of proportional representation, although the operation of the present system had lost them many seats only three years earlier.

(4) Proportional representation would cause a great increase in the number of candidates and members whose programmes were limited to special hobby-horses. This would make a farce of Parliament – and it would still be unrepresentative, for the more entrenched it became, the more certainly it would turn representatives into mere delegates.

(5) The independent men would in practice represent local interests. Everyone with good qualifications for political life can enter it through one or other of the major parties, for their bases are broad. If proportional representation were to succeed, the House of Commons would come to resemble France's Chamber of Deputies under the 4th Republic, when a stable government with a settled policy was almost unknown, because there were so many groups and sub-groups which could be got to work together only after much horse-trading and intrigue. This state of affairs was undoubtedly responsible in large measure for the French voter's temporary abdication of his constitutional rights in 1958.

(6) There are so many varieties of the system that deductions cannot be made from successes reported from abroad, where conditions are very different from those in this country. The complexities of voting and counting confuse the voter and are

and are, changed democratically, they usually enjoy stability. In France, which uses the second ballot and not proportional representation, the need for inter-party bargaining between the two ballots, to gain other parties' support for remaining candidates, inevitably entails compromise on many issues.

(6) There are several different forms of proportional representation, some less far-reaching than others. The single transferable vote, for instance, has already been embodied in many Acts of the British Parliament. In Eire, there have been several elections under this system. The political campaigns there are nation-wide; there are no uncontested seats, and the polling is high. A party which fails to obtain a clear majority over the other parties cannot govern alone, which avoids such situations as that which threatened Britain's Labour Government after the first general election in 1974.

(7) The greatest corruption occurs in small single-member constituencies in which the result can be turned by those electors who, seeking their own sectional interests, are influenced by demagogic promises. The adoption of proportional election by New York City is considered to have diminished the corruption which formerly reigned there to a startling degree.

sometimes unfair to candidates. Second ballots would remove the only real cause of complaint and are much simpler.

(7) While petty bribery might vanish, subtler forms of currying the favour of constituencies would be developed. There would be a general campaign to obtain the votes of small sections which ran no candidates. The wealthy or astute man would be at a greater advantage than before in being able to canvass a huge area. Expenses, already prohibitive for all but the chief parties, would increase. Not mechanical devices but education and a better spirit are the cure for political evils.

(See also *Liberal Party: Is it Unnecessary?*; *Second Ballots*.)

Psycho-analysis

(The three main schools of psycho-analysis are the followers of Freud, of Jung, and of Adler. Other people have proposed a combination of the teachings of these three. The common doctrine of them all is that many of our states of mind and many of our actions, if not most, are largely determined by 'unconscious' wishes and memories. The Freudians have stressed the importance of our love and sex relationships, Jung and his followers the general idea of the 'libido' or life-force, and Adler the instinct of self-preservation and self-expression, which, when thwarted, produces an 'inferiority complex'. Needless to say, the whole subject is difficult and technical, but there are several general arguments worth mentioning.)

Pro: (1) Many of our actions and emotions cannot be accounted for by causes we can ourselves discover. They are clearly influenced by other things unknown to us consciously. Psycho-analytic technique shows that there is an active part of our mind of which we are not aware, and that this affects even those of our actions for which there appears to be adequate motive in our conscious life. This 'unconscious' mental activity comes out in a confused form in our dreams, etc., and from these we can get back to it and learn *how* it acts.

(2) 'Unconscious wishes' are potent causes of mental instability and even insanity. By applying psycho-analytic technique, they can often be made 'conscious' to the patient, so that he can face them squarely and often be cured of his affliction. A large number of cases have been successfully treated by this technique.

(3) The principle of determinism, i.e., that everything that is or happens is a result of a series of causes which can be discovered, at any rate in theory, is a successful hypothesis in physical science, of which it is, indeed, the foundation; it is also true of psychological occurrences and phenomena. If it were not true, then there could not be any science of psychology at all, for we should be quite unable to say that one thing will always follow something else, other things remaining the same.

(4) The main theses of psycho-analysis are supported by a world-wide examination of the myths, customs, beliefs and practices of primitive and other peoples. In these we see the results of unconscious forces on a larger scale.

Con: (1) Though we may grant the importance of the 'unconscious' activities of our minds, they are not to be regarded as determining our character and actions. Psycho-analysts are wont to find what they set out to find, especially in dream-interpretation. This is shown by the different interpretations that different analysts put on the same dreams and the same symptoms.

(2) Psycho-analytic treatment has upset the mental balance of quite a number of people. The cures might have been obtained by other methods, especially by suggestion. In fact, though psycho-analysts claim not to use suggestion, the prolonged treatment the most eminent of them employ cannot but be suggestive. A great deal of ordinary medical treatment depends for its success on suggestion, a phenomenon which cannot be avoided, however much we desire it.

(3) There is reason to suppose that psycho-analysis is based on the unprovable assumption that mental phenomena occur in a deterministic fashion. It is not at all certain that they do.

(4) If we adopt the theory that the various cultures in the world grew up independently of one another, the argument from anthropology might hold. But there is a growing school of thinkers who argue that they are causally related one to another. If their arguments hold, the anthropology of Freud, Jung, and their followers becomes untenable, as the facts on which they rely will prove to have definite historical causes, and so cannot be the product of the 'racial unconscious'.

(5) Psycho-analysts do not agree among themselves over the most essential points of their theories. The

(5) The discrepancies between the psycho-analytic theories are partly due to the fact that it is a new science whose data are being collected only gradually, and partly because the theories are often incomplete and stress one side of the matter.

(6) Psycho-analysis aims at establishing man as more completely master of his own mind and character. This is a perfectly moral and wholly admirable purpose. Those who attack psycho-analysis often have a vested interest in keeping man the slave of ignorance and prejudice. The psychiatrist is well established, and his services are constantly used by such bodies as the Forces, the school medical services and universities.

majority concern themselves with the abnormal. Psychology as a science would make better progress if more effort were directed to the study of the normal and the perfecting of experimental technique for that purpose.

(6) By exalting the importance of the unconscious, psycho-analysis aims a blow at the idealism of mankind and tends to undermine morals by making it appear that men are automata. Many so-called analysts are charlatans.

Public Opinion Polls

Pro: (1) The public opinion poll or 'straw vote', in which selected samples of the public are invited to give their opinion on questions of public policy and interest, and the results are analysed statistically, has become an important feature of present-day life. Run on scientific lines, these polls are capable of yielding very accurate results, and most of those taken prior to general elections in Britain have proved, in the event, remarkably near to the actual result. There is no reason to suppose that the findings of polls on general questions are any less accurate.

(2) Inaccuracies are rare enough to be of little importance and can in general be allowed for by statistical adjustments based on mathematical principles. It is possible to get a broad picture of the majority view of a subject and also the prevailing view of a particular section of the population – according to age, sex, social standing, etc. The degree of importance which the public attaches

Con: (1) It is a fallacy to suppose that public opinion on general matters can be ascertained with complete reliability in such a mechanical manner. The system is subject to considerable inaccuracies, resulting from such factors as the inadequacy of some of the questioners, the nature of the questions asked and the way they are framed. The only answers possible are generally 'Yes' or 'No'. Qualifications and reservations have to be ignored. There is thus a risk that they may reflect the conscious or unconscious prejudices of those who formulate the questions, even to the extent of being 'angled' to produce a desired answer. In some cases, further questions have revealed that the original question was entirely misunderstood.

(2) A vague or undecided answer might well indicate that the person questioned has not had time to make up his mind. It is not possible for most people to give snap judgments on every question, and the practice

to a given issue can often be judged from the number of undecided answers.

(3) Any changing trends in opinion, on any question, can easily be established by a further poll. At present, the only opportunity the public has to express its views on many questions is at elections, which may be at up to five-year intervals. The questions then presented for its consideration are often more susceptible of misunderstanding and inaccuracy than those in a poll. Since referenda and the Initiative (*qq.v.*) are not used in this country, opinion polls can even serve as a safety valve – far more desirable than political strikes or other disturbances – by giving members of the public an outlet whereby their views on crucial issues are brought home with immediacy to the powers-that-be.

(4) The only question now raised by politicians against public opinion polls is whether they should be banned just before elections, on the ground that their findings might influence voters unduly. It is argued by some that, if the polls show one party to be well in the lead, supporters of that party might become complacent and not bother to vote. Alternatively, supporters of a party which is trailing in the opinion polls might be led to make more effort than they would otherwise have done. But such arguments cancel each other out and there is no evidence at all that opinion polls have ever had any real effect on an election result.

of trying to make them do so is one of the main flaws of opinion polls. Considered opinions are based on a variety of causes, not all of them purely intellectual; an opinion may be changed overnight by some new argument or event, and the record will become completely inaccurate.

(3) Owing to the method of sampling on which public opinion polls are based, very few members of the public have the chance to express themselves in person. (The number of people questioned, even by the best polls, is rarely more than 1,500 or so.) The value of such polls as a safety valve is therefore negligible. The use of opinion polls by aggressive or unscrupulous bodies might lead to the lobbying of legislators which is one of the curses of American political life. Most questions of national importance can be settled at elections.

(4) That anxiety on this score cannot be so lightly dismissed is emphasised by the ruling that no public opinion polls may be published later than 24 hours before an election. Even at this last-day stage, the polls have had some notorious failures: for instance, President Truman's re-election in 1948, when all of them forecast his defeat; and similarly, the British general election in 1970, when only one out of the many opinion polls caught a faint hint that there had been a last-minute swing to the Conservatives. Rather than risk any such potentially misleading influences on the voter, it is surely better that all opinion polls should be barred throughout the official election campaign periods.

Public Schools

(The term 'public schools', in Britain, denotes educational establishments which are anything but public. They are private, fee-paying schools, nearly all of single sex. The Public Schools Act of 1864 listed these nine: Eton,

Harrow, Rugby, Winchester, Westminster, Shrewsbury, Charterhouse, St Paul's and Merchant Taylors. There are now about 200 recognised public schools in the country, the term being applied to schools financed by bodies other than the State, the headmasters of which belong to the Headmasters' Conference. Several of the boys' public schools date back to the fifteenth century, and one – King's, Canterbury – to the year 600. Most of the leading public schools for girls were founded in the nineteenth century.)

Pro: (1) The British public school system has been the source of many of our country's most valued traditions and reputation for high standards of honesty and service in public life. It is a unique institution, without which our social and cultural development would be infinitely poorer.

(2) Among the many advantages of public schools are the high academic standards of the teaching staff they are able to attract and the relatively small size of their classes – much smaller than in State schools – which thus have something of the beneficial character of tutorials at university, permitting more individual attention to each pupil.

(3) The fact that so many parents still make considerable sacrifices to ensure that their children get a public school education is proof that they consider it well worth while. If people did not believe that public schools gave their children benefits unobtainable at State schools, the economic difficulties prevailing nowadays would have long since ended the existence of most public schools. The crux of the matter is whether people who can afford it, or who make strenuous efforts to do so, should be entitled to give their children the best that is available. Since we live in a free enterprise society, the answer must be Yes.

(4) Although most public schools take day boys (and a few, in fact, have hardly any boarders), the great majority of them are boarding schools. From the community feeling thus engendered, the children acquire an instinctive awareness of

Con: (1) Public schools represent one of the last bastions of class and financial privilege. Despite a few marginal reforms, they are completely out of keeping with majority opinion today and should be abolished or absorbed into the State system.

(2) It is now widely accepted that all children should have equality of educational opportunity (i.e. that each capable of reaching the highest levels should have full facilities to do so, irrespective of parents' ability to pay), and the trend of official policy has moved increasingly towards achieving this. In the past, the financial resources of the public schools gave them an undoubted edge. Today, though, the academic records of public school pupils are, in general, no better than those from the upper reaches of the State schools – and, in some cases, it may be doubted whether their facilities are now even as good.

(3) People with money will always use it to try to buy things which, they think, give them (or their children) an advantage over others less fortunately placed. It makes no difference whether such things are not actually superior to those generally available, as long as they believe them to be so. The crux of the matter is whether, in a supposedly egalitarian society, people who can afford it should be entitled to buy privileges not open to everyone else. Where the education of the nation's children is concerned, the answer should be No.

(4) All too often, the cloistered life of boarding schools is out of touch with the realities of day-to-day

how to live more easily with their fellow-men in the larger community of the adult world.

(5) The majority of public (boarding) schools, again, are situated in the country and have facilities for sport and country life generally which exist only in the more privileged homes. This is one reason why public schools remain in great demand, particularly among middle-class parents. Another is that public school education is concerned not only with academic standards but with developing the children's characters as future citizens. Both work and leisure time are used constructively to foster physical and mental health and to produce young people with wide interests, a sense of service to the community, and a well-rounded, balanced attitude to life.

(6) Only a very few public schools are co-educational at all ages, but the level of demand shows that there are enough of them to meet the requirements of parents who prefer this system. Although the single-sex nature of most public schools is criticised by some people, it does in fact reflect the overwhelming demand. Indeed, at the age they go to public schools, many children themselves would rather be without the society of the opposite sex – in school surroundings, anyway. The total seclusion once customary at public schools no longer applies, since older pupils at most boys' schools nowadays have a modicum of association with girls' schools – through dancing classes, orchestras, joint dramatic productions, etc.

(7) The first and perhaps the most important lesson learned by any child entering public school is the practice of mutual tolerance. From this, in turn, develop the qualities of loyalty, decision, and natural leadership – which explains why most of Britain's national leaders (of what-

existence in the outside world and engenders its own artificial values, the disillusionment of which comes as a rude shock when the children leave to take their place in adult society.

(5) The privilege enjoyed briefly by public school pupils – merely because their parents have been able to pay for it – presents the danger of them acquiring snobbish attitudes of the worst kind (especially if the leisure facilities of the school are of a nature unknown in their own home lives). Without discussing the issue of boarding *v.* day schools, which is another argument, the fact remains that day pupils at public schools tend to be less 'snobby' than boarders. Their comparative freedom to explore the world outside school gives them mental and emotional advantages which make them more immediately fitted for adult life.

(6) Children in their very young teens will nearly always prefer the company of their own sex, but those from the mid-teens onwards need to learn how to comport themselves naturally with the opposite sex, without silly self-consciousness. Many public school boys, when they leave, are still far too immature in this respect. The argument for single-sex schools has in any case been partially shattered by the fact that a good number of well-known boys' schools, in recent years, have accepted girl pupils as well – in the sixth forms, at least. Nearly all the State schools are co-educational, and their children certainly emerge with much more understanding and recognition of the opposite sex's attitudes and natures than do those from public schools.

(7) The impossibility of escaping from school influence and atmosphere, during term-time, frequently entails the stifling of individuality. The regimentation imposed by public schools is overtly inimical to independence of judgment. Against

ever political party!) have usually been educated at public schools.

the highly dubious advantages of the 'old boy network' – the implicit favouring, in later life, of people who went to the same school – must be weighed the fact that too many products of public schools are instantly recognisable by their dull uniformity and lack of initiative.

(See also *Comprehensive Schools*; *Co-Education*.)

Public Transport, Free

Pro: (1) Nationalised road and rail transport undertakings suffer from governmental demands which are incompatible. On the one hand, they are obliged to run many uneconomic routes and services, while being restricted in the charges they may make; on the other, they are still expected to show an overall profit. Experience proves that, in those circumstances, they are almost certain to register heavy losses. It would be more realistic if the State recognised that passenger transport should be a public service, in the fullest sense, and therefore met all the costs. Free public transport would not apply to freight, nor to long-distance travel, but it would be appropriate for the bus, underground and suburban commuter services used by the great majority of the public – and it would enable those undertakings to provide the standards of service which people want.

(2) 'Pilot' schemes for free public road transport have already been tried abroad, with some success.

(3) Public service is a misnomer unless travel is free. While encouraging greater use of public transport, it would permit savings in other ways. Since booking-office clerks, ticket collectors and the like would not be necessary, such staff could be transferred to more productive functions. As a result, operating costs per mile

Con: (1) Even if a very limited form of public transport could be operated without payment of fares, which is highly doubtful, its costs would still have to be met – and that means extra taxation. No new tax burden for the purpose could be fair, since people who normally need to use public transport rarely, if at all, would be helping to pay for those who use it every day. Why should people who live on or near their place of work, as in the country, meet a similar share of the costs, in tax, as suburban commuters? Clearly, the only equitable system is for each traveller, like any other consumer, to pay *pro rata* for what he or she uses. This is borne out by the nationalised airlines, which do frequently show an annual profit because they are able to set their fare and freight charges at realistically high levels.

(2) The schemes concerned, from all accounts, were one-day wonders and resulted in chaos; little more has been heard of them since.

(3) This takes no account of the increased fuel costs, nor of the basic problem that recruitment of the extra staff needed, even now, is hamstrung by the high costs of living and accommodation in the towns. Bus and underground services are already running at much lower frequency than in the past because,

would be lower if public transport were free than under the present system.

(4) (Some) Other ideas for improving transport facilities, such as the pool of battery-driven bubble cars for city centre travel in Amsterdam, usable on a co-operative subscription basis, have failed to catch on. Existing means of public transport are more efficient, and there would be far greater enthusiasm and support for them if they were turned into a free service. This would also help to solve traffic congestion problems, because there would be a corresponding reduction in the number of people using private cars to take them to and from work each day.

with cheap housing unobtainable, they cannot attract enough new employees for their present requirements.

(4) (Some) Many people regarded the Amsterdam scheme as an admirable, idealistic experiment, but concluded that it was impracticable and unbusinesslike. It was opposed not only by the local taxi drivers (predictably) but also by the police, because of the traffic problems caused. Even if such schemes were taken over by the authorities and operated without charge, they still wouldn't succeed.

(See also *Motor Traffic: Should It Be Restricted?*)

Rating Reform

Pro: (1) The English rating system has been altered only piecemeal since it arose from the Poor Law of the seventeenth century, and a thorough overhaul is long overdue. It has been said that 'taxes are paid in sorrow but rates are paid in anger'. This almost universal resentment stems from the inequities and anomalies of the present system – not only the ever-increasing burden on ratepayers, aggravated by inflation, but the lack of uniformity in assessments from one local authority area to another (whereby, for instance, a property in one district can be rated three times as high as a similar property in an adjoining district).

(2) Expenditure by local authorities has risen so rapidly that their total budgets have become ever more dependent on the annual grants they receive from the Exchequer. It is estimated that, on average, Treasury

Con: (1) Piecemeal alteration to allow for changing conditions is a feature of all English legal and administrative systems and has the advantage of permitting greater flexibility than the systems applied in other countries. Uniformity of assessment is impossible in a country with such a wide variety of communities, and the idea takes no account of the widely varying benefits and public services enjoyed under different local authorities. One way or another, services like education, road maintenance, public health facilities, and so on, have to be paid for; and despite prolonged study of other ways to raise local government money, no one has yet been able to find a fairer method than the present system.

(2) The cost of maintaining local government services has increased to a much higher level than anyone

grants now meet 60 per cent of local authority spending. This greater dependence on Whitehall, intrinsic to the inadequacies of the present system, inevitably entails a decline in the independence and vitality of local government.

(3) One basic reform which has been proposed is that the rates should be replaced by a system of local taxation, enabling authorities themselves to raise *directly* a much higher proportion of the money they need to spend. This could take the form of a percentage levy on incomes, similar to National Insurance contributions and payable by employers, employees and self-employed people. The British Labour Party, in its manifesto before the October 1974 general election, stated: 'Public services have to be paid for by the public – the only argument is about how to share the costs, not how to avoid them'. The Conservatives' manifesto said they would abolish the domestic rating system 'and replace it by taxes more broadly based and related to people's ability to pay'. Both parties, therefore, recognised the need for rating reform. The suggested percentage tax on incomes could meet the ideas of each, from their different standpoints, and would be fairer and more rational than the present system.

(4) Among specific measures, immediate steps should be taken to remove the cost of some local authority services from the rates, with the central government taking over full financial responsibility for them. A prime candidate for this is education, which is by far the biggest single local government expense. Relieving them of the burden would cut local rates by nearly half.

(5) Further ways to relieve the rates include: (a) crediting the proceeds of capital gains and land development taxes to the locality in which they originated; (b) giving

would be willing to finance solely out of local property taxes. Yet the financial limits imposed by the central government, as part of its drive to combat inflation and revive the national economy, still leave local authorities with very considerable freedom of action. Far from undermining that freedom, the Government has taken an essential step towards allowing the authorities greater exercise of their own initiative, by its recent reform of the local government structure so as to create fewer (and bigger) local authorities.

(3) Experts have been studying alternative methods of local taxation since before the last world war. If any had been able to devise a new local tax which conformed to certain essential criteria, it would have been adopted long ago. Among the necessary conditions for such a tax, it would have to be: available to all local authorities; capable of being both levied and collected locally; relatively cheap to administer; appropriate as a local tax; and socially acceptable. In addition, local authorities' freedom to fix and vary the rates of the tax would need to be set within limits acceptable to the management of the national economy. No new tax proposal has succeeded in meeting all these criteria (nor, perhaps, is ever likely to). It is significant that the pledge to abolish the rating system, made by the present Conservative leader, Mrs Margaret Thatcher, when she was Opposition spokesman on housing and the environment, has since been modified; the party now stresses that 'local authorities must continue to have some independent source of finance'.

(4) Local authorities cannot expect to 'have their cake and eat it'. Even if they remained the agents for implementing educational policy, the price for transferring the cost burden to central government (i.e.

local councils, rather than central government, the right to levy stamp duty on property transfers and to raise extra revenue by such means as planning fees, taxes on animals, and possibly even a 'bed' tax on tourism; and (c) giving councils most of the revenue from the existing motor taxes, i.e. vehicle and driving licence fees (which are already collected locally, anyway) and the duty on motor fuel (which could be collected at bulk storage depots).

(6) The methods cited in the previous section are already employed by some European countries, most effectively, in raising money for local services. In West Germany, the main burden of local taxation (about 80 per cent) is borne by business and industry rather than by householders. The local tax is levied on all businesses, from a hot dog stall upwards. Local authorities are also empowered to levy a tax on land sales, on dogs, and on bars and places of entertainment. Compared with their British counterparts, most German cities are well off financially. In France, all the financing is centralised. A citizen is liable to pay several of hundreds of varied taxes, depending on his job and social position; but every centime paid through the local tax collector's office goes to the State, which decides how and where to allot the money.

(7) (Some) Several reformers urge the introduction of a system of partial rating, under which people would not be compelled, as now, to pay for public services they do not use, such as education or public libraries.

to national taxation) would be the loss of their present relative freedom to control education in their own areas.

(5) The revenue produced by such expedients would still be inadequate to meet the full bill for essential local government spending. Measures of this kind would also tend to worsen the imbalance between local authority areas, widening the gap in the quality of public services provided in different areas – higher in some, lower in others. As an example, a less well off local authority could not collect enough from its own motor tax revenues to pay for the costs of new national motorway construction cutting across its area. In general, there would be a continued need for centralised finance to even out differences in local authority resources, to stimulate the provision of certain services and, when necessary, to provide for national standards.

(6) Population densities and other conditions differ so greatly, from one country to the next, that methods used successfully in some would be a failure elsewhere. Because of the aversion to direct taxation and the high rate of tax-dodging in several Continental countries, their governments have to rely much more on indirect taxation than is necessary in Britain. Hence, for instance, the wide variation in the VAT rates imposed. The same factors apply to local revenue raising. Eventually, the EEC aims at the harmonisation of indirect taxation, and this will pose other member-countries with far greater problems than will the present British system.

(7) Such a device would be contrary to the fundamental principles of all taxation, including rating – and it would be virtually impossible to administer efficiently.

Recall of Representatives

Pro: (1) The Recall of Members of Parliament is a necessary complement to the theory that Parliament should be subject to the will of the people. If it were possible for re-election to be forced on Members at the petition of a certain number of the electors, politicians would become more responsible and more serious. Elections would be conducted in a better spirit and a distinct check would be given to the operations of party machines and unscrupulous election propaganda.

(2) The Recall would give opportunities for showing the feelings of the country towards Government policy. At present, between general elections, this depends solely on the fortuitous occurrence of by-elections. It would also enable voters to deal with MPs who, once elected, repudiate the view of their voters, or of the party on whose programme they were elected, and thus in effect disfranchise their electors.

(3) The Recall is very popular in the USA and the USSR, where it is held to be a necessary item in the machinery that expresses the sovereignty of the people.

(4) (Some) The principle should be applied more widely. Not only elected representatives but semi-elected people – officials, judges, and important functionaries – should be liable to it. Only thus can satisfactory public service be assured and the likelihood of corruption be eliminated. It should apply to both State and municipal affairs.

Con: (1) The doctrine of the Recall is wrongly based. It applies properly to delegation, whereas representation is superior. Unless representatives are given a measure of responsibility, only inferior candidates will come forward; these will indulge in the wildest demagogy, and no coherent public policy will be advanced. The Recall might too often be exercised on trivial grounds and could lead to incessant elections.

(2) The Recall would not be an occasion for manifestations of popular feeling on general policy. There are always enough by-elections during the life of a government to show the trend of public opinion, and a hundred other ways of expressing it.

(3) The Recall was instituted in the USA to satisfy people who had little faith in their local political leaders. But it does not secure its ends: for example, in Oregon it was made a weapon by which corrupt interests got rid of their opponents on public bodies. In the USSR, where the individual candidates are chosen beforehand by the Party and only one list is presented to the voters, the procedure more closely resembles the dismissal of an official for inefficiency than the expression of disapproval of a political policy.

(4) The Recall is a desperate measure. It is not conducive to the development of a responsible, trustworthy public service. Judges would lose their independence. Corruption would still prevail, and the work of officials acting with care and foresight could be imperilled by public criticism that was both inexpert and uninformed.

(See also *Delegation v. Representation*; *The Initiative*; and the next article.)

The Referendum, More Use of

Pro: (1) More use of the Referendum would be a check upon hasty legislation; it would ensure that vitally important measures could not be passed by a Government against the wishes of the majority of the electors; it is the last step in the process of making the voice of the people effective. The efficient operation of Britain's Referendum on Common Market membership proved that the system would work well in this country.

(2) The compulsory Referendum, and possibly the Initiative, would be the greatest possible safeguard against sudden tampering with the constitution. It would be chiefly applied to questions of constitutional change and so would not involve serious changes in the routine of government. In America and elsewhere, it has generally been used in this way.

(3) The representative system has largely broken down. British statesmen, though professing to serve their constituents and the will of the people, are becoming more and more independent and out of touch with ordinary people, except at elections. They can hardly object to becoming more subject to popular control. Under the Referendum, it is not necessary for a Minister to resign when one of his department's schemes is rejected. The system thus permits able men to remain in office even if the public votes against them on a particular policy issue.

(4) The heart of a whole policy is often contained in some single resolution or law, and if the doctrine of the mandate has any place in democratic theory, it is applicable on these pivotal occasions.

(5) The electors would have to

Con: (1) Checks on hasty legislation are abundant. In general, legislation is years behind the times, and the Referendum, which is an appeal to conservative tendencies, usually puts off the day of reform. It is impossible to prevent the Government from deciding which questions are to be considered important and which not. The most important measures are not necessarily those most talked about. Britain's Common Market Referendum was mainly a political manoeuvre to overcome the Labour Party's internal dissension and cannot be regarded as a valid precedent.

(2) The British constitution has the advantage that it is largely unwritten and thus flexible and open to change whenever needed. The Referendum is workable only under a written constitution, and all written constitutions grow out of date and harmful long before anyone dreams of changing them.

(3) The central theory of the constitution is the responsibility of Ministers to the House of Commons. The Referendum would seriously affect that position. A true democracy is representative and does not depend solely on the counting of heads.

(Some) The British constitution is too democratic already. Final decisions should not be placed in the hands of the populace, which is too often uninformed and swayed by passions.

(4) It treats policy in fragments. When a law is one part of a policy, to submit each part for separate acceptance or rejection is to present the issue artificially and out of perspective. The most intelligent electors will not accept an inconvenient measure on the grounds that it is part of a larger policy of which they approve.

vote for measures and principles, not men. This they are perfectly competent to do. At present, they are asked to decide between two or three complicated policies, which touch every foreign and domestic interest of the State, without a chance of exercising a critical selection between the good points and the bad. They can surely decide on the advantages or disadvantages of a single legislative proposal. The merits of voting for 'men, not measures' are disproved by the steady degeneration of the type of candidate elected. The reason why voting is so small in many referenda is that the considerations of party and personal passion and prejudice are absent. Those who do not vote are presumably indifferent to whatever happens, and so those who are concerned are rightly allowed to decide.

(6) It would be politically educational and would free people of the habit] of thinking on party lines. Measures would then be considered from the point of view of the community and not of the interests of parties, creeds, sects or classes.

(7) The House of Commons would still deal with unimportant measures and would have to draw up each measure to be referred, settle all the details connected with it, and finally present the best result it could reach.

(8) The adoption of the Referendum would lessen the evils of the party system, because the certainty that party support meant party victory would vanish.

(9) A partial or trial application of the Referendum might be made. There is no logical or necessary connection between the Referendum and the Initiative, which, of course, may be desirable for its own sake. Nor, it should be stressed again, would it be feasible for Britain to use

(5) The disadvantages of the Referendum are like those of voting for candidates. It is possible to accept or reject, but not to select or amend. The advantage lies with voting for a candidate, because other influences may afterwards be brought to bear on him, and it is easier to weigh up the merits and demerits of a number of items taken as a whole than of one item consisting of various closely related parts. The unsatisfactory nature of the Referendum is shown by the fact that, in very many cases, the total vote for and against a policy has been less than one-third of the total vote for and against the advocate of that policy.

(6) Political education must be gained less expensively and more thoroughly. The Referendum would not abolish the party or the section. Rather, it would unite discontented and dissatisfied parties of every sort into an unnatural alliance *against* any measure. The Referendum is the great and fatal device for maintaining the *status quo*.

(7) The House of Commons would become even more an object of disrespect than it is now, as its debates and amendments would have an air of futility. It would labour in committee over every clause of the enormously complicated measures which are now the usual form of legislation, knowing quite well that the electorate would presently have to say Yes or No to the whole without proper consideration of the parts, because it is mechanically impossible for a Referendum to sift the good from the bad.

(8) The party system would remain; the mass of voters would follow one party or another, for in most cases one party would be identified with adoption and another with rejection of the measure. Each side would make the usual promises as the price of support, and voting

the Referendum on a regular basis – only on key issues involving drastic change, which necessarily occur at infrequent intervals.

(10) The Referendum would put more vigour into political life and would give the electorate the sense that they really controlled their destinies.

(11) In some States of the USA and in Switzerland, it has been tried with great success. So far from being an un-English institution, its origin was English (seventeenth century). When used in America, it has served as a substitute for the veto, which is a cardinal feature of English constitutional theory. Although British monarchs still have the power of the 'royal veto' in theory, it is no longer applied; nevertheless, it remains necessary that some form of a sovereign remedy should exist. No fewer than 1,600 instances, at the least, are known in America; if the system had been a failure, it would have been dropped. It is a common enough feature in trade union constitutions in Britain, and has worked well; decisions to call strikes are nearly always subject to it, and those in which it is not used very often fail because of the discord which follows lack of agreement about the policy adopted.

(12) It keeps the legislature and individual members in touch with opinion in the country during the interval between one general election and the next. It helps to ensure that a Government cannot carry through, unchecked, a policy different from that for which it was elected. It would also serve as the decider when the two Houses were in head-on disagreement over a measure.

(13) The expense need not be greater than the Government wished. If a simpler organisation were adopted, it would cost much less than a general election.

would still be swayed by the popular idols of the day.

(9) A partial application would not prove whether the system would be appropriate in its complete form. If the Referendum is to be adopted, its complement, the Initiative, will have to be adopted, too. When voters are called to the polls more often than for normal elections, they soon get bored (as experience in France showed under de Gaulle).

(10) It would make political life more dependent on mechanical devices and lead to a further decay of popular interest in politics. Elaboration and complication in political institutions is both a symptom and a cause of apathy.

(11) In Switzerland, the results have usually been ambiguous, while in the USA the Referendum has been confined to simple State issues. Trade union experience has not proved its great superiority to other methods, but rather suggests that it gives freer play to the transient whims of the moment. A strike is a simpler affair to decide on than an Act of Parliament.

(12) By-elections are sufficient to keep the House alive to popular opinion. Shorter Parliaments would be preferable to this device. The Referendum would give the House of Lords an excellent excuse to block every measure it disliked and, for this and other reasons, the already unduly slow parliamentary procedure would become even slower.

(13) The expense of this succession of minor general elections would be excessive, probably even prohibitive.

(14) Each Referendum would be accompanied by an outburst of all the worst features of political campaigning in the Press and by the parties.

(14) Laws thus sanctioned receive greater respect than otherwise. They could not be said to be the result either of party or of class legislation.

(See also the preceding article; *The Initiative*; *Delegation v. Representation*; *Parliament, Reform of*; *Written Constitution*.)

Registration, National, in Peace-Time

Pro: (1) Britain is one of the few countries which in normal times has no registration system and thus no continuous record of its citizens. National registration served to increase the flexibility of administration in wartime and was useful particularly in the management of rationing. It can be used at any time for such useful purposes as the revision of voting lists, and avoids much cumbersome procedure.

(2) Identity cards help to prevent crime, to catch criminals and to detect illegal immigrants or undesirable aliens. During the Second World War, one mass inspection of identity cards was apt to give the police more information than weeks of searching.

(3) In these days when there is so much necessary regimentation and recourse to documents, an identity card is a much simpler means of identification than the set of documents which would otherwise be necessary to establish an individual's *bona fides* at any time. Impersonation becomes impossible; the identity card was found very useful as a means of preventing Post Office frauds, for instance. No innocent citizen need object to carrying his papers with him; they are, in fact, a convenience, since they may avoid lengthy questioning. They are no more a threat to liberty than passports, the necessity for which is now generally accepted.

(4) The French, long renowned

Con: (1) Registration is only one more example of the increasing regimentation that is threatening the liberty of the British public today. While it may have some value in a police State, in a democratic country in peace-time there is no excuse for it. Machinery already exists for dealing with voting lists and census-taking, and rationing is not a feature of peace-time life in Britain – not normally, anyway.

(2) They are utterly useless for catching criminals, for, when identity cards are introduced, the forging and stealing of them becomes an industry. Only with the addition of fingerprints could they be completely reliable as a means of identification; but the use of such documents, and especially the finger printing of innocent citizens, is repugnant to a free community. A false identity card is otherwise accepted without question and police investigations have often revealed that it is quite possible for a man to get away for years without possessing one at all.

(3) Since ordinary identity cards are no danger to the criminal, their main effect is the harassing of the respectable citizen, who can be required to produce them at any time, even where there is no shred of evidence that he is involved in crime. The same applies to passports, which, so far from being accepted, are generally detested and have been the subject of repeated governmental promises to abolish them.

for their love of liberty and independent-mindedness, are among the nations which have used identity cards for many years, without regarding them as irksome or an infringement of individual freedoms.

(4) The French are so liberty-loving that all their policemen carry guns on everyday duty ... As a nation, in fact, they are far more regimented and bedevilled by petty bureaucracy than the British people have ever been.

Religious Teaching in Schools

Pro: (1) One dictionary definition of religion is: 'Belief in a personal God, controlling the universe and entitled to worship and obedience; the feelings, effects on conduct, and the practices resulting from such belief'. It is surely incontestable that this is a subject which it is not only appropriate but a duty for schools to teach. Even the advocates of strictly non-denominational teaching will recognise that religion, in this context, is a fundamental part of human knowledge – and therefore an essential ingredient of education, *per se.*

(2) Except in specifically denominational schools (e.g. those for Roman Catholic children), religious teaching is not simply about worship, nor does it centre on any one particular faith. Its purpose, above all, is to instruct children, in their most formative years, about morals and the code of conduct to be followed by self-respecting people in adult society.

(3) Young children themselves, without any prompting, nearly always feel a desire for a religious 'anchor'. In later years, the perspective offered by lessons in religious history gives them a better understanding of the way mankind has developed over the centuries and, thus, a better understanding of humanity as a whole in our own day. At whatever age, indeed, all of us need yardsticks by which to judge our own and other people's actions. Religious teaching is by far the best source of such guidance.

Con: (1) The principal objection to religious teaching in schools, even those which are supposedly non-denominational, is that these lessons are usually made obligatory for all pupils (up to a certain age, anyway) and there is, equally, compulsion in attending morning prayers, etc. At many boarding schools, children may have to attend prayers up to three times a day, plus compulsory church attendance on Sundays. This is contrary to the spirit of the times, which leans increasingly towards freedom of choice, both socially and educationally. Whether for religious lessons or observance, all children should have the right to decide – initially, through their parents, if need be – whether they wish to take part.

(2) One of the most important functions of school life, as a community in miniature, is to lead children to follow a social code which will stand them in good stead throughout their lives. They learn more about this from the everyday experience of how to co-exist tolerably under school conditions than from any amount of Bible stories.

(3) Guidelines of this nature – as, indeed, the morality imparted by religion – are all embodied in the legal code. It is not necessary to learn them from religious lessons. Teaching children an understanding of the law, with an appreciation of how its past development reflects man's social progress, would be much more practical.

(4) All religious faiths aim to improve human society, to help alleviate social injustice and to express ideals from which, sooner or later, necessary social reforms emerge. Accordingly, when schoolchildren receive a basic grounding in religious knowledge, their horizons are broadened and they are introduced to issues which are crucial to society in general. It follows that religious teaching in schools will not only combat the scepticism and indifference which afflicts so much of the world today but, morally, can help to counter the pernicious attitudes of the so-called 'permissive society'.

(4) This confuses the role of religion, as such, with the question implicit in the present debating issue: whether religious teaching in schools should be compulsory. Some people hold that the Church is no longer relevant because it is out of touch with present-day needs – but that is another, bigger argument. The plain fact remains that awareness of the problems of society can be imparted to children quite effectively enough without any dependence on religious knowledge.

School-Leaving Age:
Should It Be Lowered Again?

Pro: (1) Even though childhood may be recognised as a privileged state, a time comes when most children are tired of learning in isolation and begin to feel a desire to take part in the working life of the community. Except for those who wish to acquire higher qualifications or to make the pursuit or imparting of knowledge their life work, education after that time should be carried on as an adjunct to paid work in factory, office, or by evening study. Raising the school-leaving age to 16 has led to increasing frustration among a majority of children who, maturing earlier these days, derive no real benefit from the extra year's enforced schooling and, waiting ever more impatiently to enter the adult world, often cause serious problems for the overworked teachers. The age should be reduced to 15 again. Children aiming for higher academic levels would stay on anyway.

(2) The increasing need for technicians goes hand in hand with a need for mass production workers who may be unskilled or semi-

Con: (1) It is now generally recognised that a child has not finished his or her development even at the age of 16. At one time, it was thought that children of 5 or 6 were sufficiently mature to work a full day in factories! The descendants of those who held this view are the kind of people now most in favour of reducing the school-leaving age again. Although changes in school population levels and new trends in educational systems have caused some problems, raising of the leaving age to 16 has been highly beneficial overall. Many children receive technical training in their last year or two which helps them to get better jobs, in fields that interest them, once they leave. Many others have suddenly spurted ahead educationally in their final year and have been able to go on to higher education, even university – which would not have happened if they had left school at 15.

(2) If the country is to acquire the advanced technicians it needs in ever greater numbers, they must be freed as children from the disability of

skilled. Moreover, many children have neither the capacity nor the inclination to reach a high level of technical efficiency. Allowing such children to leave school at 15 need not be a bar to them reaching whatever standard they are capable of, since most progressive firms now sponsor day-release courses for their young workers.

(3) The present school-leaving age is unpractical and harmful to industry, because young people need to begin technical or industrial training as soon as they are capable of it, especially now that older people are tending to retire earlier from working life. A child of 15 is sufficiently developed to start such training, without physical or mental strain.

(4) Improvements in technical education and equipment at school have not yet been carried out as fully as planned, through lack of money for new buildings, etc., and through inconsistencies in the supply of teachers – too many in some years, shortages in others. (Or rather, shortages in some areas, like London, because young teachers cannot afford the prevailing high prices for accommodation.) Raising of the school-leaving age to 16 has greatly aggravated such problems and put extra strain on what facilities do exist.

having to leave school before their capabilities are truly known. At present, the majority of children who wish to continue their education after the age of 16, but are unable to remain at school to do so, are forced to undergo the strain of working by day and studying by night. Reducing the leaving age to 15 would aggravate this situation immeasurably – and would be a retrograde step for which later generations would find it hard to forgive us.

(3) Many children fail to take advantage of the present facilities for higher education because of economic stress in the family; the numbers of children remaining the full period in grammar schools has increased considerably since all secondary education was made free. Before the universal leaving age was raised, there was always a temptation for parents with low earnings to sacrifice their children's education for temporary economic advantage.

(4) Modern theories of education need a longer period of school life to be successfully worked out in practice. Without this, any scheme of improvement can remain only a pious hope, sketchily applied. Raising of the leaving age has also increased the supply of children willing to qualify for teaching, and thus will be self-balancing in the long run. The popularity of colleges of further education and similar institutions shows that there is an undeniable demand for more prolonged schooling.

School Sport, Compulsory

Pro: (1) Schools have a duty not merely to educate their pupils in an academic sense but also to lay the foundations for them to become rounded individuals in adult life. Sport is a valuable, even essential ingredient of this process. Apart

Con: (1) Most people have a tendency to resent any activity which is compulsory rather than voluntary, especially if it impinges on their spare time (as school sport frequently does). In these circumstances, sport is as likely to produce

from its obvious advantages in maintaining and improving young people's physical fitness while they are at school, it provides implicit lessons in the importance of teamwork, initiative, imagination, the need for hard work and continual practice to achieve higher standards, and many other qualities which contribute to good citizenship.

(2) Schoolchildren who are unwilling to take part in sports, at first, often discover to their surprise that they are above-average at a particular sport – and it ends by becoming a lifelong enthusiasm. Even among the ultra-devoted athletes who reach Olympic Games status, quite a few started this way.

(3) Children are naturally energetic and need plenty of activity to let off steam; but adults also require a certain amount of physical exercise to ensure their well-being. It doesn't have to be strenuous, nor a team activity; plenty of walking in the fresh air (rather than motoring everywhere) will suffice! Sport at school helps to inculcate the habit of exercise, so that it becomes second nature to try to keep reasonably fit.

(4) Children have the habit of obedience at school – or, at least, automatic acceptance of the curriculum drawn up for them. In this sense, therefore, few pupils regard organised sport as any more unfair than, say, lessons in history or maths; it is simply part of the scheme of things. Moreover, the point should not be overlooked that, for the great majority of children, a games period provides a welcome break from classroom lessons.

an excess of frustration and aggression as to encourage any theoretical spirit of good citizenship. The advantages claimed for it can equally well be gained in other ways – and more effectively so, above all, when the activity is undertaken by young people of their own free will.

(2) Those responsible for running school sporting activities have a tendency to concentrate unduly on children who are good at them. A competitive spirit is right and natural in games; but some teachers' desire for their school's success – particularly in matches with other schools – can be so excessive that it sets a thoroughly bad example.

(3) Adults, particularly those in sedentary jobs, are fully aware of the probability that they will start getting out of condition and make up their own minds about the extent to which they try to keep fit – or not. But they're much more likely to maintain interest in a sport they chose for themselves originally than one with memories of being reluctantly compelled to take part in it at school.

(4) Acceptance may be automatic among young children; as they grow older, though, they are supposed to be taught increasingly to think for themselves. More enlightened schools give older pupils, at least, the right of choice – and this is the crux of the matter. The opportunity to choose between a number of available activities is a key facet of modern educational trends.

Science:
Is It a Menace To Civilisation?

Pro: (1) It is more than doubtful whether the advantages of scientific progress are not counter-balanced

Con: (1) In some respects, obviously, the risks of modern life are greater than those of a few genera-

by the evil that it does. In particular, scientific research as applied to mechanical inventions is fast becoming a menace to the world. We travel at continually increasing speed in our trains, motors and aeroplanes; yet, on the roads alone, the number of people killed in this country in a single year exceeds that of all the British soldiers killed in the whole of the Boer War.

(2) Science has enabled us to manufacture engines of destruction for use in war – tanks, submarines, high explosives, poison gas and atomic bombs – which are so devastatingly effective that very little of our civilisation is likely to survive if another war between the big powers were to break out.

(3) In industry, scientific inventors are continually improving the machinery of production, with the result that fewer and fewer men are required to do the same amount of work. Thus the advance of science is one of the main causes of unemployment, because the rate of increase of productivity is so great that reorganisation cannot keep pace with it. At the meeting of the British Association in 1934, Sir Josiah (Lord) Stamp seriously advocated that attempts should be made to slow down the rate of scientific progress and invention because society could not readjust itself sufficiently rapidly to the changing conditions.

(4) One of the greatest dangers of science today is the opportunity it offers to those in power to create a race of robots. Not only can they subdue their victims by force. They can subdue their minds by radio and television propaganda, by control of the Press, and by a subtle use of the knowledge of psychology in education and public affairs. There is a growing and sinister gulf between those who have the knowledge to build space ships and atomic reactors and the rest of the world.

tions ago. But it is by no means certain that the proportional accident rate is any higher. There are more people in the world, and there are more vehicles on the roads. Life is less static than it used to be. Besides, where a few hundred people are killed in accidents nowadays, thousands used to die in epidemics before science had taught us the laws of health and hygiene, or in famines before science had been applied to communications and transport.

(2) It is not science that is to blame for this, but man's evil nature. There would be no war but for the greed, jealousy, fear and quarrelsomeness of man. The scientist rarely has an axe to grind. He works disinterestedly to increase the sum of human knowledge, because he feels the urge of the quest for truth. If his discoveries are seized upon by politicians and by governments and used for harmful purposes, that is not the fault of science or the scientist.

(3) The improvements in methods of production certainly enable fewer men to do the same amount of work, or in other words to produce the same amount of wealth. Therefore, the same number of workers can produce far more wealth. If this increased wealth were satisfactorily distributed, as it might be by rational reorganisation, the general standard of living could be raised and hours of labour could be reduced. The chief obstacle to this is not science but capitalism, which blocks the way to the necessary reorganisation.

(4) Against these possibilities we must set the effects of science in the past on the human mind – the liberation of thought due to the work of Galileo, Copernicus, Darwin and other pioneers of learning. Science has changed man's outlook from superstition to an enlightened understanding and has substituted the

concept of natural law for a state of ignorance in which, for instance, a comet was thought to be a sign sent by an angry god.

Scientific Management

Pro: (1) Scientific management eliminates grounds of contention between workers and employers by giving an independent standard to which disputes can be referred. It determines, through accurate analysis, the proper task, wage and working day for each individual, the results being calculated according to the laws of human nature and in a spirit of fairness and liberality. It introduces a positive teaching that harmony and mutual understanding should be cultivated between management and men. Trade unions become superfluous and strikes are prevented. Suitable men are raised to posts of responsibility.

(2) It greatly increases output by systematising piece-work, by setting tasks based upon time-and-effort study, by encouraging the standardisation of tools and equipment, by careful choice of managers, foremen, etc., and by greater opportunities for specialisation. In some cases, the increase in productivity is 100 per cent, and the workers are not fatigued because suitable rest-periods are allowed. With the general adoption of scientific management, production would be increased so as to provide enough for all, without increasing cost.

(3) In firms where it has been adopted, the results all round are excellent. The best possible working conditions are provided, the men are contented, and the industrial problem may be considered solved. Though there may be certain divergencies between labour opinion and management principles, co-

Con: (1) The essence of scientific, or, as it is sometimes termed, psychological management, is that men are to be treated purely as productive machines, completely dependent on the expert. Management and men might agree, provided they were the only parties in industry, but the policy of industry still remains controlled in the interests of profits by outsiders. Trade unions are necessary to protect the less efficient workers from a low standard of life, reflecting their low industrial worth. Their policy is for a high level, not a fluctuating standard. In practice, only a few 'efficiency engineers' have any real responsibility or independence.

(2) Scientific management cannot be applied on a national scale to all forms of industrial activity. In practice, it tends to overwork employees and turn them into automata, for it is most successful in fields of work that can be resolved into repetitive processes. The reduction of the need for skill is an insult to the best tendencies in the workers' nature. At the level where scientific management itself operates, it is incapable of increasing or rationalising the activity of a man's brain.

(3) It is usually an excuse for union smashing, and its introduction serves to break up the natural association between men working in the same shop and industry. No matter how benevolent it may appear, a powerful concern cannot be allowed to get free of all restrictions put on it by unions, or cease to

operation and reasonable compromise have enabled both to operate together in some plants. It will restore the morale which all observers declare is deserting the industrial world.

have them as potential checks on its actions, without grave dangers to the liberty and welfare of the workers; for power, even more than profit, is the aim of the industrial overlords. It is a device to perpetuate and make the most of an evil system.

(See also *Industrial Psychology, Applied.*)

Second Ballots

Pro: (1) The system of second ballots, by requiring the successful candidate to have a clear majority of the votes polled, would lead to a truer representation of the people.

(2) Candidates frequently and notoriously are returned by minority votes (i.e. out of the total poll in a constituency). Second ballots would always elect the candidate most favoured by the constituents as a whole.

(3) They would destroy the arguments against third-party or independent candidates which now embitter political life and lead to caucus manoeuvres on a large scale.

(4) The greater the number of candidates, the greater the choice of the electorate, while the deposit system checks 'freak' candidates.

(5) They would reduce the power of party managers and break up hide-bound parties. Candidates could afford to be more independent.

(6) In France, where second ballots have long been the practice, the system requires a candidate to win an overall majority (i.e. over all the other candidates in his constituency) to gain election in the first ballot, which normally happens in only a few instances; but in the second ballot, he needs only a simple majority over the other principal candidate(s) remaining in the field. The outcome, therefore, is a genuine

Con: (1) Taken on the whole, the people are fairly represented; if accuracy is wanted, second ballots are inadequate.

(2) This is not so frequent as to make the system seriously at fault. The candidate preferred by the majority of electors in any given constituency is produced just as often by the present system.

(3) Intrigues for support in the second ballot would give rise to the same phenomena.

(4) In Parliament, we would have a multitude of parties and splinter-groups, with all the inevitable intrigues and confusion they cause. The deposit introduces a property qualification which has ruled out excellent candidates already; second ballots would add to the already heavy cost of candidature.

(5) Party discipline is a valuable factor in stabilising our political life. Independence of candidates would vanish at the second ballot. Where it has been tried, the results are not encouraging.

(6) One of the most dubious features of French politics is the inter-party bargaining in the period between the two ballots, whereby one party agrees to support another party's man and withdraw its own less successful candidate in one constituency, in return for a like favour in another constituency. This is bound to entail compromise over

reflection of the predominant views of the entire electorate.

policies and the soft-pedalling of plans for needed reforms. And the system still motivates against some parties (e.g. the Communists need roughly twice as many votes as the Gaullists for each parliamentary seat they gain).

(See also *Proportional Representation.*)

Single-Chamber Government

Pro: (1) The tendency of all modern governments is to centre in one Chamber. The only result of having two Chambers is a pendulum swing between the obstruction of any reforming government and what is tantamount to single-Chamber government (since Second Chambers are always conservative and give almost unquestioning support to governments of like view). This happens invariably in Britain.

(2) There is no danger of a single Chamber's prolonging itself in power indefinitely under a democratic electoral system. The single Chamber is elected by the people and is therefore always under their control. The bi-cameral system is a slow and cumbrous way of conducting public business and is unjust to the electorate.

(3) No Parliament which represents a people like the British, predominantly averse to sudden change, is ever likely to be guilty of precipitate legislation.

(4) The House of Lords has often been responsible for the withdrawal of men from useful public service in the Commons, especially where progressive governments have seen the need to strengthen their power in the Lords, and has thus ended many a promising political career.

(5) No other country besides Britain has a Second Chamber assembled on such haphazard principles, with no regard to intellectual

Con: (1) Wherever democratic countries have tried the single-Chamber system, the Second Chamber has almost always been restored subsequently. The consensus of educated opinion in Great Britain is in favour of a Second Chamber.

(2) A popularly elected government is not proof against the temptations of absolute power. Many tyrants have rested their tyranny on the people. The only safeguard for the State is a balance of power among the different organs of government.

(3) The chief value of a Second Chamber is to provide security against hasty legislation; it gives an opportunity for reflection and further, more objective consideration.

(4) The House of Lords has secured for the nation the continued service of men who, for various reasons, would be unable or no longer wish to take part in contested elections, but whose experience entitles them to a voice in the national councils. If the Lords were abolished, the House of Commons would lose much of its own distinctive character.

(5) Conditions prevailing in other countries are not necessarily applicable to Britain. New Zealand is a small country with a homogeneous population and without the extreme conflicts of interest which give rise to ill-considered legislation. Russia has her Soviet of Nationalities, but

or physical fitness. New Zealand manages her affairs without a Second Chamber, and so do the Socialist countries of Eastern Europe. In Norway, the Second Chamber is chosen from members of the Lower House already elected.

(6) If a Minister is a member of the House of Lords, he is rendered less amenable to criticism than if he were a member of the Lower House; this is especially felt when the Minister is of Cabinet rank.

(7) No institution ought to be allowed to continue in existence unless it can be proved to fulfil a useful purpose. The value to be put on the Lords is shown by the scant attention its proceedings receive from the public – and from the majority of its own members.

(8) Reform of the Lords would not meet the chief criticisms against it, unless such reform were so radical as to involve a complete break with our constitutional tradition and procedure.

(9) The Labour Party's return to power in 1945 raised the problem in its acutest form, since Conservative-minded Lords promptly attempted to use their power of temporary veto in the interests of the section of society which they most reflect, to nullify measures of nationalisation for which the Labour Government had duly received majority backing from the electorate. Although the degree of confrontation has lessened in recent years, the fundamental conflict still exists.

in any case the extent to which her single Chamber and those of the satellite countries actually govern is severely limited, and so no comparison is valid.

(6) A Minister in the Lords will always have a No. 2 in the Commons, who has to deal with questions about the department concerned – and criticisms made there about the Ministry's conduct of affairs are fully effective as criticisms of the Minister himself.

(7) Any existing institution, especially if it can point to an ancient and honourable career, has *ipso facto* an argument for its continuance. The vitality and importance of the Lords have been demonstrated frequently.

(8) It is undesirable to abolish the Second Chamber, even if we do not approve of the present one, because the increase in the scope and volume of business dealt with by the State renders it impossible for one body like the Commons to cope with it all. Reform, or a new type of Second Chamber, is necessary to prevent the Executive from becoming supreme.

(9) The Lords stand for a more permanent element in the country than a Commons majority and, consequently, are entitled to be cautious about approving proposals that might well be countermanded after the next general election. The fact that some of the legislation hastily passed by the 1945 government was immediately reversed by its successors is a proof that some check on its activities was needed.

(See also *Lords, Reform of the House of*; *Parliament, Reform of*; *Devolution*.)

Social Credit

(This title indicates the principles put forward for social reconstruction by Major C. H. Douglas and writers following him. The proposals may be summarised thus: Credit should be granted for production simply on the basis of the capacity of production exercised by manufacturers, farmers, etc. Prices to ultimate consumers, i.e., the public, should be based on the relation between the Production (increase in assets of all kinds) and the Consumption (depreciation of all kinds) in the community over any selected period. If Production is the greater, prices should be proportionately lower than the Cost Price as now ascertained by firms as the basis of their charges; if Depreciation is greater, there would be no reduction. The difference between the price charged to the consumer and the Cost to the producer or retailer should be made up to the latter by a credit – not a subsidy – from the Government. All future Capital Development should carry a dividend with it, which should be distributed per head over the community. As the country developed its resources, the dividend would become larger and form a substantial part of the income of everyone.)

Pro: (1) The chief cause of trade crises and of poverty in this country is the inability of manufacturers to find a market easily for their maximum possible output. This indicates an error in our financial system of distributing the goods, as there is a *natural* demand for all they can produce.

(2) The present financial system has grown up accidentally and bears no relation to the physical processes of making and using up wealth. It should be replaced by a scientific mechanism. The defects of the current system have been sufficiently shown by the financial and industrial crises that many countries have suffered at intervals.

(3) The retail prices charged to consumers have to cover a large proportion of costs which represent wages, etc., paid out so long ago that they have been spent and so are not available to buy the goods now on sale. Consequently, the great bulk of purchasing power has to come from wages and salaries now being paid in respect of production not yet ready for sale. Owing to the development of industrial processes, this proportion tends to increase all the time. Owing to the permanence of capital equipment, this system is constantly breaking down. It is absurd not to be able to distribute the wealth available except on the condition of making a great deal more goods

Con: (1) The causes of our economic troubles are various. They comprise some or all of the following: Capitalism (see *Socialism and Communism*), over-population (see *Birth Control*), inefficiency in industry (see *Scientific Management*), ca'canny on the part of Labour (see *Trade Unions*), insufficient savings of capital, and land monopoly (see *Land, Nationalisation of*).

(2) The present financial system has been built up by centuries of experience and is a marvellously efficient and self-balancing instrument. Unnatural pressures placed on it recently have not altered the fact that, despite international calls for large-scale reforms, only relatively minor amendments have proved feasible or necessary.

(3) If prices do partially involve costs which can be paid for only by new production and the wages, etc., paid to those who produce it, this process is continuous. It has always existed and will continue. The hitches which occur are due either to such causes as those in (1), or to other causes which set on foot trade cycles, or to the mistaken policies in respect of currency pursued by various governments.

(4) The present system of covering all financial costs in prices accurately represents the debts incurred by various parties in industry which must be paid. The manufac-

which may or may not be wanted and which in any case leave the problem no nearer solution.

(4) As the fresh credits depend on charging *lower* prices, there cannot be inflation. The principle of taking a national balance-sheet would prevent over-issue.

(5) Bank credit is a continually renewed stream of inflation, which hits at the consumer through increased prices. The fact that industry would immediately grind to a halt, if all bank credit ceased, merely serves to show that the system is unsound.

(6) Besides the unused capacity everywhere observable in industry, and the innumerable wastes which go on, the potentialities of production through improvements in technique are enormous. The results now are inadequate, because the prospects of reward, in the widest sense, are so doubtful.

(7) A system by which financial profits would depend more and more on effective turnover in production would minimise the evils and maximise the good in the present system. Thereby, too, the self-seeking tendencies of human nature could be harnessed to the common purpose.

(8) The dividend is the logical successor of the wage. This is demonstrated not only by the unemployment problem and the tendency for the brains of the community to enter the selling rather than the producing branches of commerce, but also by the steady growth of dividend receivers. Even Socialists now encourage the wage-earner to try to save enough to become a dividend-receiver in his old age.

(9) We depend far more on the state of the industrial arts than on any of the other factors of production. This is an accumulating inheritance, beginning from the earliest civilisations. Every inheritor, as a matter of justice, should receive

ture of credits by the Government, as proposed, would mean a mass of paper money and all the consequences of inflation.

(5) The issue by banks of credit for production is only a superior and economical development of old methods. It has enabled the greatly increased production of the present day to come about and is absolutely necessary for its continuance.

(6) The whole idea is based on the assumption that a vastly increased production is possible. This may be true in certain small departments but is not true of industry as a whole, and especially not of agriculture. There are quite sufficient inducements already operating to secure that people shall do their best, though some minor adjustments are doubtless desirable.

(7) The principle of 'production for profit' is the chief source of our difficulties; until 'production for use' replaces it, no progress is possible. A different relationship between employer and employed is needed.

(Some) Human nature must alter before any such scheme can be a success, as it calls for closer co-operation and complete honesty in those working it.

(8) 'He who will not work, neither shall he eat.' The dividend is the hall-mark of social parasitism and will inevitably breed a nation of *rentiers*, as the Dutch were in the eighteenth century.

(9) Land, Labour and Capital are the only factors of production, and the proper reward of each is determined in the long run by the operation of supply and demand. The proposal for a national dividend is an attempt on the one hand to outwit economic laws and on the other to abolish that competition by which alone mankind can survive and evolve.

(10) A Socialism of producers is

from it a concrete revenue. A developing dividend system would turn 'exploiters', 'profiteers' and 'wage-slaves' into citizens working together less and less from compulsion and more and more from inducement.

(10) The idea of Social Credit would unify the nation, for it would give everyone an immediate interest in the common prosperity. It would promote international peace by making the economic system of each nation self-balancing, and so end the unnatural struggle for markets and resources.

(11) The solving of the Financial Riddle is the first step in any form of social reorganisation whatever. Finance is the great instrument for securing co-operation in the modern world, and it is the first obstacle now met with in putting through any reform, large or small.

(12) It would make the poor rich without making the rich poor.

a nobler ideal. There can be no solution of our social problems while some have access to the means of production and distribution while the majority have not. Social Credit, or any other system, could not promote international peace unless every country adopted it – and even then, some nations would always strive for a more dominant role.

(11) Finance is but one of the implements of society. Social co-operation can be attained by goodwill and the determination of everybody to avoid waste and ostentation.

(Some) A revival of religion in the widest sense of the term is what we most need.

(12) No scheme of social reform is acceptable which leaves the rich in possession of the good things of life and the plutocrats masters of the community.

Social Service Conscription (For Both Sexes)

Pro: (1) It is well known that the majority of young people, of both sexes, have a deep-seated desire to do work of benefit to their fellow-humans. That desire could be put to more effective use, for the general good, if all young people underwent a limited period of social service conscription. They should be given the choice of various kinds of social work, should have the assurance of being able to find a place in one or another of the fields most of interest to them, and could also be given the opportunity to decide whether to do their service here or abroad.

(2) Although peace-time military conscription (or National Service) was unpopular, it did have its advantages for the development of

Con: (1) This commendable trait in young people normally finds expression in their late teens or early twenties, when many of them do in fact seek voluntary social work. Unhappily, the desire is all too often stifled or made impracticable, before long, by the pressures and responsibilities of adult life. To harness it to the machinery of official conscription would even more quickly stifle the spontaneity of young people's desire to serve. The very act of formalising it would make their contribution less effective.

(2) It is doubtful whether many young people would welcome any form of service that is imposed rather than voluntary. Nor is there any proof whatever that more than

young men's characters. Few would wish the military aspect to be restored, but its beneficial effects could be fully equated by conscription for social service. Young people would accept this much more willingly than military service. An important reform should be to make social service conscription applicable to girls as well as boys. Most girls are just as willing – often, even more so – to devote themselves to useful work of this kind, and they would welcome the wider opportunities for it which an official scheme would offer them. (The only necessary difference would be that the conscription of young women would have to be restricted mainly to single girls, with married women entitled to obtain exemption, if they wished.)

(3) The period of social service conscription would not cause such interference to young people's careers as National Service did, because its timing could be more flexible. Those training for professional or technical qualifications would either be able to complete their studies beforehand or, in many cases, regulations could be amended to permit their social service to be incorporated as part of the practical work required before they qualify. Since full-time social workers need considerable training – as, of course, do the teachers, medical staff and many others involved in various fields of social service – the proposed arrangements would help to ensure higher standards among the conscripts. Moreover, once they had completed their 18-month or two-year period of service, many might well be motivated to carry on with it of their own accord.

(4) A period of obligatory social service could become regarded as payment by students for the university or technical college education they had received. This would mollify public opinion at large and a small proportion of girls would be glad of this particular equality; a greater probability is that there would be a sharp increase in the number of girls getting married in order to avoid conscription. If young husbands are to be called up (as they were for military service), usually obliging their wives to manage on lower earnings than before, why should the wives be entitled to exemption, anyway? Unless they are bringing up babies, such differentiation would merely add to the resentments in these egalitarian times. Illogicalities of this nature serve to demonstrate just how unpractical the whole idea would be.

(3) Non-interference with young people's careers could be only a pious hope. Most would find social service conscription just as much of an interruption as military service was. Even among those who had just qualified, few would yet have the necessary skills for some of the often difficult and diplomatically delicate work entailed (particularly in the developing countries). Much of this work requires continuity, and the endless turnover would be harmful in that respect. Moreover, only a small proportion of those conscripted would be at the level of professional or technical qualifications; the majority would have to be used for less skilful work. But if these were obliged to spend 18 months or two years doing social service at a lower level (e.g. painting old people's homes for them, reading to the blind, playing with mentally handicapped children), they would not be fully engaged and would soon suffer the frustration of feeling that much of their time was being wasted or inadequately used. Another snag: the logistical difficulties of providing enough accommodation for the conscripts (especially the new residential centres necessary for the girls) would be almost insuperable –

silence most of the present, ill-informed criticism of students.

and far too costly in present economic conditions.

(4) Should students be expected to pay, anyway? Doesn't the nation have a duty to educate its children?

(See also *Military Training, Compulsory: Should It Be Restored?*)

Socialism and Communism

Pro: (1) The fundamental fact of human life is that men are drawn into association with one another. It is to take the fullest advantage of this natural characteristic that a Socialist society should be established. It is not to be denied that individual and sectional interests have been dominant of necessity at various periods in the past, but human history is a long succession of changes leading up to a general reconciliation of the interests of the individual with those of society at large. The State is not necessarily the organ of integration.

(2) Men are not entirely selfish, nor entirely altruistic. In the past, however, society has rested its conscious policy solely on the first impulse, with the result that excellent moral codes have existed side by side with the triumph of the strong, the brutal and the cunning. If freedom, or rather the power to do whatever one wishes, is limited by society, the interests of all are enhanced and freedom is much more secure and much more extended.

(3) The alternative to Socialism is chaos or a slave State. The present system is breaking down in the spheres of morals, economic efficiency, and culture.

(4) The economic development of capitalist production has divorced the producers almost entirely from all property in or control over the instruments of production, creating

Con: (1) The evolution of society does not move in the direction of the Socialist State. The self-regarding impulses are more fundamental than the associational. The only way in which advantage is likely to be taken of the latter is by putting everything under the despotism of the State.

(2) True individuality and freedom can obtain only where the individual is left as much freedom as is consistent with the safety of the State. Humanity has no collective mind; human progress is due to the free play of rivalry between man and man.

(3) The main spur of economic and social progress in the past has been individualism. The same force is the only one capable of carrying mankind forward in the future. Civilisation always depends for its cultural development on a small class, which is supported by the profits of individualism. That class has also been the standard-bearer of freedom in politics and morals.

(4) (Some) The trend of development does not divorce the worker more and more from the means of production. Side by side with the big factory, there constantly occur chances for small people to start independent trades. The peasant proprietor in most parts of Europe is as strong as ever. It has been shown that small-scale production can secure practically all the advantages of large-scale and, in terms

a proletariat on the one hand and a non-working capitalist and propertied class on the other. The surviving independent craftsmen are an unimportant exception to this general rule and have an increasingly difficult task to maintain themselves. Peasants and farmers are very often only nominally the owners of their holdings, exploited unmercifully by mortgages or in the hands of transport or distributing agencies. Peasants manage to maintain themselves only by exploiting their families. Though idealised by some people, they are, in fact, physically, morally, intellectually and culturally inferior even to the town proletariat. Shopkeepers are rarely independent; they are tied down to the wholesale firms, whose paid agents they often are. The only places where independence survives are in the interstices of big industry.

(5) The measure of individual wealth should be the amount of work done by the individual; this being impossible to apply, the best maxim is: 'From each according to his ability, to each according to his needs.' The present system secures a distribution that approaches neither principle. The capitalist exploits the labour of the producers by hand and brain, from the unskilled labourer right up to the manager, not by virtue of his transcendent services but because he has inherited stock from an ancestor or can limit production, or secures a mortgage, or can maintain prices – in fact, by means of any successful application of the principle of obstruction between the production of goods and their distribution to those who need them. A 'pull' is more certain of gaining wealth than great genius or singular powers of organisation.

(6) Lack of an assured purpose breeds despair; hence the inefficiency of the chronically casual worker. Man loathes boredom to

of relative efficiency, is often superior to very huge organisations.

(Some) Even if it were possible to put an end to the economic and social process of differentiation, and to all its causes and effects, such a consummation would not imply an advance in human culture.

(5) The capitalist could not exist without the labourer, nor could the labourer without the capitalist, who supplies the sinews of industry with which the former produces a commodity. Besides this function, the capitalist often performs that of directing production. Most of the profits are the earnings of managerial ability. The distinctive feature of capitalism today is the complete withdrawal of the men of exceptional intellect from the business of performing or directing any labour of their own and the concentration of their powers in organising the labour of others, with the result that the mental capacities of the few, instead of being confined to the task of guiding their own muscles, lend guidance to the muscular operations of the many. The profits of the capitalist employers have their origin in the fact that, in this way, commodities are multiplied as they were never before, their individual values remaining unaltered in proportion as this multiplication is general; and the sum of the values thus added to the general product forms the funds from which profits are drawn.

(6) Socialism, by guaranteeing to all a livelihood, takes away the chief incentive to exertion. Saving becomes useless. Private enterprise has been the best prerequisite of progress everywhere; wherever there are traces of Communism, it is only as men get away from it that they become energetic and progress is possible.

(7) The labourer has shared proportionately in the increase of

such an extent, and has such an instinctive aversion from futility, that in a properly constituted society, where a few men could do the work with the machines to hand, there would be competition to get work rather than to avoid it.

(7) The luxury of the rich increases faster than the comfort of the poor. Though better off than his great-grandfather, the worker has not received a proportionate share of the vast increase in the country's wealth. Terminologically, the theory that wages sink to the level of 'bare subsistence' may need restatement: its substance – that the workers receive only enough to keep them efficient – remains fundamentally true. This is the latest scientific wage theory of capitalism – the economy of high wages. All the advances the workers have made have been gained despite capitalism, not because of it.

(8) Individualism is a theory that does not fit the present facts. The industry of the country is passing rapidly into the hands of a few men, as great firms diversify their interests. Smaller concerns are usually helpless in the face of takeover bids. Interlocking directorships are held everywhere. The shareholder has to have blind faith in two or three of the board of directors. Financial and industrial magnates influence the stock, produce and raw material markets in their own interests. The result is a nation of serfs on the one hand and a few industrial and financial overlords on the other.

(9) The creation of a great body of unemployed is an invariable accompaniment of capitalism. When advances in invention or foreign competition render an industry obsolete, whole regions are left high and dry, with no prospect of better times, and nothing is done to help them beyond pious exhortation. The men affected are neither idlers nor wastrels, though constant disturb-

wealth; he has shared very probably to a greater degree than capital. He also now has shorter hours and better conditions. The statistics magnifying the disproportion of the wealth of different sections of the community are fallacious. If the national income were shared out equally, the addition to the workers' wages would be negligible. Under a free, individualist social system, none has a fixed status; the same men are both capitalists and workers. To a large extent, men reputed to be the possessors of great wealth are simply its distributors.

(8) There is no universal tendency to eliminate the small capitalist and business man; a small, ably conducted business has a very good chance of success. Co-operative enterprises and limited liability companies secure a large field of investment for the small capitalists, who are necessary to the captains of industry. The principal gambling in shares is not done in the case of companies which are on a sound basis, so that such methods of business are generally impossible in this country.

(9) Socialism would not solve the problem of the unemployed because that problem is as much moral as economic. In every community, idlers and black sheep will always be present, yet Socialism assumes an ideal state of society in which all men will be equally good.

(10) All Socialist systems mean the minute regulation of life by statute and bye-laws, probably administered by officials. These would be so numerous that the manual workers would become impotent. All spontaneity or self-expression would cease or, eventually, escape from repression into revolution. Bureaucrats tend to develop the 'red tape', obstinately conservative habit of mind. Their conduct becomes high-handed, as they feel bound to

ances may turn some of them into black sheep. It is only in times of war, when weapons of death are produced in vast numbers and immediately consumed, or in the period after a war when the devastation it has caused gives rise to a demand for all kinds of goods for the rebuilding of normal life, that workers can be temporarily assured of steady employment. In a Socialist society, the very few who were unwilling to work could be dealt with by disciplinary measures as a last resort. Socialism demands no 'change of heart', only the enlightenment of self-interest.

(10) Society is at present minutely regulated, openly but unobtrusively, by Government officials in part, but mainly by capitalists. Socialism will endeavour to reduce regimentation and set people free individually in groups to manage their own affairs. Socialism does not mean necessarily the aggrandisement of State departments. Devolution by area and function is possible, and Guild Socialism and the Soviet system are examples of other schemes. The British official is efficient and not corrupt, and can be trusted to work in the interests of the community.

(11) Crises which render everybody's existence insecure are inherent in the capitalist system, arising from the fact that production for the world's markets cannot gauge the limits of consumption and that production is continually outstripping the effective demand. The conditions under private property have become too narrow for the constantly growing accumulation of wealth. Malthus's law of population is now obsolete. It is not the population that presses upon the means of subsistence but, on the contrary, the means of subsistence that press upon the nation. Hence the feverish race for new outlets, new consumers, profitable investments. Hence also the deliberate destroying of goods

support the dignity of the administrative machine of which they are part. The general standard of efficiency of the industries nationalised in this country since the last world war has not been impressive and has strengthened many people's determination to resist any further nationalisations. In many countries, wholesale corruption would be inevitable, and here we should not be immune. The German official in the old days used to be incorruptible and intolerable; with the coming of the Third Reich, he lost much of his incorruptibility but little of his overbearing behaviour. Nor would these dangers be avoided if some other form of organisation were adopted. For every large organisation develops the same habits; trade unions, industrial conglomerates, the Soviets and the Church can be cited as instances. Here, numerous incidents involving the Post Office, the Treasury and the Ministries responsible for health, insurance and agriculture can all be cited as showing how the jack-in-office afflicts the supposedly free citizen and enfranchised constituent. Our aim should be the reduction of administrative machinery and the freeing of choice and initiative in as great a degree as possible.

(11) The primary question which presses for solution is not the unequal distribution of wealth but the production of the wealth to be distributed. The wealth of modern nations depends upon international credit and trade. Under capitalism, the two virtues necessary in the accumulation of capital – thrift and industry – are encouraged, and the rewards for the effective and punishments for the non-effective direction of labour are automatic. Under Socialism, the detection of the misdirection of labour becomes a practical impossibility, and thus capital must waste away while the

which would have been of use to the community, in order to maintain the level of prices at times when purchasing power has fallen. Under Socialism, such crises would be avoided, for production would be adapted to national consumption, and the needs of the nation could easily be ascertained. The mere production of great wealth is no test of social and industrial well-being; distribution is the real test.

(12) The regulation of production is not incompatible with freedom of choice of profession. If it were found that too many people were turning in any one direction, it would always be possible to increase the inducements in other directions by offering more favourable conditions of work, e.g. increased remuneration, shorter hours or other privileges. The dirty work would be remunerated in proportion to its unpleasantness. Short hours, long holidays and generous treatment should be the portion of those who do it.

(13) No regulation of individual consumption would be necessary, for modern labour is so productive that it could satisfy all needs of a civilised society. Moreover, Socialism, by broadening the basis of consumption, would give individual freedom also to those classes which, under the present conditions, are poor and obliged to limit very strictly their individual consumption.

(14) Socialism would have no need to abolish competition, but would leave men free to compete not only for 'service' but for high salaries, for position, for authority and for leisure. Socialist competition is a well-known feature of life in the Soviet Union. Under capitalism, while competition among workers for the means whereby to earn their daily bread becomes keener, competition among capitalists gives way day by day to co-operation. The more production gets into the hands

primary cause of its waste is unknown and therefore not remedied.

(12) The management of the entire production would force the Socialist State, in order to prevent overproduction, to abolish the right of the worker freely to choose his profession. Everyone would have to act in accordance with orders. Otherwise, everyone would flock into those professions which afforded the pleasantest way of life.

(13) The regulation of consumption destroys all freedom of choice and enslaves everybody; only through regulation can production be made exactly to meet consumption – otherwise, the old difficulty must recur. Moreover, everybody would want the best things, which, by their nature, are limited.

(14) Socialism would abolish competition and establish a huge monopoly, which would soon be that worst of tyrannies, a mob tyranny. Free competition is the only real freedom in industrial matters, as well as the only guarantee to the consumer that he gets what he wants. The law should make and enforce regulations to ensure that fraud is not perpetrated on the consumer, but nothing more. Honesty pays in the general run. Given a number of labourers equal in productivity, working for an equal number of hours, and receiving as their rewards equal shares of the total product, no single group of labourers could augment their own gains in any way except by a successful attack on the gains of all the others. However an individualist community might be socialised, all the elements of industrial conflict would survive in it. The only way in which the position of any group of labourers could be improved would be by the advent of some exceptional man. He would demand his special bargain. The bargain which a Socialist State would, in the inter-

of the big companies, the easier do capitalists find it to form rings, etc., to keep prices up. No legislation can prevent secret agreements. Again, the practice of advertising warfare and misleading half-truths condemns the competitive system. Dishonesty is an essential part of present-day competition. The consumer is not in a position, under the complex conditions of modern life, to know a genuine article, or to know what is compatible with health in food, dwellings, etc. He cannot be a universal expert. Such measures of inspection and regulation as have been taken are insufficient to deal with those whose intention it is to defraud or mislead.

(15) There need be no such thing as confiscation. The tendency nowadays, especially in Britain, has been to give compensation to the former owners of nationalised industries, generally in the form of State bonds. Although this involves a charge on the State, the curbing of the practice of investing in subsidiary industries or abroad should provide sufficient funds for improvements in working hours and conditions, as well as wages. The large, near-monopolistic industrial groups have shown how enormously production can be raised, and the great difficulty of the capitalist – how to limit production so as to sell the products at a profit – would disappear. In a transformed society, when all the private capital of production and exploitation has been socialised, the compensation that former capitalists have received will enable them to buy the products of social activity but not to control their production.

(16) The existence of idle classes is a direct social evil – whether the idle rich or the idle poor. The so-called services of the former to society are for the most part the merest dilettantism, and their social influence is pernicious in every way.

ests of the majority, have to strike with its exceptionally efficient citizen would be in its essentials the same as that made under a system of free exchange and competition.

(15) Socialism would involve wholesale confiscation; confiscation would create universal mistrust and prevent all progress. Theoretically, the State might confiscate all such resources as exist at any given moment, but no one, if it aimed at making this confiscation permanent, would ever accumulate any such resources again. The idea of buying out the whole property-holding class would spell bankruptcy and, moreover, bring no advantages. It would simply turn what are, in many cases, active workers into pensioners of the State. Socialists would soon find that people would not work if assured of a living; hence production would soon fall off. Destroy confidence in the future and the great driving forces of the economic processes are paralysed. The continued progress of Socialism, if translated into a national policy, must drive the owners of liquid capital to domicile elsewhere. On the other hand, the owners of fixed capital and the population who live on their own personal labour would suffer from the consequences of excessive taxation and the attrition or flight of capital in abnormal quantities. As ninety-five per cent of the industries of Great Britain are conducted by credit, any interference with that confidence which is the basis of credit necessarily drives the injured industries to foreign countries which are our competitors in the world markets.

(16) The so-called idle classes do much valuable social and philanthropic work, which could not be done by any paid official with the same disinterested love. They are, moreover, the upholders of culture and patrons of art. From these

Their artistic taste, even when sincere, is based on false values and is often mere ostentation. Inclined strongly to superstition, belief in luck and so on, and to barbarism in their amusements, blood sports, etc., they speedily degenerate. The political leadership of the propertied classes tends more and more to fall to men whose social origin is different from theirs. Their philanthropy, where felt, degrades the proletariat, as their patronage degrades art. It is not denied that this class has in the past performed a certain social function, though badly; but it has now become superfluous and noxious.

(17) Social progress and social evolution are different from natural selection and natural evolution. The present system has produced an inferior population out of a sound stock. The successful men are the cunning men, those with a commercial instinct. Given economic and social equality as far as may be, the best types would come to the front. The type of person who has a talent for prospering at the expense of others is not necessarily the 'fittest' human being.

(18) The present marriage system is still a reflex of the property system. Socialism would determine whether monogamy suited humanity by making everyone freer than he or she is at present. Recent trends in the USSR, with tightening up of marriage and divorce laws, suggest that monogamy would be found to be the best system; the example of the USA, on the other hand, suggests that monogamy is not an essential feature of capitalism. Socialism is in any case an economic doctrine which bears on the sex question only where it is complicated by money matters.

(19) By making work obligatory for all, Socialism would reduce work to a minimum for all alike and would set free the worker to enjoy his

classes our greatest statesmen have sprung.

(17) Socialism, by stopping the competitive struggle for life, puts an end to the process of natural selection for the elimination of the unfit, and thus brings progress to a standstill. Those who fail are less desirable types of humanity than those who succeed, since they are physically, intellectually and even morally inferior. The growth of medical science reinforces this tendency. Socialism encourages the survival of the unfit.

(18) The Socialists teach that existing marriage relations are simply the outcome of property. Property in children under Socialism would soon cease to exist, and marriage would be an association terminable at will by either party. Thus the family would disappear. If society guaranteed subsistence to all its members, it must regulate the number of citizens for whom it would have to provide.

(19) Socialism would have no leisured class; and since we owe a great deal of our art, literature and science and the refinements of everyday life to this class, cultural progress would cease. The Socialist society would maintain a constant level of dull materialism.

(20) It is almost impossible to conceive how work is to be remunerated, save on a competitive basis. Under Socialism, all kinds of work would have to be valued on a common basis, which could only be the amount of time spent in the production of commodities. Socialism would be possible only if all men were not only equally good but equally gifted. One of the chief incentives to labour would be removed if parents were deprived of the wish and ability to provide for their children's advancement. The Christian doctrine of the equality of man is an ideal, not a working

leisure, to develop his cultural equipment, or to express himself in more personal methods of work. The culture that depends on a leisured class and is the monopoly of the few cannot be very valuable.

(20) The competitive reward of labour is a fiction in present-day society. The worker was never rewarded in proportion to his toil but only as allowed by the market rate, determined by factors outside his control. Collective bargaining by trade unions has ended the theory. The best work has never been done out of consideration for money. Though inequalities may persist as between different classes of workers until society has achieved a sufficient abundance, ultimately equality of income will be general. Socialism would secure free play to the better side of humanity, i.e. pride in one's work. Socialism is designed for a humanity that has not been repressed and thwarted by economic serfdom.

(21) (Some) Socialism is the social interpretation of Christianity, and though some individual Socialists may be atheists, there is no connection between atheism and Socialism.

(Some) Socialism has nothing to do with religion, which is a private affair. It is a sociological programme. Capitalism has equally little to do with religion, though its theories and practices are repugnant to most of the leading religions of the world and some of them have been specifically condemned by the Church. Socialists are generally anti-clericals because most of the clergy, especially in the higher ranks, have always been on the side of their enemies in the past.

(22) Socialism will abolish war by mitigating the frenzies of nationalism and preventing the capitalist developments which make for international competition for foreign markets and resources. The patriotism of a Socialist society will accord with

system. Character must be the mainspring of the State; an atmosphere of potential inequality gives free play to all the passions and active powers of man. Socialism presupposes men not only more perfect but of an entirely different nature from what they will ever be.

(21) Socialism is atheistic. This is clear, not only from the doctrines and philosophy of the leading Socialist thinkers but also from their policy and action when in power. Marx and Engels said that religion was 'the opium of the people'. Socialists everywhere desire the secularisation of the schools and the educational system.

(22) The international doctrines of Socialists are absurd. The real causes of war are nationalist ambitions and over-population. Socialism might well be intensely nationalist. The main driving force of Russian resistance to German invasion in the Second World War was the desire to drive out the foreign aggressor, and many British Socialists today have shown themselves to be excessively nationalist (e.g. the left-wing opposition to Britain's new role in Europe). Socialised industries would have to enter world competition and, as the whole might of the State and political machine would be brought into play to support them in their struggles for markets and the sources of raw materials, the danger of international rivalries and feuds would be as great as under the most rapacious private capitalism. The class war is more hateful than international war and, on a world-wide scale, could work even more damage than international wars. Socialists often condemn strife between nations and at the same time extol strife between sections of a nation.

(23) The horrors of Socialism in practice are illustrated by Russia under the Bolsheviks. The cultured classes were extirpated, production

justice and benevolence. No Socialist regards the class war as desirable, though some believe it to be inevitable; all strive to gain their ends by the constitutional methods of modern political democracy. The conflict of classes is recognised by Socialists as inevitable until economic democracy has supplemented political democracy.

(23) The Bolsheviks were not typical Socialists; nor are present-day Russians. The state of the country at the end of 1917, after the Russian Revolution, and the widespread hostility it has had to face since for most of the time, are largely responsible for the special features of Socialism as now practised in the Soviet Union. In each country, indeed, the form of Socialism would be modified by the economic and cultural development of that country.

as a whole fell off enormously after the Revolution, and distribution was poor. As time went on, the Soviets found themselves obliged to abandon more and more of their original doctrines, in practice if not in theory.

(See also *Christian Socialism.*)

Soft Drugs, Legalisation of

Pro: (1) There is no legal bar on the purchase of alcoholic drink and cigarettes, though both are often addictive. No logical reason exists, therefore, for the continued ban on soft drugs, which, despite assertions to the contrary, have not been proved to be addictive.

(2) The open availability of soft drugs would help greatly to reduce the incidence of alcoholism and addiction to hard drugs. It could also lead to a reduction in cigarette consumption, thus lessening the incidence of lung cancer from tobacco, since the smoking of soft drugs has far less harmful effects on the health than cigarettes.

(3) Public alarm has been stirred up more by the undesirable side-effects of the illicit trade in soft

Con: (1) There is no proof whatever that soft drugs are non-addictive. On the contrary, the evidence points entirely the other way. That alcohol and cigarettes are available to all, despite their admittedly harmful effects, is no reason for the legalisation of soft drugs as well – merely an argument to restrict the sale of alcohol and cigarettes.

(2) Even if irrefutable medical evidence were eventually to prove that the majority of soft drugs are not addictive, which is highly unlikely, this would still not overcome the greatest danger in these drugs – the likelihood that they will lead on to far worse substances. When people find that soft drugs are no longer giving them as much satisfaction or pleasure as before, the first

drugs than by any knowledge about the drugs themselves. Since the law bans them, it is inevitable that a black market should have grown up to meet the considerable demand that exists. If their sale was made legal, at officially-controlled prices, the black market would disappear overnight – and with it would go the theft, blackmail, drug-pushing and other evils which surround it at present.

(4) Soft drugs merely induce a sensation of being mildly 'high' – much less so than with alcohol – and a pleasant feeling of well-being. The predominant characteristic among people taking such drugs is their peaceful attitude to all fellow-humans; violence is abhorrent to them.

reaction is usually to increase the intake (which can be serious enough); but the most probable outcome is that they will progress to hard drugs, which are killers. That this tendency has become all too common is shown by the ever-increasing number of young people dying in Britain each year from the effects of drug addiction.

(3) Since the word side-effects has been used, it should be mentioned that among those known to result from addiction to soft drugs (and not just hard drugs) are impotence and sterility. One of the most pernicious social effects of drug trafficking is that addicts, particularly the young, are led into crime in order to obtain the drugs for which they crave. They may commit thefts to get the money required; they may break into a pharmacy or doctor's surgery to steal drugs; when unable to pay the trafficker on whom they rely for supplies, they may well be enrolled as 'pushers' themselves. All these cases figure frequently in the drug trials one can hear in the courts every week. Legalising the sale of soft drugs would not end the problem. Addicts unable to pay for them would still resort to crime.

(4) The process of 'coming down', as the effects of the drug wear off, can be anything but pleasant. Drug addicts have a tendency to live in a sub-culture world utterly removed from the realities of life. Indeed, their refusal or inability to face the real world is often the reason they resorted to drugs in the first place.

Space Exploration:
International Only?

Pro: (1) Two main forms of space exploration are now in prospect: (a) the unmanned probes, pushing ever

PC–H

Con: (1) The two super-powers, the USSR and the USA, have hitherto been the only countries with the

farther outwards into the universe (and including attempts to discover whether any hint of elementary life exists on other planets); and (b) the closer study, from space, of the Earth's resources and environmental problems (notably through the American 'space shuttle' – a reusable vehicle, half spacecraft, half aeroplane – due to come into service in the 1980s). To ease the huge and ever-growing costs, to avoid wasteful duplication, and to prevent future political confrontations, the time must come when all such explorations cease to be conducted unilaterally but are carried out on an international basis.

(2) As a first step, an International Space Agency should be formed, its members comprising not only the two super-powers but all nations which already have a lesser scientific role in space exploration (like Britain) or are likely to make an increasing contribution to it in future (like China and Japan). The initial purpose of the Agency would be to co-ordinate all space activities, but ultimately it would become the controlling body.

(3) Proof that space co-operation is entirely possible, given the political will, was provided by the Apollo-Soyuz project in July 1975. It did not represent any significant advance in the technology of manned space flight; its greatest achievement was one of organisation, in overcoming new, different kinds of problems – language, getting the control centres and tracking networks operating closely together, making the two spacecraft compatible in many various ways. In short, it was an important first step towards true space co-operation, though only a first step. As an example of the immediate possibilities arising from it, one result of this initial collaboration is that all Soviet and American manned spacecraft in future will use the

resources to embark on large-scale space programmes. But their motives were not altruistic, nor even a matter of simply trying to gain prestige over each other. The principal spur behind their space exploits has been militaristic. (One has only to think of the large but unpublicised number of space satellites now in orbit for intelligence and other military purposes.) Until the powers achieve such mutual trust that all threat of war is removed at last – and with it, the potential instruments of war, wherever they may be – there can be no hope of anything but relatively limited co-operation between them in peaceful space affairs. International space exploration is a fine ideal; so is the concept of World Government; but conditions are unlikely to be ripe for either of them in the foreseeable future.

(2) Such a body would have all the defects of present UN agencies in other fields. It would inevitably be dominated by America and Russia, and thus still subject to the political strains and rivalries between them – with the customary undesirable line-up of their respective supporters behind them. No measures envisaged by other members, however wise, could be enforced unless both the super-powers agreed. It should also be recalled that China, now a nuclear power, has refused to sign any of the treaties restricting nuclear tests or weapons; how long would she decline to co-operate in space affairs, too?

(3) Despite its world-wide impact as a symbol of *détente*, the Soyuz-Apollo project merely underlined the enormous gulfs to be bridged before international space exploration could even begin to seem a practical possibility. For instance, Soviet and American engineers did not develop the compatible docking mechanism jointly; they agreed on dimensions and on how the system

compatible docking system developed for the Apollo-Soyuz link-up. This means, for instance, that Soviet spacecraft of the 1980s will be able to dock with the US space shuttle, without any of the elaborate modifications required for the 1975 mission. Equally, since the Americans will have an airlike atmosphere in the space shuttle instead of the low-pressure pure oxygen they have used hitherto, there will be no need for airlocks.

(4) The financial savings which could be effected by pooling resources for space exploration are indicated by the fact that the Apollo-Soyuz project was one of the cheapest in American space history. It is estimated to have cost the USA only $250 million.

(5) There is already one area of the world, Antarctica, where the nations have kept their word to reserve the territory solely for peaceful purposes, to co-operate in scientific investigation and research, and to preserve the *status quo* with regard to territorial sovereignty, rights and claims. Now, Apollo-Soyuz has proved that in space, too, nations with political systems widely different in values, outlook and purpose *can* co-operate in a peaceful project. There has long been international co-operation as well in such fields as communications satellites and the obtaining and sharing of information for purposes like astronomy and climatology. In short, precedents have been set, and the gap between individual national and general international operations in space will be much easier to bridge than many people imagine.

would work, etc., but built their own mechanisms quite separately – and along completely different lines (hydraulic for the Americans, mainly mechanical for the Russians). Technologically and psychologically, the USSR derived most from the project. The Americans provided the bulk of the know-how – the Russians had little or nothing to offer, technologically, that was not already known to American scientists. Again, though the Soyuz was ten years behind the Apollo, as a spacecraft, the venture made the two nations appear as equals in the field of space research. Politically, too, any future co-operation depends on how far the Russians are willing to maintain it. The Americans had been advocating this type of co-operation for years; the Russians accepted it only when, after their initial headstart had worn off, the fact could no longer be disguised that the US had forged far ahead. If Moscow decides that it has derived sufficient benefit for the moment, the Soyuz-Apollo project may yet have to be classed as only a flash in the pan.

(4) The cost was so low (comparatively!) only because the Americans used a starter rocket and an Apollo capsule which were already in existence (and which would otherwise have been scrapped). The design and construction of new material, which would doubtless be required for any major joint space exploration, might well be more expensive for each nation than its own space programmes.

(5) In Antarctica and the other examples cited, the co-operation is relatively superficial and each nation continues to go its own sweet way in its researches, etc. To give an analogy: two car manufacturing companies might agree to standardise tyres, but this is very different from jointly producing a car. In practical terms, we have a good idea

of American space plans for the next ten years or so; the Russians have talked about putting very big space stations into orbit round the Earth, but their actual plans for the future have been kept as rigidly secret as ever.

Speculation, Suppression of Commercial

Pro: (1) Gambling in goods, shares or land disturbs ordinary trade and business.

(2) Dealers and investors are thereby exposed to more risks than need be, while an army of parasites does nothing useful and gets rewarded for doing it.

(3) Prices fluctuate and expenses increase, and for both it is the general public that has to pay.

(4) Trade, inevitably, is full of risks, but the gambler increases them. He excludes much talent from legitimate commerce.

(5) 'Rigging' markets is made easier by the liking of many traders and investors for deals with a prospect of excitement (and of big profits almost overnight), and this tendency provides ready opportunities for unscrupulous business men.

(6) During the world's present precarious economic conditions, commercial gambling is one more obstacle to reconstruction on sound lines.

Con: (1) Speculation is inevitable in commerce, for nothing else brings the present into connection with future needs and supplies.

(2) Middlemen are a necessity for securing efficient distribution. Without readiness to take large risks, large results cannot be obtained. All business has an element of gambling in it.

(3) In the long run, the free play of business brings about the lowest possible level of prices.

(4) There is no way of making, in a business context, a clear distinction between what is gambling and what is not.

(5) 'Rigging' would occur anyhow, and steadiness might even promote it.

(6) Free opportunity will bring about the results desired more quickly than red tape and restriction. Beyond a certain point, efforts to make trade conform with rigid systems result in far more harm than good.

(See also *Gambling, Morality of*.)

Spelling Reform

Pro: (1) The spelling of English, which became finally fixed by pedants only as late as the eighteenth century, bears little relation to the spoken language. It is a logical absurdity. Its substitution by a

Con: (1) The present spelling of English is an integral part of the language. Few languages have phonetic spelling, and there are sufficient rules for English spelling to make it reasonably easy to master adequately.

phonetically consistent method would be of enormous value.

(2) Correct spelling is looked upon as a *sine qua non* for an educated person, so that an enormous expenditure of time and effort is involved in teaching it to children and to foreigners – who, on the average, take five times as long to learn to spell reasonably well as they would if the language were spelt phonetically.

(3) The time taken to learn to read is similarly extravagant. Because of the difficulties, many people lose all interest in reading as soon as they leave school, and thus remain inefficient workers and citizens. The form of phonetic spelling taught in some junior schools in recent years has been very successful; the children learn to read much more quickly and they have had little or no difficulty in coping with conventional spelling at a later stage.

(4) The superiorities of English as a language, on the scores of grammatical ease, logical syntax, expressive idiom and magnificent vocabulary, warrant an effort to relieve it of its quite inessential difficulty. If this were done, English would be accepted without question as the world language for purposes of international communication.

(5) Phonetic representation would be unnecessary, though not unduly difficult if the international phonetic symbols were used. The use of a conventional but sensible system, employing simply the ordinary letters, would meet all requirements. American is already so different from English as to be ranked in several countries as a separate language. In any case, if we wish to take American English into account, it has already set us an example in spelling reform.

(6) The aesthetic argument against spelling reform is merely a plea that what is novel is ugly, what is old is

(2) Phonetic spelling would not make it any easier for the child or the foreigner to learn English. Our alphabet contains five vowels. At least twenty symbols would be required to represent the various ways in which those vowels are pronounced in spoken English. Would this simplify the task?

(3) Those who want to read will surmount the difficulties. The remainder would not be any more interested in acquiring ideas through reading under a new spelling system than they are now. Reformed spelling would mean that children would have to learn two schemes until all our literature could be reprinted, at the risk of being cut off from the great writings of the past. Many adults would not learn the new system at all. That the recent phonetic spelling experiment at some schools has fallen short of success is proved by the fact that it has not been adopted generally.

(4) As the Basic English experiment showed, English is too rich a language for fully satisfactory 'rationalisation' and is thus unlikely to become the world language; nor are national susceptibilities likely to permit it. An International Auxiliary Language (*q.v.*) is much more hopeful for this purpose.

(5) Spelling reformers are not agreed on what system to adopt. The only sensible one, a phonetic system, would be extremely difficult to apply to English, with its many vague sounds and numerous diphthongs, and would cut us off from writings in other varieties of English, such as American, which differs dramatically at times from our own language in pronunciation as well as spelling.

(6) The NU Spelling is incurably ugly. To see the English classics transliterated into it gives our aesthetic sensibilities a shock. It also largely obliterates the indications of the derivation of words which the

beautiful. The meanings of words are by no means usually to be discovered from their derivations. Many words give no obvious clue to their origin and history.

(7) There is no real difficulty in choosing which pronunciation to use. The accepted pronunciation is given in any standard dictionary. Local dialects and variations of pronunciation would continue to exist, as they do now, independently of spelling.

present spelling gives, and so weakens the interest we take in them and the understanding of their true significance.

(7) If spelling is to be made to fit pronunciation, whose pronunciation is to be chosen? Would the Scots, the Irish or the northern English accept the decision of a committee of English dons? They would more probably prefer to set their own standard pronunciation.

Spiritualism

Pro: (1) Mankind has always believed that death was not the end of human existence and that the dead were sometimes able to communicate with the living. Many religions are based on this belief.

(2) In history, there are many authenticated instances of spiritualistic phenomena which cannot be dismissed as baseless or given any 'normal' explanation.

(3) In modern times, multitudes of sober and reliable people have witnessed marvels. Though sometimes they may have been mistaken or deceived, it is incredible that they should all have been deceived all the time.

(4) Eminent public men and, more especially, eminent scientists, such as A. R. Wallace, Lombroso and Sir William Crookes, have conducted impartial and scientific investigations, which gave conclusive results. Many people who have made themselves famous for intellectual qualities and sound judgment, such as Sir Oliver Lodge and Sir A. Conan Doyle, and certain shrewd journalists with no axe to grind, have been convinced of the truth of spiritualism. We may have confidence in the conclusions of a variety of people of first-class intelligence.

Con: (1) The belief in spiritualism has not been universal; even if it were, that would be no proof of its truth, as men have always believed firmly in things that were baseless.

(2) Most of the historical evidence is untrustworthy and is based on incorrect observation or prejudiced theories. Much of it refers to happenings which would now be ascribed to disorders of the subjects' minds, while the best of it contains indications that the original story has since been elaborated.

(3) Mediums work under the most propitious conditions, as they choose the time and circumstances, e.g. darkness, and their audiences come in an excited frame of mind, prepared to accept any occurrence as the work of spirits. Some years ago, members of the Magic Circle staged a 'seance' at which they reproduced many of the reputed phenomena of spiritualist seances. Although people in the know were allowed to search the demonstrators at each stage, beforehand, they did not discover any of the methods used – and, until afterwards, not one of the ordinary spectators present knew that the seance was in fact spurious!

(4) Only a few investigations can properly be described as scientific,

(5) There is good evidence for otherwise inexplicable physical manifestations. D. D. Home's phenomena were unexceptionable. He courted investigation, he was never detected in trickery, and the witnesses are numerous and of the highest standing. Stainton Moses was, for years, the centre of phenomena recorded at the time by people with no motive for deception. The Boston medium 'Margery', the Belfast Goligher circle, and the Austrian mediums Rudi and Willi Schneider are cases in point.

(6) Numerous messages have come from the dead, giving information for the living that no one else knew.

(7) Spirit photographs give permanent and objective proof of survival. The conditions generally preclude fraud, as sitters are unknown to the medium.

(8) It is not sufficient to cavil at items in the evidence, as the mass of witnesses and the multitudes of separate instances establish a solid case. Evidence for spiritualism is much more abundant and of better quality than that for the origins of the Christian religion.

(9) Mediums, as a class, are as good as the average man or woman. A few black sheep are not sufficient to establish a general charge of fraud. Even then, it is not impossible for lax morals to go with psychic power; geniuses are not noted for moral perfection.

(10) Spiritualism gives mankind a great hope, and more than hope, at a time when traditional religion is decaying and unsatisfactory. It is morally uplifting, does not promote nervous disorder and, indeed, is much healthier than fervid religion, which is often accompanied or followed by mental or moral decadence.

(11) The marvellous in spiritualism should not excite incredulity,

and they give only negative results. The scientists commonly cited were not investigating their own subject-matter under their own conditions, and a physicist is no more qualified to investigate problems involving psychology and conjuring than a psychologist is to investigate physics. Their evidence shows the same gaps and faults as other people's. The scientific specialists most fitted for the task, the psychologists, include hardly any adherents of spiritualism.

(5) Nearly all mediums in whose presence physical phenomena have occurred have been detected in fraud when sufficiently shrewd observers have sat with them. Home's career is not free from suspicious events, and it is to be noticed that he always chose his audience carefully. It is quite possible that he had the power of causing hallucinations in his sitters. The evidence in his case is so incomplete and unsatisfactory that it cannot be properly appraised. Moses was undoubtedly a pathological character in some ways. His phenomena took place in a very select circle and were reported only by himself and his friends. In reporting or discussing other people's phenomena, he was credulous to the last degree. 'Margery' has been declared fraudulent by certain experts of weight, and the Golighers would never accept the presence at their seances of Psychical Research Society investigators. The Schneiders survived a number of tests, but judgment on all such cases must be suspended until the mediums involved have been subjected to investigation under the strictest scientific control.

(6) Messages from the other world are generally incapable of verification. Those which seem most promising usually turn out to be guesses or derived from hints thrown out by the sitters. The state of mind

for it is no more astounding than the ordinary phenomena of human life, or such discoveries as wireless telegraphy and telephony. Much has been done to advance and prove its cause in the past, and much more will be done in the immediate future.

(12) There is nothing in spiritualism which makes it hostile to Christianity on either the moral or the theological side. Many earnest Christians have been convinced of its truth, but remained Christian. The established churches believe it threatens *their* prerogatives and oppose it just as they have always opposed what they thought would damage their worldly position. The Roman Catholic Church does not deny the phenomena of the seance room but holds that they are the work of devils or evil spirits.

(13) (Some) It is well to keep an open mind and pursue investigations. Indubitable data of supernormal phenomena are still not available in sufficient quantity to permit of a scientific or logical examination. Spiritualism has at least the advantage of a ready hypothesis, which we should not reject merely because we are used to scientific phenomena which demand more mechanical and materialist theories.

of the bereaved sitters must be taken into account.

(7) No spirit photographs have yet been accepted as genuine scientific proof, because conditions lend themselves to deceit. It is a proof of the credulity of believers that the very evidence of double exposure, etc., is passed over without remark. It is significant that the best known 'spirit' photographers insisted on using plates and avoided using roll films, which can give just as good photographic results but are nothing like so susceptible to fraudulent manipulation. The most famous 'spirit' photographers have been exposed one after another.

(8) A multitude of bad links will not make a strong chain, and the accumulation of bad evidence does not prove a good case. Evidence of the trends in human thought which led to the foundation of Christianity (as distinct from documentary evidence about Jesus Christ himself) is substantial and irrefutable.

(9) Spiritualism is the great arena for fraud, and the majority of professional mediums are deceitful – some to a small extent, perhaps, but others on a large scale.

(10) Spiritualism promotes insanity and minor nervous disorders, and encourages a disastrous indifference to the affairs of this life.

(11) Analogy is not proof and does not make up for the absence of definite and conclusive evidence. Great progress was expected when the Society for Psychical Research was founded. Except for a wider knowledge of the abnormalities of the mind, no progress has been made since then.

(12) Spiritualism's beliefs go too far to be compatible with Christianity. Its teachings simply give what the teachers think their followers want.

(13) It is precisely the need for keeping an open mind in the present

state of our knowledge that should lead us to reject 'ready hypotheses' based on such inadequate observation. A section of mankind is as ready now to accept assurances of communication with the other world as it was in former ages to believe that objects of daily use buried with the dead in their tomb would be made use of after death. Desire to believe in spiritualistic phenomena can be simply explained by the desire for personal immortality.

State Medical Service

Pro: (1) The present system, under which doctors are still paid according to the number of patients on their lists, reproduces the evils of the old, since they are obliged to attract custom just like any other tradesmen.

(2) Enthusiasm which varies with a money incentive is valueless in a profession which is supposed to have as its aim the service of humanity. At present, a financially successful doctor has no time to give adequate attention to his patients. Under a salaried service, he would be relieved of the burden of overwork without suffering financially.

(3) The public authorities already maintain a salaried service in the county and borough health departments and in the hospitals. No one in either of these branches of the profession complains of lack of freedom or incentive, and the service given is often better because of the greater facilities, which individual doctors usually cannot afford. Hospitals have been freed from the degradation and distraction of begging for funds and, through the reorganisation resulting from complete control, have improved the scope and performance of their work.

(4) A State-salaried service is alone able to practise preventive

Con: (1) The present system is intended to ensure that doctors give satisfaction to their patients or lose financially by it. Under a salaried service, there would be no such incentive and the attitude of slackness which is notorious in the Civil Service would prevail. Doctors with full lists (notably when they are the only GPs in the area) have become so busy that many can give only two or three minutes' time to each patient visiting their surgeries. The need is for more doctors – and State control would worsen rather than remedy the situation.

(2) Both doctors and patients would object to any further regimentation. Both complain already of the excessive formalities involved in the National Health Service, but at least the patient has at present the right to change his doctor and the doctor an equal right to refuse a patient.

(3) While it is possible that hospitals may benefit from national or regional control, the case is different from that of a general practitioner, who usually has the whole work of diagnosis, treatment and after-care in his charge. In many instances, doctors have found themselves obliged to refer more and

medicine on a wide scale, and does so very successfully both in school and maternity clinics and in the armed forces. It is not disputed that, through the work of the maternity and child welfare clinics, recent generations of infants are the healthiest ever produced in Britain.

(5) There is little freedom at present for the newly qualified practitioner, who cannot even settle in an area without the permission of his potential competitors. Under a salaried system, he would at least be assured of an income and be freed from the financial anxiety involved in starting a business. Doctors' sons are still given preference in the succession to their fathers' vacated practices, and tend to be trained with this end in view, sometimes in disregard of their own preferences and capabilities.

(6) Under a properly graded system, a young doctor would have prospects of promotion, possibly to more rewarding and responsible types of work. At present, a general practitioner is almost always obliged to continue working as such to the end of his career.

(7) What is proposed is simply control by the State of the services of doctors. No one suggests that their work should be supervised in detail. General practitioners would be protected in great measure from the occasional frivolous or malicious complaints to which they are now exposed. Patients would have extra safeguards against careless or over-hasty treatment.

(8) With a wholly integrated system, provision could be made for research on a much larger scale than at present. The general practitioner could take his place in the system and provide clinical information arising out of his daily experience. Nowadays, this can usually be obtained only by special research projects or by erratically answered

more cases to the hospitals because of limitations on freedom of treatment, and this would be aggravated under a fully integrated, State-controlled system.

(4) These bodies and such services as the mass X-ray units are adequate for the purposes of preventive medicine. Actual diseases remain to be diagnosed and treated, and the complete control of the doctor implied in a salaried service would destroy the valuable concept of the 'family doctor'.

(5) Before the National Health Service was established, a young doctor could settle anywhere he wished, with no further formality than that of putting up a plate. This freedom has already been curtailed, and the loss should not be aggravated by yet more government control. Complete freedom is as necessary to a doctor as to an artist, if he is to do his work in a creative way. When a doctor dies or retires, the patients usually prefer his son to a stranger.

(6) Promotion in any Civil Service sphere is slow and hedged about with formalities. A junior would be compelled to wait, perhaps indefinitely, without any prospect of escape into other avenues. At present, a competent doctor is able to rise to consultant status by his own efforts.

(7) Even under the present modified system, too much power is wielded by the central authority. Diagnoses and treatment have not infrequently been disputed – and by persons remote from the scene and unfamiliar with the patient. Doctors are already protected by the British Medical Association and various legal defence bodies; patients with justifiable grievances are protected by the disciplinary powers of the Ministry's Executive Committee and by their own freedom to change doctors.

(8) Research pursued under com-

appeals to individual doctors. Medicine is often said to be an art, but contact with work in the more strictly scientific branches of the profession can do nothing but good to its practitioners.

plete government control is generally stultified and frustrated. Only an ideal government department would allow the complete freedom necessary to research workers. But research, while obviously valuable, is not the only object of the profession. The emphasis on this aspect ignores the physician's role as guide and counsellor, which cannot be fulfilled in a regimented way.

(See also *Private Medicine.*)

State-Registered Brothels

Pro: (1) Prostitution is often called 'the oldest profession in the world' – which points to a fundamental truth. There have always been men, and probably always will be, who are led to seek the company of prostitutes because of inexperience, inadequacy, as a relief from domestic problems, to ease the tensions of over-sexuality, or whatever the cause may be. However much the Church condemns its immorality, however much we deplore it socially, it is a basic trait in human nature and nobody will change it. The State should recognise this fact of life and accept the urgent need to protect both the women and their customers from the disease, crime and other evils which surround prostitution in Britain today. The only effective way to do this is to sanction State-registered brothels, with legislation to ensure regular medical inspection and other necessary supervision.

(2) Since the street offences legislation, prostitution in Britain has become a hole-in-the-corner business of tatty bars and clubs, 'call girls' surreptitiously advertising their phone numbers, and other such shoddy means of making contact. Nobody would want the streets to become infested with prostitutes

Con: (1) The fact that vice and immorality exist is no justification whatever for the State to condone them. Even if we must recognise the weaknesses of human nature, the State has a prime duty to try to set and maintain standards of behaviour which all decent people would wish. By allowing officially-controlled brothels, it would not only give an appearance of participating in the trade but would actually be legalising permissiveness and encouraging promiscuity. State-registered brothels would also open the way to other forms of corruption (involving the police, etc.), which might well prove even less desirable than some of the present evils.

(2) Before this legislation was passed, the level of prostitution had become so serious that people could not walk down some thoroughfares in our main cities without being accosted every five or ten yards. Since then, the problem has not simply been swept under the carpet; all the evidence points to the fact that, overall, prostitution itself has decreased sharply. Immorality has a cumulative effect; so do measures to stop it. We may not be able to stop men seeking out vice, but we certainly shouldn't make it easier for

again, as they were formerly, but an evil is always easier to control if it is in the open. A system of 'tolerated houses' (to use the French phrase) would provide this element of control and eradicate much of the present shady nature of the trade, while keeping our streets free of it.

(3) Venereal disease is rife – and getting worse. An essential condition for State-controlled brothels is that, as is the practice in Continental countries which permit them, the prostitutes registered for work there would all be subject to strict medical inspection not less than once a week, thus cutting down the dangers of disease.

(4) Among the chief hazards faced by prostitutes are the violent, evil men who bully and threaten them into carrying on the trade and who live off their earnings in exchange for supposedly 'protecting' them. If the women worked in officially sanctioned brothels, they would be safeguarded from these menaces.

(5) Before France abolished its 'tolerated houses' – a move intended principally to protect Frenchmen from the rise in disease consequent on the successive presence of three foreign armies – it was not unusual for poor country girls to work in a brothel for a couple of years, to save up for the dowry which was then necessary before they could make a good marriage. Nobody despised them for it. Similarly, if there were State-registered brothels in Britain, many prostitutes would feel that there was less stigma in working for such establishments; and this in turn would lead to a sharp reduction in the number of 'call girls' and other tawdry expedients for prostitution now current.

(6) The 'social approval' of brothels, in effect, would greatly reduce the incidence of sex crimes, such as rape. That has been the experience in all Continental coun-

them to find it. By tolerating brothels, the State would be abnegating its moral responsibilities – *and* encouraging a renewed increase in the total level of prostitution.

(3) The rise in VD is due to the increased permissiveness of our age and stems almost entirely from the 'amateurs', not the professionals. Most young women who become full-time prostitutes are already in the habit of getting themselves checked by a doctor regularly, for their own sake. In any case, experience in Continental countries has shown there is a danger that, because official medical inspections in brothels soon acquire the character of a weekly 'chore', they often become cursory and inadequate.

(4) Anyone who imagines that pimps would cease to batten on women, just because they worked in an official brothel – or, indeed, that no prostitute ever gives money to her 'boy friend' of her own free will – simply does not know the harsh realities of life.

(5) Whatever the initial reasons may have been for the closure of France's brothels, the plain fact remains that they have not been resanctioned even now, some thirty years later – which shows that other moral and social considerations had greater weight. Nor can anything alter the fact that, however cosily you try to wrap it up, prostitution entails the degradation of women. And a British Government which permitted the opening of State-registered brothels would not merely be condoning but furthering such degradation. Moreover, the assertion that the existence of official brothels would cut the amount of other prostitution is sadly naïve. Human nature being what it is, there would much more probably be a considerable increase in the number of 'freelances'.

(6) The customs and experiences

tries which allow brothels. It has also been established beyond question that, in the Scandinavian countries which permit the open sale of pornography, the local people soon lose any interest they might once have had in the subject – to the point that, nowadays, the pornography shops rely almost solely for their trade on foreign tourists from countries where such wares are banned. Similarly, it is recognised that the State-tolerated brothels in West Germany are well-ordered, clinical, and frankly boring. In short, it is human nature that vice should be most attractive when it is illicit but rapidly loses its appeal once it is openly available.

of Continental countries do not provide a valid yardstick; through differences of temperament, climate and many other factors, conditions and standards in Britain are quite different. Even the most permissive British 'liberals' have not raised protests against the crack-down on purveyors of hard-core pornography which has been carried out since the uniformed police took over the anti-vice responsibility from the plain-clothes branch. There was general public approval of the moves to stamp out the seedy 'bookshops' which so disfigured Soho and other city backstreets. By the same token, the great majority of the British public would strongly oppose any attempt to establish official brothels in this country.

Sterilisation of the Unfit

Pro: (1) There is now conclusive evidence that certain types of mental deficiency and certain physical defects and diseases are transmitted to offspring according to known laws. The sterilisation of persons liable to transmit such defects would help substantially towards the eradication of these maladies, at a small cost and with the least possible interference with the present defectives' liberty and experience of life. (Modern sterilisation methods prevent them from having children but do not otherwise affect their enjoyment of love-making.)

(2) Moral and religious duty impels us to take such a simple step towards ending a source of great suffering and degradation.

(3) Degeneracy is largely responsible for the worst social problems. A particularly high proportion of these unfortunates, for instance, is found among slum dwellers. It is cruel and

Con: (1) Sterilisation is an unwarranted interference with personal liberty and an infringement of the dignity which should be preserved even in the least fortunate of human beings. Moreover, sterilisation involves a major operation for females, though it is simple enough for males. Geneticists have shown that most of such defects are transmitted to offspring only when both parents, who may themselves be normal, carry the weakness (a 'recessive gene'). Sterilisation of actual defectives would therefore only touch the fringe of the problem and, under random mating, would only slightly reduce the proportion of defectives in each succeeding generation.

(2) It is against all religious standards and scruples. The tradition of Christianity is hostile to such interference with the workings of nature.

(3) To a large extent, this confuses

absurd to try to palliate evil results, while leaving their sources unchecked.

(4) Owing to the greater security of life in modern times, this problem becomes worse, because defectives survive in a higher proportion than formerly, while people of intelligence above the average have smaller families than ever. This is a most serious matter for the future of civilisation in Britain and other countries.

(5) Great care must necessarily be exercised in carrying out the proposal, but doctors, who are traditionally and professionally jealous of the rights and well-being of their patients, and lawyers, who are notoriously cautious in their outlook, can be relied on to prevent abuses.

(6) The advance of civilisation comes from the superior stocks. The production of an occasional genius is not sufficient compensation for the harm done and suffered by an increasing number of defectives in the community.

cause with effect. Much degeneracy is due to bad social conditions, inadequate attention and education during childhood, and poverty.

(4) The most promising attack on this problem is by way of scientific research into the effects of diet, sunlight, and the activities of various glands on the mental and physical growth of man. As our present social system favours the prosperity of those who can make money rather than of those who can contribute to the development of culture, the infertility of genius is not to be wondered at. (Plus the fact, of course, that people of intelligence deliberately have small families nowadays, in recognition of the environmental problem.)

(5) The administration of such a measure lends itself to great abuses. In Nazi Germany, where liberty of opinion and conduct was little valued, sterilisation was a punitive weapon against people who departed from the beaten track. It will always be used against the poor, never against the rich.

(6) Many of the geniuses to whom the world owes much of its culture belonged to families in which other members were defective. For the progress of mankind, sterilisation might well cause more losses than gains.

Suicide:
Is It a Crime?

Pro: (1) Suicide is wrong because man's life, being a gift from God, belongs to Him, and only God has the right to decide how long a man shall live and when he shall die.

(2) It is opposed to natural human instincts; healthy-minded men take pleasure in life and regard even the worst difficulties as challenges to be

Con: (1) Many religions, several Christian sects and some philosophers have praised and practised suicide. The Christian Church did not denounce it until the Council of Arles, A.D. 623.

(Some) A man is not responsible for the obligation to go on living, which he did not undertake of his own free will.

faced and overcome, not as reasons for abandoning the struggle.

(3) It is a dereliction of duty, since 'we are all members one of another' and should make ourselves useful in the community to which we belong. Misfortunes, such as apparently incurable disease, are not sufficient excuse for deserting our posts.

(4) Struggling with adversity moulds one's own character and at the same time sets a good example to others. The suicides of older people, when more or less condoned by a weak public opinion because they appeared to have some form of understandable excuse, can have a disastrous effect on a number of adolescents, who magnify petty disappointments into incurable tragedies and kill themselves instead of facing their difficulties.

(5) The law should continue to punish attempts at suicide; it deters the culprit from other attempts and prevents others from following his example.

(2) We do not know for sure what is natural or instinctive in man. Many 'instincts' are incompatible one with another. Civilisation has developed through the repression of instincts. What may be culpable in a healthy-minded man could quite well be natural to a sick mind, and most suicides are neither healthy nor happy.

(3) Suicide is often a relief (albeit not openly admitted) to the suicide's family and friends, and not infrequently to the community.

(4) To commit suicide, a healthy man must have received great provocation and possess great courage.

(5) The laws against suicide should be abolished. They do not punish suicide but lack of success in attempting it. Just when some unhappy human being is most in need of help and sympathy, the law threatens prosecution for a crime. Suicide is not anti-social, and the law should deal only with things that are.

(See also *Euthanasia: Should It Be Legalised?*)

Sunday Entertainment

Pro: (1) There is a widespread demand for the lifting of all remaining restrictions on Sunday cinemas, the staging of professional football matches, and the opening of theatres and other forms of public recreation on Sundays. People quite naturally desire the most wholesome form of rest – that is, not inactivity but a salutary change from their normal occupations. The opposition to this demand comes from a minority of Sabbatarians, whose outlook is centuries behind the times and who wish to impose their views on the whole nation.

(2) In Roman Catholic countries on the Continent, full facilities for

Con: (1) Where Sunday games and cinemas are the general rule, people are tending to discard all religious observances and Sunday has become a day of noise, frivolity and irreverence. If fewer people attend places of worship and fewer children go to Sunday School, there will be a general decline in morality. There has, in fact, been a continual lowering of moral standards contemporaneously with the decline in Sunday observance. Besides, the opening of places of amusement on a Sunday deprives those engaged in them of their day of rest.

(2) Notwithstanding the discipline imposed by Roman Catholicism

Sunday entertainment have been the practice for many years – and the Church makes no objection provided people go to Mass beforehand.

(3) The Act permitting the Sunday opening of cinemas makes the express provision that those employed on Sunday in places of entertainment shall have a complete day's rest on another day each week.

(4) In a complicated society like our own, it is impossible to prevent all labour on a particular day. Trains and buses must run. Electric power must be generated for lighting and transport. Postal and telephone services must be available. Monday morning's newspapers and Monday's bread are largely provided by Sunday labour. Few Sabbatarians would care to dispense with the protection afforded by the Sunday labours of the police, the fire brigades and the medical profession.

(5) No one contests the Sabbatarians' right to observe the Lord's Day in their own way. They should not try to interfere with other people's rights.

and its attempt to ensure at least the essential minimum of religious observance among its adherents, the so-called 'Continental Sunday' is among the reasons why, in many ways, the trend away from religion has been even more marked in some of these countries than in Britain.

(3) A day off during the week is not equivalent to a free Sunday. It gives no opportunity for attending church or chapel, or for family reunion.

(Some) Sunday should be kept as a day apart. 'Remember the Sabbath day, to keep it holy.'

(4) It is not feasible to stop all labour on Sunday but at least there should be as few people employed as possible, and these only on essential services. No one can maintain that Sunday cinemas are a necessity. Many professional football managers doubt whether matches would attract any larger crowds on Sundays than they do now on Saturdays (which would be the only advantage for such managers).

(5) Sabbatarians are fully aware that their views are now unpopular and in a minority, but they believe sincerely that they have a duty to uphold adherence to the 'traditional' Sunday, in the hope that (as has happened before in history) the majority of people will eventually want to come back to God.

Taxation, Indirect, Abolition of

Pro: (1) Indirect taxation violates the first principle of taxation, for it causes more to be taken from the taxpayer than it brings to the State. Direct taxation can still be extended, while its greater imposition on all classes would make them more eager to check extravagant expenditure by the Government.

(2) Indirect taxation can be trans-

Con: (1) Direct taxation is already so heavy, for peace-time conditions, that very little extension of it is feasible. It is very unpopular with the working classes, who, nevertheless, ought to pay their share of the national expenditure. Though theoretically direct taxation may be better for the psychological health of the taxed community, moderate indirect

ferred easily from the shoulders of one class to those of the class or classes below it. The consequence is that the poor, who are least able to bear it, have to pay most – or, at least, to meet the heavier share of the burden, in proportion to their earnings.

(3) It restricts consumption and hampers trade.

(4) The revenue is uncertain and fluctuating.

(5) The expenses of collection are heavy.

(6) Even before VAT was made general under the EEC, most European governments had for many years applied indirect taxation on a much broader scale than practised in Britain, and their methods have always worked with success.

taxation is to be preferred, as it is not felt so much.

(2) The transference is not so systematic as is often asserted; and in practice the trend is usually the other way round, with efforts to reduce the burden on the poorest classes. That being said, it is nevertheless only right that the poor should contribute to the cost of the benefits they receive.

(3) Some of the articles on which it is imposed are not suitable for the unlimited encouragement which removal of all indirect taxation would give them (e.g. alcohol and tobacco).

(4) Revenue from all forms of taxation is uncertain and fluctuating.

(5) Evasion is minimal, under the well-organised and incorruptible Customs and Excise Department.

(6) In some Continental countries, dodging income tax is almost a national hobby, and governments therefore have to rely on indirect rather than direct taxation for the bulk of their revenues. In Britain, this problem does not apply.

Taxation of Single People

Pro: (1) Under the British taxation system, single people normally pay a higher proportion of their earnings in income tax than do married people with the same level of income. There is nothing inequitable about this, since single people generally have only themselves to support and can afford to pay more than those with family responsibilities. Taxation should always be based on the resources of the individual citizen.

(2) A family bringing up healthy children is automatically contributing to the welfare of the State, and it is only right that the parents should accordingly benefit from taxation relief. There is an equally good case,

Con: (1) It is implicit in this debating issue not simply that single people should be taxed but that they should be taxed more highly – and the argument opposite recognises that they already are, indirectly, through the granting of extra allowances to those who are married and have children. While such allowances are fully justifiable, it is nevertheless inequitable to impose a relatively heavier burden on single taxpayers, because this is, in effect, double taxation (which is contrary to the first principles of taxation). Moreover, it lacks sense from the national economic standpoint, since high taxes impair their ability to save money, at the very period of

therefore, for the proposition that childless single adults, above a given age, should actually be taxed at a higher rate than they are at present, i.e. a new, additional tax on single people. Among its desirable effects would be the encouragement of marriage and a sharp reduction in the number of irregular unions, now all too prevalent.

(3) Official statistics show a marked increase in the number of illegitimate children. Higher taxation of single people would not only curb immorality but would improve the lot of many children who now suffer from the lack of a true family life.

(4) Marriage is natural to mankind and the unmarried state is, in itself, undesirable. Most men are better for the responsibilities and influences of married life; all but a tiny handful of women desire to get married and have children.

their lives when they are usually most free to do so.

(2) The theory that citizens exist for the benefit of the State finds favour only in totalitarian countries. No democracy should base its taxation on such exploded ideas, which represent gross interference with the liberty of the subject. Far from framing taxes to encourage marriage, present-day environmental problems – in particular, the need to combat over-population – make a strong case for giving people incentives to stay single longer. If the nation faced up to its environmental responsibilities properly, the taxes imposed on single people should be proportionately *lighter* than on anyone else.

(3) To suggest that higher taxation would prevent immorality is unrealistic, to say the least. Even if it did lead more 'illicit' couples to decide to get married, which is extremely doubtful, marriage contracted under such economic threats would rarely make for a happy family life.

(4) The unmarried state is undesirable only for people who want to get married but are unable to do so. A growing number of people nowadays, women as well as men, prefer to stay single, as a matter of deliberate choice. Why should they be penalised?

Teaching Machines

Pro: (1) The supply of competent teachers is so far behind the ever increasing demand for knowledge that teaching machines are a necessity. Classes, both in schools and universities, are so over-crowded that many students end with large sections of their knowledge incomplete or distorted. No one has time nowadays to read all the books published on any particular subject.

Con: (1) No machine can replace a human teacher. The admitted shortage of good teachers, especially of the sciences, should be met by a great extension and improvement of training. Any authority which persuades itself that true education can be obtained from machines is merely shirking its responsibilities.

(2) While machines may be useful in impressing both grammar and

A machine can store available knowledge in a digestible form, and students can test, by playing back, whether they have in fact assimilated the knowledge correctly.

(2) Machines are particularly useful in the learning of languages, which is an important necessity in Britain today. By imparting a sound knowledge of grammar and a reasonably good accent, and by allowing each student to proceed at the pace which suits him, they should help to overcome the prejudice against foreign languages and the admitted inadequacy of language teachers in Britain.

(3) Machines are not meant to replace teachers altogether. Where they are used for the groundwork of acquiring facts, there is more time for discussion and tutorial guidance, both of which are of more value if they are based on a sounder knowledge of facts.

(4) Constructive thinking and development of ideas are easier if they are not obstructed by imperfect knowledge of the premises from which they start. The teaching machine is an aid that should no more be mistrusted than a short-sighted person would despise spectacles.

accent on the memory, the true learning of a language involves the give and take of conversation. Any idea that a language has been learned from either books or machines is an illusion. The best commercial companies in the language training field, while using language laboratories, tape recordings and so on, all include a proportion of face-to-face conversation in their courses.

(3) There is already a tendency in young people, particularly those who specialise in science, to confuse true education with the mere acquisition of facts, and universities are having to take special measures to contend with this obstacle to their aims. The function of teachers is to give a meaning to this collection of information and, by training students in habits of thought and reflection, to show them the way towards acquiring true knowledge.

(4) The facts for assimilation are chosen by those who set up the machines. The result of the widespread use of teaching machines would be a dead conformity in knowledge and thought.

Terrorism

Pro: (1) The essential point to bear in mind is that one man's terrorist is another man's patriot. People who resort to violent protests, such as time-bombs and the hijacking of aircraft, are not sadists or otherwise morally depraved; right or wrong, they believe that they have genuine political or social grievances, which governments have refused to recognise or remedy, and that a campaign of terrorism is the only way to overcome the apathy of the general

Con: (1) One could more readily understand a terrorist's motives – however much one disagreed with them – if his acts were directed against the military or against armed police. While no revolt or violent defiance of law and order can be condoned, this would at least have some character of openly declared warfare. As it is, though, most present-day terrorism involves the jeopardising or actual deaths of innocent civilians. Nothing can

public and of the authorities concerned. They decide on this course of action as a last expedient, when all conventional political or legal means have failed or are barred to them.

(2) In the words of a Russian terrorist, Zlelyabov, in 1879: 'History is terribly slow; it must be pushed forward.' History does, indeed, provide many examples of sustained terrorism achieving objectives which governments had previously been unwilling to grant (e.g. the Jewish militancy which helped to expedite Britain's decision to leave Palestine, thus leading to the creation of the State of Israel in 1948; and similarly, the four-year Arab terrorist campaign which brought about independence for the Republic of South Yemen in 1967).

(3) By threatening the lives of selected victims (e.g. aircraft passengers or diplomats in an embassy they have occupied), terrorists have frequently been able to win specific concessions - such as the release of jailed colleagues. More broadly, by creating a climate of fear and disrupting everyday life, they keep their viewpoint continually before the public eye. Eventually, this *can* succeed for them – either because public opinion gradually becomes convinced of the justice of their demands and swings behind them, or because more and more people grow so sick of the violence that, to have done with it, they force recalcitrant governments to give way.

(4) There was a considerable body of support among young people in West Germany and Britain for the aims of the so-called Baader-Meinhof gang and the 'Angry Brigade'. Their disgust with present-day society, and their desire to change it fundamentally, was shared by many – even if they did not go along with the extreme violence espoused by the groups concerned. The police themselves recognised

justify that. But terrorists become so obsessed by their supposedly righteous cause, so eaten up by their sense of grievance, that all moral judgments are excluded from their thinking, which is the worst form of perverted arrogance. They do not resort to terrorism out of desperation, as their apologists claim, but because its methods appeal to their own warped characters. They are not selfless heroes but criminals.

(2) On the contrary, the weight of historical evidence shows that terrorism rarely succeeds in its ultimate objectives. In Aden and pre-1948 Palestine, a virtual state of war existed and the terrorists' targets were, first and foremost, the British soldiers stationed there. When ordinary people are the main victims – as in South America and Northern Ireland – the terrorists end by alienating many sections of the population who might otherwise have had some sympathy for their aims. Most of those Middle Eastern countries which formerly supported the hijacking exploits of Arab guerrillas, if only tacitly, have now turned against them openly, recognising that the adverse reaction provoked by such acts, in other countries, does the Arab cause far more harm than good.

(3) Governments have a duty to protect human life, which always adds to the controversy over their decisions on how to deal with terrorism. If they resist, they endanger the victims held captive by the terrorists; if they yield, they lay themselves open to further terrorist attacks subsequently. It is a harsh dilemma – though, on balance, those governments which have refused to surrender to terrorist demands, even at the risk of the victims' lives, have usually proved their case. Such governments were able to take this course because majority public opinion in their own countries was behind them. And that is the crux of

that members of these groups were not criminals, in the ordinary sense.

(5) When a cause is just, the end justifies the means.

the matter. If terrorism's bluff is called, whatever the immediate price, the fundamental lack of justification for its methods will lead to its collapse.

(4) The terrorism adopted by these would-be social revolutionaries was self-defeating, because it lost them whatever public sympathy their idealistic objectives might once have had. History is a natural evolutionary process, and any attempt to force extreme reform by violent means will succeed, at the most, in producing short-term changes which are swiftly followed by other upheavals. Changes, in short, which are without durability or permanence. Whether socially or politically motivated, this is the basic flaw in all terrorist philosophy.

(5) It doesn't, and never will.

Theatres:
Are They In Need of Reform?

Pro: (1) The theatres of London have fallen into the hands of businessmen who openly admit they are concerned with nothing but profits. Many of them know little of dramatic art and work on the principle that the largest profits are to be obtained from plays and entertainments which pander to the lowest tastes of the public. In the provinces, matters are worse than in London.

(2) Landlords have put up rents to such an extent that serious producers can embark on new ventures only if they have a virtual certainty of packed houses or are backed by enormous capital. Even when these rare conditions are fulfilled, they may not be able to obtain a theatre for more than a very restricted period, if they get one at all. Plays or spectacles which achieve success are kept on for absurdly long runs, and many new plays never reach London

Con: (1) Theatres are *not* worse than they were. They give the public what amusement it wants, which is their proper function. Good plays are provided in sufficient numbers by the commercial theatre to satisfy those who wish to see them, and the present very high standard of drama in Britain is esteemed throughout the world – as shown by the many new British plays which are produced soon afterwards in the USA and other countries. As for 'popular' shows, the not infrequent failure of very vulgar but expensive productions shows that the public has a remedy in its own hands.

(2) If theatres are reformed as some people wish, many of them will fall into the hands of cranks who seem to believe that the only proper subjects for drama are gloomy and unsavoury treatments of moral problems. One of the reasons for the

at all. Many actors who wish to do good work are forced to remain performing drivel, unless they are content with the limited audience of a suburban 'little' theatre.

(3) The prices of seats in West End theatres are prohibitive for the majority of people, and this factor has obviously contributed to the large number of theatres which have gone out of business.

(4) The commercialised theatre is infested with unscrupulous men who would not be tolerated in any other business. As the profession is over-crowded, young actors and actresses are grossly exploited by managers and agents, especially in the provinces.

(5) The stage has a much deeper and more long-lasting influence than that of the screen, but many of the people running it have failed to measure up to their responsibilities, and the inadequacies of their present policies have driven increasing numbers away to other forms of entertainment.

commercial conservatism of managers is the already excessive taxation to which they are subjected. Rents are admittedly high, but the remedy for this does not lie in further harrying of theatrical managements.

(3) Grants from the Arts Council, and the Entertainments Tax remissions for plays of educational value, ensure a constant supply of works of high cultural standard, in both London and the provinces. The majority of people like theatres near their homes, and many of these small theatres in the suburbs or in towns near London are among the most thriving and progressive.

(4) The exploitation of young actors is much less common nowadays, and any abuses are dealt with by British Equity and the leading managers. The growth of trade union organisation among actors has brought them into the same social atmosphere as other workers.

(5) Television and the cinema are much more important than the theatre as an industry and a social influence, but the special impact of a 'live' performance must never be underestimated; theatres will always have this particular appeal and be sure of attracting a public, albeit possibly smaller than in former years.

Tied Cottages

Pro: (1) In feudal days, farm workers lived on the lord's land and gave him work in exchange for accommodation and protection. Ever since then, they have been accustomed to expect free or very cheap accommodation from their employers, with a little land where they can supplement their income by growing food for themselves. Farming is already suffering from a labour shortage, which will be further

Con: (1) Tied cottages constitute a survival of serfdom, since a farm worker is prevented from voicing dissatisfaction, or views distasteful to his employer, by the additional fear of eviction. He is thus deprived of one of the elementary rights enjoyed by all other workers. It is partly the effort to escape from these feudal restrictions on their liberty, which have weighed longer on them than on any other section of the

aggravated if farmers are no longer able to offer this inducement.

(2) Tied cottages are situated on the employer's land, which is more convenient for the workers, since they have easy access to the farm without having to travel several miles from their homes. It would be grossly unfair if a dismissed worker were able to continue in occupation, or if a local authority were able to let these cottages to people quite unconnected with farming, while new workers on the farm were forced to live at a considerable distance from their work. When workers resign or are dismissed, hardship caused to the men and their families (in having to leave their tied cottages) is part of the general rural housing shortage and would not exist if adequate alternative accommodation were provided by local authorities.

(3) Rents in tied cottages are either low or non-existent. If a farmer were deprived of control over his tenants, he could hardly be expected to charge an uneconomic rent. Similarly, if a farm worker lived in a house away from his farm, he would be obliged to pay a rent equal to those paid by other people, so that he would not benefit from any freeing of tied cottages, any more than would the employer.

(4) Because of the objections listed above, many MPs are continuing to resist proposed legislation to abolish the tied cottage system.

community, that has led so many of the younger farm workers to desert the land for other occupations. At present, it is estimated that there are some 70,000 tied cottages in England and Wales, housing about half the total farmworker population, and that evictions average about 1,000 a year.

(2) Living close to his work is not an unmixed blessing for the farm worker. It is often made the excuse for calling upon him to work at any hour of the day or night, and the tacit threat of dismissal and eviction looms in the background, to coerce him. If there are no tied cottages, then the accommodation in a district can be made to correspond with the probable needs of its inhabitants. Providing alternative accommodation for workers who might or might not be evicted means, in effect, duplicating the housing problem in a district.

(3) The bad state of repair and lack of amenities in many farm cottages are such that, were it not for their special status, they would be condemned by the authorities. Freeing them from restriction would encourage improvements, or, in some cases, overdue demolition and replacement. Increased rent for better housing accommodation would cause no hardship to farm workers who were properly paid, as they are gradually beginning to be now that they have come into the scope of trade union organisation.

(4) Despite the resistance of some Tory MPs (mostly representing rural constituencies), a Government Bill to end the tied cottage system passed its second reading in May 1976.

Tied (Public) Houses, Abolition of

Pro: (1) The tied house system deprives the licence-holder of full control of his house, which remains

Con: (1) It is as much in the brewer's interest as in the tenant's that the public house should be

under the aegis of a third party, although the licensee himself still has to take all responsibility in name.

(2) Those who own tied houses impose strict terms on the managers and, by making their tenure terminable at short notice, keep them completely under their own control.

(3) The brewers are able to sell whatever beer they choose to their tenants, who in some cases are bound by agreement not to return any. Moreover, for the beer thus sold to them, many tenants have to pay a higher price than the owners of free houses pay.

(4) The tendency of some owners of tied houses is to extend the system to wines and spirits, as well as beer.

(5) The uncertainty of tenure and the onerous terms oblige the tied house licence-holders to increase their sales to the utmost, so that they may make money while the business remains in their hands. Thus the system is a direct incitement to excessive drinking.

(6) The system is actually illegal, since a licence, which is granted to one man, is granted to him alone, without power to assign it, so any such transfer would be null and void. Accordingly, a brewery owning a tied house would, following such a transfer, be guilty of a breach of law if it sought to turn out the original licence-holder.

(7) Brewers very often fix the rent at a lower figure in order to lower the assessment, and thus are able to evade their fair share of taxation.

(8) The drink trade, being a licensed one, cannot be compared with any other, and the publican should be regarded more as a public servant than as a tradesman.

(9) Brewers cannot complain if their 'rights' are ignored since, knowing the law, they yet choose to risk their money and trust that the strict letter of the law will not be applied. The publican himself has

conducted in a proper manner, so that the licence may not be endangered. Tenants of tied houses usually take a great pride in seeing that they are well run.

(2) No publican need take a tied house, nor would he if the terms were too onerous; the eager competition for the tenancies of tied houses disproves all assertions as to the tyranny of brewers. Tenancy agreements nowadays normally provide for at least one year's notice on either side.

(3) No brewer would willingly or knowingly sell bad beer in a house under his own name. Most brewers allow their tenants to return beer if not good; and if the tenant has to pay a higher price for his beer, he receives an excellent *quid pro quo* in that he has to pay nothing for the goodwill of the business and gets possession for a lower rent than would be possible under any other system.

(4) Even where the tie extends to wines and spirits, these must be good or the public would not buy them. There is no tie on tobacco or food, which the licensee is free to buy wherever he can get the most advantageous terms for his own profit.

(5) Few customers want to get drunk; the vast majority drink only as much as they wish, and no more. They are not likely to increase the amount at the bidding of the publican.

(6) If the tied house system is illegal, why is it necessary to introduce an Act of Parliament to say so? Magistrates have, as a rule, declined to interfere with the system. Brewster Sessions are held twice a year at which licences are renewed to existing tenants and transfers are approved.

(7) It is a matter for the authorities to see that the assessment is put at a fair figure, and it cannot be charged as a fault against the tied

never been recognised as having a 'right' to renewal of his licence.

(10) The system has often ended in throwing the trade of a whole district into the hands of one brewery, or in the amalgamation of breweries, thus destroying all competition.

(11) The evils of the system are felt by all connected with the trade, and the system is almost universally condemned.

house system if they fail in their work.

(8) The tied house system prevails in every country business where large firms have branches, and there is no reason why a distinction should be drawn between the drink trade and others.

(9) Much money has been spent by brewers in improving their properties; no one could expect them to hand this over to the publican without a measure of compensation or safeguard. By the nature of the trade, it is only right that a publican should reapply for his licence every year.

(10) No district is so completely monopolised by any one brewery that competition is altogether destroyed. Brewery companies now make 'swap' agreements with each other in various towns (particularly those where one firm has a high percentage of the pubs), to ensure that customers get a choice of more than one brewer's beers.

(11) If the system were universally condemned (which it is not), it would be quite possible for the big breweries to combine to put an end to it.

Trade Unions:
Should Their Powers Be Restricted?

Pro: (1) By their power to stage strikes as and when the leaders call for them, the more powerful unions hold industry up to ransom and injure the country in numerous ways. A secret ballot on any strike issue should always be enforced by law, and it should be carried out by public officials so as to avoid trickery. The public authorities might even be empowered to control the form of ballot paper.

(2) They should be prohibited from authorising or financing strikes

Con: (1) Strikes are never called unless the leaders have the most overwhelming evidence that their members wish to strike. Most unions have elaborate machinery (including secret ballots, in many cases) for determining what their members want, and the influence of trade union leaders is more often exercised nowadays in moderating rather than in provoking the desire to strike. To impose excessive restrictions on workmen's freedom to withdraw their labour would be an

on such frivolous questions as the demarcation of crafts or compulsory membership of one union rather than another.

(3) Pressure on workers to become members should be prohibited, and any coercive steps which unionists might take against non-unionists should be heavily penalised.

(4) Trade unionists often claim that employers are guilty of much more irresponsible acts than their own. But because one set of people engages in malpractice, there is no justification for another set to imitate the example.

(5) 'Peaceful' picketing should be prohibited, or at least surrounded with greater safeguards. Trade unions should be liable for the unlawful acts of their members, as their present legal privileges render them a danger to the community.

(6) The practice of 'contracting out', by which members who disagree with the political affiliations of their unions are forced to take special steps to retain their political levies, should be reformed so that such workers may exercise the right more simply and without fear of the consequences from their workmates. Many workers are forced to acquiesce in the encouragement of political acts far removed from the legitimate purpose of a trade body, on pain of victimisation.

(7) Unofficial strikes, originating on the shop floor and often called on frivolous pretexts, have destroyed the confidence which should be at the base of sound industrial relations. Dominating personalities gain power as shop stewards, often with purely political aims. Union leaders are powerless to prevent these incidents and are often reluctant to deal with them when they occur, especially when such leaders have themselves gained power for political ends. Some have not scrupled to use this power illegally in tampering

infringement of their legally recognised rights.

(2) Union leaders have themselves recognised the existence of this issue by initiating discussions on demarcation problems in general.

(3) The reaction against those who accept all the benefits that their fellow-workmen secure for them, but do nothing whatever to assist in getting them, is natural. Here again, though, opponents of the unions tend to exaggerate the extent of the few abuses which do occur.

(4) The whole idea of crippling the unions, on the pretext of keeping them to their legitimate functions, is promoted by those who practise the same sort of abuse in their own interests and against the community – forming rings for the restriction of output and raising of prices, suppressing inventions, withdrawing investments to foreign countries, etc.

(5) The history of trade unions provides sufficient justification for their legal privileges. Any attack on their legal status will boomerang on those who engineer it.

(6) A trade union has as much right to further the interests of its members in the political sphere as in the industrial, especially now that industry is so closely affected by legislation. The overwhelming majority of trade unionists support their unions' political affiliations – agitation against which is mainly conducted by Conservative elements who object to the increased power thus given to the Labour Party. Any member is free to 'contract out' and no compulsion can be laid on him.

(7) Unofficial strikes are inevitable while union leaders remain inaccessible to the rank and file, but this is a matter of internal organisation which the unions should tackle themselves. Apparently frivolous pretexts are often merely the latest incidents in a long history of bad

with union rules and voting procedures.

(8) Trade unions should be obliged by law to invest a given proportion of their money (pension funds, etc.) in their own particular industries, which would lead to readier co-operation between unions and managements *and* be a further aid in discouraging unnecessary strikes.

relations with the management. The remedy for infiltration of unions by unscrupulous people lies with the membership and, in cases of illegal conduct, with the courts.

(8) Many trade unions already do just that. But no amount of investment could exceed the biggest stake that all hold in their own industry – the mere fact that their members' livelihoods depend on it.

(See also *Closed Shop*.)

Unemployment, State Remedy for

Pro: (1) Unemployment is one of the worst misfortunes that can befall a person or family and has many harmful influences on industry and society at large. As in many cases it is a direct result of government decisions at home or political changes abroad, and tends to afflict whole regions whose workers were dependent on a particular superseded industry, the State should step in to help. It is unjust that workers should suffer for conditions which they cannot in any way control. America's unemployment problem during the Depression of the 1930s is a classic example. It was dealt with by President Roosevelt as a matter of national urgency – which indeed it was – with a considerable measure of success.

(2) Only the State can provide facilities, on the scale now needed, to train the increasing number of redundant workers for new jobs in other industries. Only the State's ability to pay National Assistance (or 'dole', as introduced in 1918) has prevented large-scale unemployment from swelling into civil strife – at the same time, saving wages and conditions of work from deteriorating and preventing adolescent workers from being forced into industry on a pittance.

Con: (1) The evils of unemployment are admittedly great, but they are due to conditions and circumstances which cannot be ended or mended quickly by any State action. Only by patience and the slow rebuilding of international trade can we look for relief. On the other hand, matters would be much improved by the withdrawal of trade union restrictions on rates of output and on the sort of job a tradesman can do, by the freeing of industry from the multitude of restrictions which hamper it, and, in the opinion of some experts, by the re-introduction of import quotas to protect our own manufacturers.

(Some) The unemployment situation, especially in the export trades, has been distorted by international political considerations and the present world-wide economic recession. Were it not for these, the problem would right itself without the need of further State intervention.

(2) It might be a help if more men agreed to such re-training and were willing to shift to new jobs in other parts of the country where labour is needed. As it is, too many try to stay within their own shrinking industries and, despite above-average unemployment levels in their own

(3) Unemployment cannot be made a direct charge on industry, because all sections of industry are not affected by it in the same way. Nor could this apply in the case of a whole industry which has become obsolete or contracted. There are also many workmen, chiefly unskilled, who shift about from one industry to another. Above all, the fact must be faced that, because of international economic conditions generally, the unemployment problem has reached a pitch where full-scale governmental action offers the only hope at present, if not of solving it, at least of palliating it.

(4) Thrift is not a virtue when the family income is inadequate to satisfy present needs. If unemployment were dealt with properly, trade unions would be willing to relax their regulations about permitted levels of output and so on, for these are mainly designed to secure that their members are not thrown out of work owing to redundancy or temporary gluts on the markets. It is well known that a period of unemployment decreases the skill and general efficiency of a worker by lowering his standard of living, so that the reduction of unemployment would raise the average efficiency.

(5) Many Conservative thinkers privately endorse the idea that large-scale unemployment is to be welcomed as the quickest way to remedy the country's economic ills. The argument is debatable; its immorality is uncontestable.

regions, refuse to move elsewhere. The remedies offered by the State, therefore, have not been a success. The 'dole' has proved the greatest single impediment to the adjustment of our industrial system to changed conditions.

(3) The State is not the proper organ for relieving the misfortunes occasioned by unemployment. Since capitalist industry depends on a reserve of labour, each industry should be made to support its own unemployed. This is a charge which ought not to be spread over the general population. If each trade has to meet its own problems, it would quickly turn to reorganisation of its production and marketing, with most beneficial results.

(4) State maintenance of the unemployed tends to discourage thrift among the working classes and actually fosters idleness and inefficiency. Even on present standards, the unemployed sometimes draw allowances of as much or nearly as much as their fellows get for a whole week's work.

(5) Unpalatable though it may be, increased unemployment is both essential and inevitable in grappling with the problem of inflation, a far graver threat to any country's future. History shows that, once the rate of inflation is brought within reasonable bounds, restoring industrialists' confidence sufficiently for them to resume capital investment, the pool of unemployed is rapidly reduced.

(See also *Full Employment*.)

United Nations Organisation

Pro: (1) In spite of the failure of the League of Nations in some fields, and fortified by the experience of another world war, the nations of the world deemed it necessary to form a

Con: (1) History is strewn with the wreckage of attempts at international organisation, of which the UN is only the latest. They have all split on the same rock of sovereignty, and the

successor organisation. A modern world without any international authority is unthinkable.

(2) The difficulties which the UN encounters in the field of high politics should not blind us to the useful work it does. It has proved invaluable in facilitating international co-operation in such matters as health, education, control of dangerous drugs, suppression of the white slave traffic and (through the associated International Labour Office) conditions of labour in industry, agriculture and shipping. Above all, despite its obvious political failures, it continues to provide a regular meeting-place for behind-the-scenes talks and negotiations between countries which are publicly at loggerheads. It has been well said that 'the mere habit of representatives of various nations meeting together and discussing matters for the general good will create a valuable habit of mind and temper which should have a wide and beneficent influence'.

(3) The UN's constitution – notably, the establishment of the Security Council and the right of veto among its Big Five members (the USSR, USA, Britain, France and China) – is far more realistic than that of the ill-fated League of Nations. While political rivalries may limit the scope of its effective decision-making, the system does ensure that whatever decisions are taken will correspond with the ability and willingness to carry them out of those Great Powers on whom such duties mostly descend.

(4) If there were no disagreements of principles between different countries, there would be no need for any such all-embracing body as the UN. The function of the organisation lies precisely in making it possible for nations to act together on the basis of whatever agreement they can eventually achieve. Widely publicised

UN, in the long run, will be no exception. Such an organisation cannot succeed because the necessary prerequisite – willingness on the part of member countries to recognise its overriding rights – is lacking. The scant respect with which its decisions on such questions as Palestine and South-West Africa (Namibia) have been treated by the States concerned; the tendency to bypass it in settling really important questions, such as the crises of Berlin, Cuba and Vietnam; the organisation's huge indebtedness, through the failure of many members to pay all the dues they owe; all these things show that the process of decay has already begun.

(2) That international regulation of various social matters is a good thing cannot be denied, but this work can equally well be carried on by *ad hoc* bodies, as has been done in the past. In fact, it is endangered by being linked artificially to the controversial discussions on political and diplomatic issues on which there is continual disagreement. Wrecking of the UN on political issues would leave its social committees high and dry.

(3) The smaller nations are resentful of the right of veto enjoyed by the Big Five and would certainly try to end it, if they could. In the meantime, some of them have attached themselves to one or other of the two big power blocs, as the best way to promote their own interests, while the so-called non-aligned countries now form a third bloc of such size that their unrealistic conduct has largely discredited the General Assembly's proceedings. At the same time, the very narrowness of the conditions under which agreement must be reached in the Security Council gives rise to an inflexibility which, eventually, might well cause the breakage of the machinery itself.

international discussions put a brake on secret diplomacy and secret alignments. The symbolic presence of a UN 'buffer' force is a crucial factor in the efforts to avoid a new war between Israel and the Arab countries. UN forces also succeeded in keeping the inter-communal temperature down in Cyprus (prior to the Turkish invasion, at least). By remaining in the former Belgian Congo (now Zaire), they could have helped in bringing about a peaceful transition to stable government and prevented the tragedies subsequently caused by tribal violence and foreign intervention.

(5) The truly international spirit of the organisation is underlined by the fact that its officials are drawn from virtually every one of its member-nations and that they work together harmoniously, irrespective of any political or ideological differences between each other's countries.

(6) Economically, the world is moving towards the breakdown of national barriers. The formation of the Common Market and the general agreement on the desirability of lowering tariff barriers are illustrations of this tendency. Conditions are likely to grow more favourable to the success of the UN, not less so.

(7) Liquidation of the UN would leave sectional bodies, such as Communists, Roman Catholics and international financiers, as the only ones internationally organised. The United Nations Organisation, essentially, defends the interests of the ordinary citizen throughout the world, without sectarian or sectional partiality.

(4) In hard fact, the nations are divided into three main camps, those of the Communist and capitalist countries, and the non-aligned bloc. At all UN meetings, decisions are taken, and arguments presented, in accord with one or other of these tendencies. But where formal international agreement is difficult, the UN is bypassed. The fragility of its role in the Middle East is shown by what happened immediately after Nasser ordered the UN force to be withdrawn in 1967. The Congo intervention was not conspicuously successful and, in overstepping the bounds of impartiality, the UN forces may actually have delayed the end of the war there.

(5) The UN Secretariat has become a top-heavy bureaucracy. Many posts are allotted on the principle of 'Buggins' turn', i.e. they go to someone from this-or-that country simply to ensure that the country in question is represented in the Secretariat – and quite irrespective of the ability, or otherwise, of the official concerned.

(6) Agreements to abolish tariffs and abide by international decisions on economic matters are apt to be flouted when conditions are unfavourable. The conclusions and decisions of the UN, as past experience shows, remain particularly vulnerable to the same tendency.

(7) Religious and political bodies are able to achieve a fairly stable organisation because they have a common purpose, and financiers because it suits their business interests. With the purposes of its members differing so widely, the UN has no such basis, to any effective extent. Nor does it operate with consistent even-handedness, any more than its individual members do.

United States of Europe

Pro: (1) The national idea was necessary in the Middle Ages to raise the world out of barbarism and help the development of modern civilisation, but it has served its purpose, and events since 1914 have finally shown that complete national sovereignty is unworkable. Ever since the Congress of Vienna (1815), the nations of Europe have been attempting to reach some form of unity. The League of Nations was wrecked on the rock of national sovereignty; if Europe is to have equal weight with other power groupings in world counsels, its constituent countries must consent to some form of federation among themselves.

(2) For various reasons, but mainly because of their sufferings as important theatres of war, the European countries lost much of the economic power from which their former dominant political influence was derived; yet European civilisation has a great tradition and a unique contribution to make to international life – and the formation of the Common Market is already re-establishing their joint economic strength. If brought together politically, too, they would become a telling force and rank alongside the so-called Super-Powers, America and the Soviet Union (and eventually, no doubt, China).

(3) Modern economics demand a larger geographical unit than can be provided by any single country in Europe. The industrial and agricultural nations of Europe are complementary, natural resources are distributed over the whole continent, and their integration is essential for their future economic survival – as the EEC has already demonstrated.

(4) There is no reason for a United

Con: (1) The idea of European Federation is not practical. There is no true identity between the various States of Europe, and national sovereignty is necessary in order to preserve the distinctions to which they cling. The League of Nations failed because it was not content with limited achievements, based on the few common interests of its members, but strove after an unreal and unattainable unity. The same possibility is inherent in the UN, could yet afflict the EEC members (who are anything but united in their views about the nature of eventual European political unity), and would certainly appear in a United States of Europe.

(2) The British Commonwealth is still strong enough and united enough to constitute a cogent force in world policy, despite occasional disagreements. A United States of Europe might benefit some other countries but has no advantages for Britain and would complicate our relations with the rest of the English-speaking world. While recognising that the EEC's objectives are not merely economic but, in the longer term, political as well, Britain opposes anything more than a loose linking which would preserve national identities.

(3) It would be over-optimistic to expect any country to weaken the balance of its economic life for the benefit of a federation. So far from wishing to rise above nationalism, most countries are striving to advance the interests of their own populations. All the Common Market's hard-fought economic agreements are still marked by forced concessions to individual self-interest among its member-nations.

(4) For the United States of

States of Europe to exclude any nation from its framework. All the nations have similar problems to face, and differences in ideology and degree of State control are of decreasing importance these days. It is already foreseeable that Communist and capitalist countries could take part without any serious difficulties arising.

(5) The idea of federation is not new. It has worked very successfully in the USA, in spite of early growing pains, and the power of the federal organisation has developed in a natural manner. Moreover, the federal structure does not prevent the exercise of the individual 'State's rights', which are still jealously guarded. In the two centuries since establishment of the USA, political education in the world at large has so much advanced that federation could be initiated much more painlessly in Europe. It has also worked well in the USSR, which is a federation of national republics, and notably in Switzerland.

Europe to succeed, it would have to include all European countries. Serious divergences of economic interest exist between Western European nations, let alone between them and the countries of Eastern Europe. The Soviet political and economic systems are too far removed from those of other countries to be easily absorbed into a federal system.

(Some) In practice, the USE idea is most popular among those who would exclude Russia and countries linked to her ideologically. A Western USE, which would in effect be based on NATO and thus tend to exclude neutral countries, would be more likely to result in renewed polarisation between East and West than to enhance their present progress towards *détente*.

During the 1975 summit meeting of the European Security Conference in Helsinki, several Communist representatives stated bluntly that the conference agreements did *not* mean a United States of Europe was possible.

(5) The USA were formed in a new and unsettled country by groups of people whose outlook and racial origins were similar at the time. In the USSR, State autonomy is slender and the federal authority overriding. Switzerland is composed of states with strong economic identity, whose local differences are more apparent than real. Europe, on the other hand, consists of old-established countries with long traditions and pronounced national differences. For Britain, entry into a USE would entail the abandonment of some of our most cherished institutions.

University Reform

Pro: (1) Universities should be national, in that they ought to provide for the highest cultural

Con: (1) Those few who can benefit from education at the older universities already have opportunities

requirements of the whole nation and no university should be reserved for one or two classes of society. The scholarship system at Oxford and Cambridge, their relatively limited contact with State schools, and the independent procedures of the individual colleges, discourage many would-be students.

(2) Some provincial universities are still without the indisputable benefits that come from residence in college. This means the isolation of the student not only from the main currents of university life outside the lecture room but also from any fruitful contact with his teachers, for the tutorial system which is such a feature of life in Oxford and Cambridge works best when followed by resident students and dons.

(3) University legislation and administration should be in the hands of the teaching staff and others who are running the academic side of the university and who know its needs and difficulties.

(4) All universities should be controlled more closely by the Department of Education and Science, because they form part of the national educational system. At present, there are too few universities to meet local needs in some regions and a surplus of choice in others. Most universities have insufficient staff for their needs. Because universities have grown too large in recent years, tutorial groups now average twelve students or more, whereas they should ideally comprise not more than six. At present, there are too many students at university who should not really be there.

(5) Conditions of entry should be revised. The present specialised requirements involve intensive cramming in school and destroy every chance of achieving a general all-round education. Candidates from State schools are at an unfair

through scholarships. There are enough places in provincial universities for other students. That the institutions of Oxford and Cambridge are sound is proved by the competition for admission. It would be more profitable to leave their unique character intact.

(2) Non-residence also has its advantages. Non-campus universities in large cities can often offer the student a rich general experience which is denied to those who enter university as inexperienced schoolchildren and remain in its rarefied atmosphere. Students who continue to live at home are spared the sudden deprivation of family life. The best provincial universities have developed tutorial and counselling systems for their non-resident students.

(3) To limit the conception of a university to a body of resident dons marks a self-satisfied exclusiveness. A true university comprises all its graduate members.

(4) The University Grants Committee has enough control to guard against abuses or eccentricities. The idea of direct control is repugnant to the traditions of academic independence which have been the special glory of our universities. The population explosion in students has led to a dropping in the standards required for entry. But this does not require more staff; it can be remedied, once the population levels out, simply by resuming entry standards which produce the right number of students for the existing staff.

(5) Students who cannot satisfy university entrance requirements are better accommodated in technological institutions. Candidates are not always assessed solely on examinations and academic records, and any falling short in other respects is likely to be the fault of the schools or the candidates themselves.

(6) A university of scientists would be a national calamity.

disadvantage compared with those from the better-staffed independent schools.

(6) Educationally and for the sake of the community, university curricula ought to be based on natural science. Furthermore, they should be so reorganised, especially in the scientific departments, as to allow more time for research. It is because universities do not give enough of the practical side that more and more money has been going to the polytechnics, who do.

(7) (Some) There are already too many universities. However small and local in character, they try to cover the whole field of university education. As a result, there is widespread overlapping and inefficiency.

Science without moral philosophy and liberal culture is a danger to the world. Many scientists, not excluding some who are distinguished, are remarkably ignorant and presumptuous about subjects off their special track. Several of the newer universities have shown their awareness of this by instituting mixed courses. In many fields (e.g. law, medicine, psychology, social sciences), university curricula do in fact incorporate a large proportion of practical work.

(7) No university is granted a charter until the institutions out of which it grows have reached a suitable status and can establish their case for the grant. Local universities, by their appeal to local patriotism, divert funds to education which would otherwise be used for different purposes.

Vaccination

Pro: (1) Vaccination, has eradicated epidemics of smallpox, world-wide, and has proved an efficient protection against other diseases. In the few cases where smallpox has occurred after vaccination, it is always modified to such an extent as not to be recognisable in its early stages. In pre-vaccination days, the mortality from smallpox, and the blindness, disfigurement and other injuries caused by it, were universally dreaded. Apart from smallpox, the efficacy of vaccinations is shown by the fact that some countries make it compulsory for visitors to have them for yellow fever and cholera as well. The very success of Jenner's discovery has blotted out these dangers from our national consciousness.

(2) Statistics show an enormous difference between the relative numbers of cases of smallpox among the

Con: (1) The only definition that can be found for 'efficient' vaccination is that which is not followed by smallpox. Even if this occurs in the individual, vaccination will not destroy the infectivity of the disease, so that a person immunised by vaccination might act as a carrier for non-immune people. This fact may easily disguise the serious nature of an epidemic at its start. In the present high state of development of preventive medicine in Britain, there is no likelihood that an epidemic will get far before control measures stop it.

(2) The Bradford outbreak was started by a child in whom the symptoms had been masked by an attack of malaria. That the outbreak did not spread further was due to the prompt measures of isolation, disinfection and tracing of contacts, in which the local doctors and authori-

vaccinated and unvaccinated, which also show far fewer fatal cases. This was borne out strikingly in the case of the troops invading tropical countries in the Second World War. In an outbreak of the disease at Bradford in 1962, during which seven people died, four of the victims had never been vaccinated, one only in infancy, and one showed no trace of the vaccination he claimed; but all the people who recovered had been vaccinated. It was generally agreed that the epidemic had demonstrated the urgent need for vaccination at intervals throughout life, especially among hospital staffs and people working at shipping terminals and airports. The great increase in air travel particularly has made it possible for a sufferer to enter the country before the symptoms of the disease have appeared.

(3) Inoculations of various kinds are accepted nowadays and have reduced mortality in many other illnesses. The public confidence in vaccination was shown by the fact that more than 100,000 people in Bradford came forward and asked for it, as well as thousands elsewhere. When Edward Jenner carried out his first successful vaccination in 1796, one-fifth of all deaths in Britain were due to smallpox. In 1967, when the World Health Organisation began a mass vaccination drive to eradicate smallpox, the disease was endemic in about thirty countries and there were more than 2,500,000 cases throughout the world; five years later, there were only 150,000 cases; by 1976, except for a last 'push' on the Indian sub-continent, the disease was virtually conquered. Similarly, in Britain, with the 'triple jab' introduced after the last world war (against diphtheria, whooping cough and tetanus), the figures speak for themselves. Deaths from diphtheria in 1941, 2,641; by 1972, none. From whooping cough,

ties, the Ministry of Health and its laboratories, all played their part.

(3) The willingness of people to be vaccinated in times of panic only testifies to the depth and strength of propaganda on the subject. After vaccination of infants ceased to be compulsory in 1946, the proportion of infants vaccinated dropped to some 18 and 10 per cent in England and Wales respectively (in 1948), and it is admitted that the areas where vaccination figures are lowest are not those to suffer the greatest incidence of the disease.

(4) Coroners' inquests have over and over again proved that vaccination has been the cause of death. Jonathan Hutchinson in his *Archives of Surgery* recorded no fewer than 679 deaths from cowpox from 1881 to 1893, or more than one child a week. There is also a definite risk of other diseases being introduced with the serum. Some tragic cases have been recorded of children dying of other diseases in the absence of any risk from smallpox itself, or even from smallpox contracted as a result of vaccination. In 1974, a pathologist giving evidence at a Walsall inquest disclosed that, as a result of the standard 'triple jab', there had been 425 cases of adverse reactions in England and Wales during a seven-year period – and of these, 17 were deaths. In the same year, it was officially estimated that, out of about 600,000 children given the 'triple jab' each year, between 60 and 80 might suffer brain damage in consequence. Professor George Dick, microbiologist at the Middlesex Hospital, put it somewhat higher, producing data which showed that permanent brain damage could follow immunisation in two out of 10,000 children. He also observed that whooping cough (for which vaccination presents the most risk in the 'triple jab') is now usually a mild disease – and that this could

between 1941 and 1949, annual average of deaths, 1,008; in 1972, down to 8. And deaths from tetanus were cut to only 10.

(4) Before antisepsis was practised, there was no doubt a small but real risk of conveying some form of sepsis. There was also some risk of inoculation by accident with other diseases. But these risks are infinitesimal since the introduction of glycerinated calf lymph, which is produced and tested in most rigorous conditions. Since direct inoculation from sufferers was abandoned, it is impossible to contract smallpox as a result of vaccination.

(5) The risk of vaccinia is extremely small. In 1958, there were only 25 cases, or one in 500,000 vaccinations, and five cases of encephalitis. Most of the few cases occur among older children and adults being vaccinated for the first time, which points to the advisability of doing the first vaccination in infancy.

(6) Smallpox, unmodified by vaccination, is one of the most infectious, contagious and fatal of all diseases. Before vaccination was introduced, it was fatal in about 30 per cent of cases and hastened death in most of the others. Few other diseases kill as quickly or cause such widespread suffering, so that priority in research and treatment given to it were justified, as are any drastic measures taken to prevent it. The small number of deaths shown in recent figures testifies dramatically to the value of vaccination, which performs precisely the function of breaking in the population to the milder form of the disease, in a controlled way which is much superior to the operation of chance contact, with all its attendant risks.

be due to the natural waning of the disease rather than vaccination. Apart from all these dangers, there is the added risk of sepsis from inoculations.

(5) In the first day or two after vaccination, there is actually an increased liability to the disease in the patient. There is also the risk of complications giving rise to vaccinia or to a severe form of encephalitis which may cause permanent invalidism and mental derangement, if not death. If most of these cases do occur among older children being vaccinated for the first time, as is claimed, it would clearly be better if the schoolchildren in question were not vaccinated at all.

(6) Smallpox is now so rare – only 10 cases were notified in the five years to 1958 – that the time, money and effort spent in combating it would be better employed in fighting the serious evils of cancer, rheumatism and tuberculosis. The cases that do occur can be treated adequately by isolation and nursing. By the theories of inoculation now current, the whole population should be given a chance to acquire the very mild type of smallpox which is now more common, for thereby they would gain a degree of protection against the acute variety far superior to that afforded by vaccination. Proper examination at the ports and airports, with less reliance on evidence of vaccination, would prevent the spreading of disease brought in from abroad.

Vegetarianism

Pro: (1) The slaughter of animals bred for the purpose is cruel and degrading. The conversion of pasture into arable land would greatly benefit the nation, as would the cessation of expensive meat imports. Artificial manures can be derived in ample quantities from coal and the atmosphere.

(2) (Some) Darwinian theories add special force to the argument against domesticating cattle for the purposes of slaughter; for artificial selection with a view to the table only is substituted for the healthy operation of natural selection, and the animal is thus deprived of its capacity to improve and rise in the scale of being. Moreover, animals in a domestic state are more liable to disease than when wild.

(3) The process of evolution teaches us that man will have less and less to do with animals, which are a fertile breeding-ground for disease, e.g. cows were largely responsible for tuberculosis.

(4) (Some) The universe is a whole; animals are just as much a part of it as man. Mankind must not violate the harmony and plan of the world by destroying his fellow creatures.

(5) The slaughter of animals is accompanied by much cruelty, as when calves and lambs are separated from their mothers. Animals also suffer much in transit and, while the cruelties at present associated with the slaughterhouse might be abated, they could never be quite abolished.

(6) The work of destruction is demoralising and the surroundings of the slaughterhouse are degrading. We ought to relieve our fellow-citizens of such employment. If everyone had to slaughter his own meat, most people would be vegetarians.

Con: (1) Unless animals are kept for food, they will die out. If they are not kept in large numbers, arable land will not be properly manured, as artificial manures are not a complete substitute for organic. Fertilisers and manures would have to be imported instead of meat if there were any large extension of arable farming. A general conversion to vegetarianism would not prevent the killing of animals. If cows are to be kept for milk and cheese, then bulls would have to be destroyed as non-productive.

(2) The only alternative to domestication in man's service is extermination by man. Either process is a part of man's survival and selection. It is erroneous to suppose that wild animals are freer from disease and parasites than tame ones, or that natural selection is not as cruel in its operation as artificial.

(3) A world in which man has left no room for other animals is inconceivable. The tendency of history is to make man more and more dependent on a rational exploitation of the lower animals.

(4) A universal harmony is accepted or desired by only a few. Destruction of one animal by another seems to be a part of the world plan.

(5) Much pain has been eliminated by the invention of the humane killer, and measures to ensure that animals are not unduly frightened have been greatly improved. A certain amount of suffering is inevitable in nature; we can alleviate but not eliminate it. Moreover, the separation of the cow from its calf for the sake of obtaining the cow's milk for human consumption also involves a certain amount of cruelty.

(6) The fact that a trade is

(7) Revelations from time to time, such as Upton Sinclair's *Jungle*, show the abuses and horrors that the meat trade abounds in. Our markets, large and small, reveal themselves to ordinary observation as disseminators of dirt and disease.

(8) Vegetarianism fosters humanity and gentleness, while a meat diet produces ferocity.

(9) The formation of man's teeth (he has no teeth wherewith to tear flesh food), the fact that he has not a rough tongue, and the nature of his intestines, which are long and sacculated compared with those of flesh-eaters, prove him to be frugivorous by nature. The apes, which are nearest to man, are wholly vegetarian in diet. Neither man's strength nor his speed is as it would have to be if he were flesh-eating by nature. If man depended on his strength and speed for his flesh food, he would have to be a carrion eater.

(10) A vegetarian diet will give as much nourishment as a meat diet; while the consumer of meat, which is mostly protein, takes in addition a large amount of starchy food, the vegetarian balances his diet by living on pulses and cereals which contain a large proportion of proteins mixed with starch. No scientific vegetarian lives on vegetables alone; nuts and cheese contain no starch.

(11) The craving for stimulants results in many cases from the qualities of meat, which induce a craving for stronger stimulants. The nations which consume above-average quantities of alcohol are the meat-eating nations. The only hope of curing alcoholism lies in a non-meat diet.

(12) Animal fats are more likely than vegetable fats to cause arteriosclerosis, leading to premature old age. Sir Clifford Allbutt has said that comparatively few people over forty do not show some such signs, so that vegetarian diet cannot be

disgusting is no reason for its abolition. Many industrial processes and sanitary services are also disgusting, but we do not abolish them. Butchers, as a class, show no signs of demoralisation.

(7) Abuses such as those referred to are not confined to the meat trade, nor to markets. They result from the consideration of profit at the expense of all else and are a question for economic and social reform. Cleanliness in markets is a matter for municipal regulation.

(8) Diet has no such influence on character. For instance, many Turks and Japanese, both peoples known for their ferocity as warriors, are practically vegetarian. A meat diet may be said to improve the temper, as a meal including meat produces in most people a feeling of satisfaction. Perhaps Hitler's vegetarianism contributed to his seeking satisfaction in other ways.

(9) It is impossible to judge of man's necessities by analogy with the ape's, but it is worthy of note that the human intestine does not resemble that of the vegetarian rabbit. Man's organs are adapted to a mixed diet; like the pig, he is omnivorous. His wits replace strength and speed. In any case, the argument from nature is weak, for naturally carnivorous animals like cats flourish on a diet almost exclusively composed of milk and vegetables.

(10) It is an advantage to the human organism to receive protein in a more concentrated form than can be obtained from vegetables. First-class protein, which is only to be found in meat, is an essential constituent of a scientifically balanced diet. Vegetables are so overloaded with starch and cellulose that they are less assimilable than flesh and larger percentages escape digestion.

(11) Special complaints naturally need a special regime. Nations which

held responsible. The peoples in all parts of the world that avoid meat are less liable to cancer than meat-eaters. Statistical studies have shown that people who have always been vegetarians tend to live longer than meat-eaters.

(13) Vegetarian diet is capable of as much variety as any that meat diet can offer. Vegetarians can take the credit for making some vegetables (e.g. haricot beans and lentils) much more popular with the general public. While costly dishes are possible, the object of rational vegetarians is to bring people to a rational simplicity.

(14) Diet should be settled scientifically, on the basis of man's basic requirements. It is natural that there should be different schools of vegetarians, but the principles remain the same. Vegetarians who relapse do so through special causes or through their own errors.

(15) A vegetarian diet ensures that adequate amounts of mineral salts and vitamins are consumed. Meat-eaters take vegetables; but they are often cooked in such a fashion as to destroy these vital substances. Appetite is also destroyed by the indifferent cooking of vegetables, when their lack of flavour can be concealed by the flavour of meat.

(16) The latest evidence goes to show that the low rating put on cereal proteins is unsound. At least one cereal – soya bean – contains 'first-class' protein. As the majority of people suffer from too great an intake of protein, this criticism of vegetarian diet is not important.

are vegetarian are given to drug-taking, e.g. opium, betel, bhang, coca. The real hope for curing alcoholism lies in the development of mental therapeutics. Vegetarians are often of a slightly abnormal temperament and vegetarian literature tends equally often to be hypochondriac.

(12) An exclusively vegetable diet is liable to produce debilitating intestinal disorders, especially if the food is uncooked. Apart from other considerations, it is doubtful whether the British climate is suitable for large-scale practice of vegetarianism. The differences in expectation of life are in any case so small as to make it hardly worth while to deprive oneself of the advantage and enjoyment of eating meat.

(13) While in theory vegetarianism offers a new and large variety of foods, in practice the reverse is the case; the food habitually consumed by vegetarians and served in vegetarian restaurants is often singularly deficient in variety and cooked in unappetising ways. The 'scientific vegetarians' who add eggs, milk and cheese to their diets are not true vegetarians, for they can only get those things if the rest of the world is meat-eating. A vegetarian diet adequate to the body and pleasing to the palate involves much expense of time and money.

(14) Vegetarians are not agreed among themselves; their varieties are numerous (e.g., VEM – vegetables, eggs, and milk – fruitarians, purin-free, unfired), and they are as opposed to one another as they are to meat-eaters. Equally good cases could be made out for Fletcherism ('chew, chew, chew again'), the fasting cure, and the exclusively meat diet. Quite a number of vegetarians take to meat again after some years.

(15) The remedy for such deficiencies in meat-eaters' diets is to

see that they eat salads and cook their non-flesh foods properly, not give up meat. Vegetarian cooking is frequently poor.

(16) The quality of the proteins in cereals and vegetables tends to be low and, since quality of food is as important as quantity, the consumer of animal foods, including cheese, scores heavily in this respect. The amount of protein in a diet cannot in any case be prescribed for everybody on one scale; it is quite possible that sedentary workers can do with comparatively little, but very few heavy workers would tolerate the idea of vegetarianism – and, in fact, most vegetarians are drawn from the middle classes (in Britain, at any rate).

Vivisection and Experiments on Animals

Pro: (1) The healing art depends for its advancement on all the sciences, but especially on biology. The laws of biology can be discovered only by observation and experiment, just as the laws of other sciences have to be discovered. Observation may suggest a law, but experiment is essential to substantiate the theory. As men can relatively rarely be observed under the strictest scientific conditions and can be the subject of experiments only in exceptional circumstances, animals which are closely similar in physiological processes have to be used. Few of these laws could have been elucidated without experiments on animals. Before carrying out any experiments, investigators have to obtain a Home Office certificate authorising the proposed study.

(2) Psychopathology depends largely on animal experiments, particularly the study of instinctive behaviour and reflex action. Vivisection has taught us much about

Con: (1) Medicine and surgery are arts as well as sciences, and the animal economy is much more than a piece of machinery which can be taken to pieces and investigated in a vivisector's laboratory. Experiments done on sub-human creatures are, when applied to man, apt to be misleading and therefore dangerous. The late Sir Frederick Treves, himself a vivisector, admitted this as regards certain of his own experiments. The artificial diseases of the laboratory are not the same as diseases occurring naturally.

(2) Vivisection has distracted medical science away from psychopathology, with the result that progress in mental science has been much slower than in other fields. Yet knowledge of how to cure the diseases of the mind is more urgent than knowledge of how to cure the diseases of the body, as it is now recognised that the mind has an enormous influence over the body.

(3) Such important discoveries as

the purely physiological side of sensation and thought. It has saved an enormous amount of suffering both for men and for animals.

(3) Vivisection has given us many facts about the functions of the body, and has confirmed or modified those otherwise discovered, e.g. the laws relating to blood pressure and the functions of arteries and nerves.

(4) The surgeon has been enabled to localise the functions of the brain and bring to perfection such operations as lobectomy. By experiment on animals during his training, he gets an idea of the effect of any measures he takes. Having the broad lines of possible results before him, he can proceed at once more boldly and more skilfully.

(5) Vivisection has not only shown us the true causes of infectious diseases but, to a considerable extent, has enabled us to prevent and cure them. The Pasteur treatment has reduced the mortality among those bitten by rabid animals from at least 15 per cent to fewer than 1 per cent. The antitoxin treatment of diphtheria has reduced mortality to nil when applied in the first two days.

(6) In war, the methods of prevention and cure by antitoxins and serum injections have eradicated the danger of typhoid and reduced the risks of tetanus and gas gangrene to minor proportions. All the methods employed are based on knowledge gained through vivisection. The very methods employed for disinfection are based on experimental results.

(7) Cancer now has a much greater recovery rate, thanks to animal experiments. Influenza is better understood and more nearly under control, and deaths from scarlet fever and measles have vanished thanks to treatment with antibiotics. Virus diseases are being conquered, poliomyelitis being an outstanding example. Sanitation has

the circulation of the blood were made not by vivisection but by clinical and post-mortem observation and inference. As for the nerves, no experiments at all are needed to demonstrate the process of reflex action, which is claimed as a triumph of vivisection. 'Living pathology' suffices for the purpose.

(4) Prehistoric man well understood trepanning. As the human brain and body differ from the animal brain and body, little is to be learnt from vivisecting the latter.

(5) Although Pasteurism has taught us much about the causes of disease due to microbes, it has been far less productive in practical results.

(6) The improved health of armies during war has been due to superior sanitation and better facilities for normal medical attention. In some cases, the injection of serums can be fatal; in others, it weakens the health and stamina of the subjects.

(7) The diseases over which vivisectionists have spent most time show no signs of being eradicated through their researches. The menace of influenza continues, despite the efforts of the vivisectionists to invent a serum or antitoxin to combat it. It is true that the death-rate from diphtheria has been reduced since vivisection was brought to bear on it. But the death-rate had already begun to decrease, through the natural waning of the disease, before the introduction of the antitoxin treatment. In other diseases such as measles and scarlet fever, similarly, the fall in the death-rate had begun long before there was any treatment due to vivisection, and it was even more marked than in the case of diphtheria.

(8) As very few medicines have the same effect on the lower animals as they do on human beings, it cannot be said that we owe any exact knowledge of the action of drugs to

undoubtedly reduced many diseases greatly, as also has a lessening of poverty. But the general advance in the treatment of all manner of complaints is bound up with the study of morbid conditions under laboratory control and with the advance in biochemistry, both of which are dependent on experiments with animals. The supply of insulin, which offers the victim of diabetes a successful life, was the work of vivisectors.

(8) The action and effect of drugs are the same on all animals; when there is a difference in the action of a drug on two animals, it is a difference of *degree*, not of *kind*. Though anaesthetics were not actually discovered by vivisection, their development is largely due to it, e.g. Simpson's discovery that parturition could take place under an anaesthetic. All new anaesthetic compounds are tried on animals first. More thorough and more carefully controlled experiments would have prevented the thalidomide tragedy.

(9) Naturally, biology is full of controversies, like other sciences. There would be small hope for it if it were not. Anti-vivisectionists select from such discussions whatever statements or opinions suit their case. Dr Walker [see Con (9)] actually criticised the use made of vivisection, not the practice itself.

(10) The greatly increased knowledge of foodstuffs, of the role played by vitamins, of the value of proteins, etc., is dependent on systematic experimentation with animals – mostly, of course, by giving them special diets and noting results. The value of experiments on animals is firmly justified and established in this field. To those experiments we owe the great diminution in the number of children deformed by rickets, the reduction of the death-rate from puerperal sepsis by some 95 per cent, from cerebro-spinal

experiments on animals. The use of thalidomide was the result of unjustified reliance on animal experiments. Anaesthetics were discovered not by experiments on animals but by Simpson's experiments on himself, and by the experiments of Morton, the dentist, on his patients.

(9) There is a minority of able doctors who themselves deny or drastically criticise the claims of vivisectors. For instance, Dr G. F. Walker, an authoritative writer on medical subjects, and holding several important hospital appointments, declared that 'vivisection, overwhelmingly on the whole, has been wasteful and futile'.

(10) The results of the biochemists' researches into food, etc., merely confirm what medical men without faith in vivisection, unorthodox practitioners, 'food reformers', and others, have said for many years, viz. we must not sophisticate our foodstuffs more than is necessary, we must buy food of good quality, we must take exercise and get plenty of fresh air. The same is true of the vogue for sunbathing. Those who could afford it have always known it to be desirable to get sea air, avoid the chemical-laden atmosphere of the industrial town, etc., and those who could not afford it have always wanted to follow their example. But the conservatism of the medical profession as a whole, with its excessive faith in laboratories, is demonstrated continually. Although a doctor in the eighteenth century proved that scurvy could be prevented by consuming fresh vegetables and citrus fruit, and Captain Cook kept his crews healthy by following this advice, British medical 'experts' still recommended a diet for the Army during the First World War which resulted in many of our soldiers suffering from scurvy.

(11) How can anyone condone the

meningitis by almost 90 per cent, and from pneumonia to under 2 per cent of cases in patients aged under 50. Can anyone maintain that the sacrifice of a few thousand mice is too high a price to pay for the saving of so many human lives?

(11) The fact that, in Britain alone, some 1,000 people die from lung cancer every week is surely a far greater cause for public concern?

(12) The anti-vivisectionist has no case on scientific grounds. His moral principles are dubious. Most 'experiments' are of a minor character that involve only slight discomfort to the animals concerned, and often not even that. Serious operations are conducted under anaesthetics, and, moreover, are only 5 per cent of the total number of experiments. The other 95 per cent are simple experiments such as inoculations and feeding tests. Other animals are beneficiaries, too, because nearly all veterinary medicine derives from such experimentation. The harrowing descriptions and illustrations circulated by the anti-vivisectionists are misleading to the public. Two Royal Commissions have decided in favour of experiments on animals. The last one, after inquiring into the charges of cruelty brought by the antis, refuted them with the finding that 'after careful consideration of the above cases, we have come to the conclusion that the witnesses have either misapprehended or inaccurately described the facts of the experiments'.

experiments, disclosed in 1975, in which beagle dogs were in effect forced to smoke cigarettes? (The precise object was to compare the irritant power of smoke from tobacco substitutes with that from cigarettes.) It is small wonder that there was a major public outcry at the disclosure.

(12) Although it is not denied that vivisection may have produced some good results, the foundation of the opposition to vivisection is moral. Not even the surest advance in knowledge justifies the infliction of excessive suffering on dumb animals. Even the serum experiments involve acute pain, while sensation experiments must necessarily be done without anaesthetics. In tacitly inviting the public to tolerate vivisection, the scientists are encouraging callousness and cruelty and are stifling compassion in the human heart.

Voting, Compulsory

Pro: (1) It is the duty of every citizen to take an interest in the affairs of his community, and to express his opinion on the questions at issue and choose between rival policies. Voting should therefore be made compulsory, under penalty for

Con: (1) Compulsory voting obliges electors to choose one out of two or three persons or measures, even though they might not approve of any of them. It endeavours to force them to give a practical assent to a system which they may not like and

failure to vote. The ballot paper can be drafted so that no one has any grievance about being made to support a policy or candidate that he dislikes. Such a measure would heighten the sense of civic responsibilities and would be a precaution against power getting into the hands of incipient dictators (whether in the State or the local municipality).

(2) In countries which already have compulsory voting – such as Australia, which introduced it as long ago as 1925 – the idea works smoothly and well, and no reasonable elector feels that it is onerous or restrictive.

may even want to change. The negative comment implied by abstentions from the poll can at times be most valuable.

(Some) If people are so indifferent to what happens that they do not trouble to exercise their rights, they should be left alone to bear the results of their negligence.

(2) It may work in a country with a relatively small and scattered population but would create vast problems in Britain and other densely populated industrial countries, with a much higher number of inhabitants. The volume of paperwork alone, in checking who had or hadn't voted and going through any necessary court proceedings afterwards, would be a bureaucratic nightmare.

War:
Is It Desirable?

Pro: (1) It might be held nowadays that no one in his right senses would deem war to be desirable. Professional soldiers are the first to say that their prime aim is to prevent war. Yet the fact remains that war does have beneficial aspects, notably as a moral influence. It develops virtues such as patriotism, self-sacrifice, efficiency, inventiveness, courage and discipline. The 'Dunkirk spirit' embodied all that was finest in our national character, but no stimulus sufficiently powerful to arouse it exists in peace-time, although the need for it is as great.

(2) Military training in time of peace brings similar benefits. It educates and disciplines, preserves from idleness and greatly increases physical fitness and mental alertness. (See *Military Training, Compulsory*.)

(3) War is necessary for the growth of powerful States. Only in these can individual capacities develop most fully.

Con: (1) Whatever may have been the attitudes of past generations (often conditioned by those of empire-building and colonialism), most people today – particularly the young – have come to regard war, of any kind, as utterly (and rightly) repugnant and immoral. War promotes cruelty, vice and stupidity, as well as untold physical and mental suffering. Most people are content to exercise their limited capacity for adventure in their working and home lives. Those who wish for wider opportunities can go in for exploration, pioneering, reclaiming of waste places or voluntary social service.

(2) Military service is generally disastrous to the individual. It uproots him from normal life and often substitutes demoralising idleness for useful occupation.

(3) Citizens of small, peaceful States generally achieve a higher average standard of living and more individual fulfilment within society

(4) Art and literature, and religion, are stimulated by war.

(5) It selects the fittest, and thus secures the progress of evolution.

(6) War is a cure for over-population. If that sounds callous, reflect how often in history the threat of over-population has been abated (in the absence of war) by massive epidemics or other natural disasters. This pattern has always been evident in nature, when any species of wild life becomes too prolific for its healthiest survival.

(7) Trade follows the flag. The prestige of a nation in war and its armed strength are the foundations of its commercial credit. Victory secures access to resources of raw materials and foreign markets.

(8) War is often undertaken to save people from oppression or aggression, when intervention becomes necessary to national self-respect. The liberation of occupied countries from their oppressors, and the punishment of the guilty, advances the moral standing of society in general. If it had not been for Britain's determination to fight on alone in 1940, against all the odds, three-quarters of Europe might still be under the aggressor's heel.

than those of big countries. Inhabitants of the most militant States usually tend to lose much of their individual liberty.

(4) Flourishing periods for art and literature are not confined to warlike nations or times of war. Some religions (e.g Buddhism) are completely opposed to war. People's fears in wartime make any religious upsurge all too understandable. And how else to explain the irony of ourselves and our enemy praying to the same God for victory?

(5) War selects the physically fittest only to eliminate them. In modern warfare, a soldier's chance of survival does not depend on his personal qualities. In the social ruin that follows war, it is the most cunning that survive.

(6) On the contrary, the birth rate often increases during and immediately after a war. But in any case, the remedy for over-population must lie in education and social change (see *Birth Control*). To regard war as a cure for anything is quite unspeakable.

(7) Nations lose more in war than they gain in the trade that is supposed to follow it; war, under modern conditions, will ruin both victor and vanquished; the Second World War resulted in the widespread destruction and paralysis of peaceful industry. The days when trade could be imposed on conquered countries are past; indeed, nations are now forced to spend time and money on rebuilding the countries they have destroyed.

(8) Though sometimes fought for such ends, wars rarely achieve them. The fruits of victory are usually wilted by compromise and intrigue between the victorious nations.

(See also *Armaments, Limitation of Conventional; Nuclear Weapons: Should They Be Banned Completely?*; and the next article.)

War:
Is It Inevitable?

Pro: (1) Mankind has always been prone to war and, to judge from the past, always will be. For every one year of peace, in recorded history, there have been thirteen years of war. Throughout the early civilisations of Egypt, Assyria, Greece, Rome, etc., war was a prominent feature of life. It was characteristic of their highest development and greatest vigour.

(2) Human nature is unchangeable – and the aggressive instinct is one of its characteristics. Virile men enjoy a fight. Desire for adventure and the struggle for existence accentuate the tendency.

(3) Nations have the same characteristics as individuals. They have a sense of national honour which prevents them from submitting to outrage and indignity.

(4) All nations are not at the same level of civilisation or strength. Weaker or more primitive nations will always be in danger of ill-treatment by more powerful nations, and rising nations will always have a temptation to go to war to establish their domination and overthrow the older powers.

(5) The commercial and economic rivalries between the various nations cannot always be displaced or removed by arbitration, international organisations, or merely good aspirations. These rivalries subsist and cause wars even when most of the world is striving for peace.

(6) A nation which does not defend its honour and prestige, or is known to be unprepared for war, will invite aggression from other more virile or belligerent countries.

(7) War may have become much more horrible, but men will not

Con: (1) The progress of anthropological research shows that war is a recent phenomenon in human history, arising a few thousand years ago, through a definite set of conditions. The earliest civilisation of all, of which the records are chiefly traditional and archaeological rather than historical, was most certainly a peaceful one. But in any case it is false to assume that the future must resemble the past. Slavery, once a flourishing and unchallenged institution, is now negligible.

(2) Man has gradually risen in the scale of evolution and should by now be able to control or sublimate his fighting instincts.

(3) The analogy between nations and individuals may be rejected. Even if it is accepted, however, it leans in favour of the disappearance of war, since individuals now co-operate more than they used to – and fight less.

(4) Wars to replace one empire by another may have been natural in the past, but today it is more difficult to succeed in a war of aggression since it inevitably raises the threat of becoming world-wide in its scope.

(5) Economic rivalry has caused war, but that is only an argument for changing the social system that causes economic rivalry. Even without changing the whole social structure, a stable arrangement of economic interests could be made. The widespread economic devastation which results from war today is more than any nation can afford, even those which are only indirectly affected.

(6) The honour of the individual once maintained the duel. Today, the duel has disappeared and, if

cease to engage in it. Mankind has an enormous capacity for suffering, but the individual always enters a fight in the expectation that his enemy will suffer more than he does.

(8) Man is doomed to unhappiness by his nature. War will always be welcomed every now and again, as a relief from the boredom of everyday existence, especially in times of economic stagnation or depression.

(9) For these reasons, arbitration, the UN and disarmament schemes will never prevent occasional wars. Since they induce a false sense of security, they might even be a danger to a country's welfare.

necessary, aggrieved parties turn to the courts. National honour can be dealt with in the same way, by substituting recourse to international law for summary action.

(7) Small wars risk growing into big ones and the horrors of nuclear weapons have rendered any large-scale war impossible, unless the human race as a whole is prepared to commit suicide.

(8) A rational system of society and a national mode of life will abolish poverty, unhappiness and boredom. People will then value life far too much to throw it away.

(9) Men have striven for international agreement since nations existed and are not likely to give up the effort at this stage. Already the principle is accepted, though not much has been achieved yet in practice. The hope for peace is fundamental, and the solution will one day be found.

(See also the preceding article.)

Women, Married, More Jobs for

Pro: (1) Married women have as much right to take part in the general activities of the community as other people. They are just as likely to do good work, and many of them do not feel fulfilled solely by household and family duties.

(2) In many cases, the family income would be insufficient if the husband alone were working. For some, marriage would not even be possible if the woman could not continue her employment or profession.

(3) While young babies may need their mothers, older children are sufficiently cared for during the day by school facilities. All responsible mothers who take a job make sure that they or their husbands will be

Con: (1) A married woman should find scope enough in looking after the home and her husband. Her first duty is to care for her family.

(2) The entry of more married women into the labour market would risk keeping wages low and harming many other women who do not have the resource of a husband's income. Generally speaking, given the taxation differences, it is nearly as easy to support a man and wife on the husband's income as it is for a bachelor to keep himself in lodgings, where he must provide for his own needs and also, perhaps, save money with a view to marriage or the support of dependants.

(3) The rise in juvenile delinquency is partly due to working mothers'

home in time to look after their children, as necessary. In other societies, the child is often felt to belong to the whole community and shows no sign of deprivation. On Israeli *kibbutzim*, children spend allotted time with their parents after working hours but are otherwise cared for separately – again, with no ill effects.

(4) Many married women lose contact with the outside world when they have nothing to occupy them but their own family affairs, and thus may become poor companions for their husbands and growing children. In some homes, there is also a danger of polarisation, whereby the husband becomes regarded simply as the provider of income, while the wife holds herself to represent the family's source of culture and refinement. Wives who take part in their husbands' business and women (many of them married) who run their own businesses are usually far more interesting and intelligent than those who vegetate at home.

(5) The only valid test for employing people, in any work, should be their efficiency. This, and not the maintenance of obsolete traditions, is also the prime interest for the community as a whole. Since the task of rearing babies may lessen a woman's efficiency (by restricting the hours when she would be free to do an outside job, for instance), it is reasonable that young wives should have 10–15 years off work, if they can, to bring up their babies. But once the children are in their teens, married women should be given every encouragement to take a job – if they wish to, that is. Women themselves (and their husbands, should their opinion be sought!) are the only proper judges of whether they should seek work outside the home. However, there is no doubt that most wives in their mid-30s – particularly those who had a job before

absence from home, which contributes to unconscious resentment, bewilderment, a generally negative attitude, and the build-up of an anti-social attitude in later years.

(4) Some women are completely absorbed by running their homes, and prefer it that way. Mothers of growing children certainly don't need to take a job to avoid vegetating or losing contact with the outside world. Vast numbers of them remain intelligent and interested in life, often using free hours in the middle of the day to help with voluntary activities in their local community. Many married women in industry – particularly those who have to carry out all their domestic work, as well as doing their jobs, but do not get as much help from their husbands as they should – quickly show signs of strain and become worn and nervous, with the result that domestic unhappiness follows.

(5) Family life is an older and more important basis of communal prosperity than any form of industrial production. Some factories run kindergartens to look after their women employees' children in working hours; but, while some may regard that as a commendable expedient, it does not alter the basic objection that industrial jobs for young mothers put unnatural pressures (of time and strain) on both woman and child. Another drawback arises when women in industrial jobs become pregnant; for monotonous factory work and sedentary occupations often produce deep-seated fatigue – even though the women may not realise it, thinking that they are so accustomed to the work that it does not particularly tax them. Nor do such jobs give any opportunity for the kind of healthy activity which is beneficial to child-bearing.

(6) It is not suggested that no married women should work in industry – that would be nonsense.

they married – welcome the outside interest of at least a spare-time job. Nor is there any doubt that women with previous working experience, especially of office jobs, are much valued by enlightened employers. For mothers of younger children who want to work in industry, more provision should be made for adjacent crèches or kindergartens to care for the children while the women are working.

(6) The 'equal pay' legislation now in force should be made truly effective by job re-evaluation and regrading, which should give proper weight (for instance) to the fact that men's physical strength is no more or less valuable, in context, than some of women's special attributes, such as manual dexterity. In addition, there should be more facilities to train married women, if they wish, for promotion to the highest levels of responsibility in factories, shops and offices, as well as in the professions.

But there can be no doubt that measures to encourage a sizeable increase in their number would be unwise, because the right conditions for it do not exist. Women still of child-bearing age, for example, need the opportunity for flexible hours, job-sharing, part-time work, re-training and maternity leave without loss of seniority, pensions or similar benefits. In present circumstances, even the most enlightened employer would find it difficult, if not impossible, to accord all these on a large scale. In boom periods, when there are labour shortages, the employment of more married women may be of temporary benefit to an industry; but any advantages are offset in the long run by the problems caused – for the industry and the women alike – as soon as an economic recession occurs.

(See also the next article.)

Women's Liberation

(The first women's suffrage committee was set up in Britain as long ago as 1866, yet it was another fifty-two years before some British women won the right to vote and a further ten years before all did. Efforts to gain equal rights for British women in other fields achieved their greatest step forward only as recently as 29 December 1975, when the Sex Discrimination and Equal Pay Acts came into force. During the previous decade, a new element had been introduced into the fight by an American writer, Betty Friedan; her book, *The Feminine Mystique*, published in 1963, led three years later to her foundation in the USA of the National Organisation for Women, which campaigned – often using deliberately aggressive means – for women to free themselves from traditional male dominance. The organisation soon had 255 branches in 48 States and, with its counterparts in other countries, has since become known familiarly as the Women's Liberation movement (or 'Women's Lib'). In Britain, the principal protagonist of this militant movement, initially, was the university lecturer Germaine Greer. By 1969, there were 12 Women's Lib groups in the London area; within three years, the number had grown to between 40 and 50 – a growth pattern certainly echoed in other British towns.

It should be emphasised that the following arguments are *not* about the merits of women's rights, as a whole; they are concerned specifically with the pros and cons of the role played by Women's Lib, as that term is now generally understood.)

Pro: (1) Popular newspapers have concentrated on extremist activities by Women's Liberation supporters, largely ignoring the fact that many of its members have thought deeply about women's role in society and have simply refused to accept situations which had too easily been regarded as immutable. Among the movement's great strengths are that its support comes from a wide range of women, from many different classes, and that it embraces numerous individual viewpoints, some less militant than others. However, one point on which all its members are agreed is that there are still a great many injustices and illogicalities to be overcome before women achieve anything like truly equal rights.

(2) The women's movements of former generations had two big flaws. First, they were open to criticism as being run almost solely by middle class, professional people. Second, the suffragists became so pragmatic in demanding political rights that they 'sold out' regarding more fundamental changes in attitude. Neither objection applies to Women's Lib. By its dynamism and questioning of basic attitudes, it has provided the main stimulus for the change in public opinion which brought about the latest sex equality reforms. It prepared the ground for popular support for these reforms from an extremely wide spectrum – not just middle class but active trade unionists, married as well as single women, and from all age groups. Moreover, Women's Lib has devoted itself above all to the removal of socio-economic inequalities, over the broadest possible range.

(3) Without the impetus given by Women's Lib, in focusing attention

Con: (1) The image of any movement, however valid its fundamental aims may or may not be, will always tend to be coloured – in the eyes of the general public – by the excesses of its lunatic fringe. The broader that fringe, the less credibility a movement can retain. Before the First World War, the violence of the suffragettes, and the ridiculous extent to which they became opposed to anything masculine, utterly alienated public opinion from what was otherwise a just cause. The suffragettes did not win women the right to vote; parliamentary resistance was finally overcome by the splendid efforts of ordinary women, during the war, in showing themselves fully capable of taking on jobs previously done only by men. Similarly, today, the aggressive attitudes of Women's Lib have lost rather than gained them support and have even threatened to jeopardise the advances being achieved by more moderate women's movements.

(2) Women's Libbers must indeed live in a fairy-tale world if they believe that, through such symbolic gestures as burning their brassieres in public, they did anything at all to change the climate of opinion in favour of legislative reform. The real spadework in creating the groundswell of popular support for changes in women's affairs was done by much less abrasive bodies, like the Fawcett Society (descended directly from the original London Society for Women's Suffrage of 1866) and the Six Point Group (founded in 1921 to work for the *emancipation*, not spurious 'liberation', of women). Such bodies have solid achievements to their credit, both through their campaigns which led specifically to

on the need, the 1975 Acts would probably still be awaiting implementation. Women's Libbers have also been foremost in pointing out that those Acts do not go anywhere near far enough. They have protested at the failure to give 'teeth' to the new Equal Opportunities Commission, which can only advise complainants on what action to take but, under the Sex Discrimination Act, has no powers itself to start legal proceedings. The commission can send a questionnaire to a person or company accused of discrimination but cannot even insist that the questionnaire is filled in. Consequently, since women will often be reluctant to go to court on their own initiative, many offenders will escape. Among other points with which the Women's Liberation movement has taken issue is the legislation's failure to give women full equality in three key areas: social security, income tax and pensions. Under employers' pension schemes, for example, men can still receive higher benefits for the same contributions. Thanks largely to Women's Lib in the USA, that disparity is now banned by American law. Similarly, US laws about maternity leave and women's reinstatement rights are much stricter than is envisaged by Britain's Employment Protection Act 1975 (the implementation of which has in any case been delayed).

(4) The year which ushered in the unsatisfactory sex equality legislation was also a year in which British law gave men a licence to rape and some MPs started moves threatening to weaken, or even scrap, the Abortion Act. Women's Lib calls for every woman to have the right to free contraception and to abortion on demand. It also urges the establishment of a network of child care centres, open twenty-four hours a day, so that women can be freed to

the new anti-discrimination laws and through their clear exposition of inequalities which still need to be remedied. What's more, unlike Women's Lib, their membership is also open to men who support their aims.

(3) Legislation cannot conjure up equality out of the blue. It is up to women themselves to make the new laws work effectively. But the shrill hectoring of Women's Lib will not encourage them; it requires, clearly, an educative process which spreads steadily without frightening people off (as shown in a parallel field by the gradual but eventually undeniable success of the Race Relations Act). In the USA, an Equal Employment Opportunity Commission was established in 1964 under the Civil Rights Act to deal with complaints concerning race, colour, religion and national origin, as well as sex discrimination. Even with this wider scope, the commission's most valuable functions still are its work of research and public persuasion. Britain's Equal Opportunities Commission, in fact, was framed after a parliamentary select committee heard evidence about the American commission's mode of operation. Too many of the Women's Lib objections display an oversimplistic approach to what are highly complex problems. (For example, while the EOC itself cannot bring lawsuits for people it advises, they *can* apply for legal aid in the normal way.) Since the 1975 Acts came into force, the more experienced women's movements have concentrated on shortcomings which can be remedied more quickly than others, getting to the heart of what is practicable at this stage. In the industrial field alone, they exposed the 'dodges' used by some employers, whereby male workers were put in new grades, so that women continued to receive the lowest pay; they

lead useful lives and not be pinned down by domestic drudgery forced on them by men. At the last count, in 1973, there were only 466 local authority nurseries, caring for 25,574 children in all – and this at a time when Britain has nearly nine million working women, representing close on 40 per cent of the country's total work force.

(5) The more education a woman has, the deeper she is committed to creative work and not the kitchen sink. Women have a right to equal opportunities in public life and worth-while careers. They must be given improved training facilities in every field, equal access to the professions, to universities (including medical schools), and to courses enabling them to obtain higher qualifications – and their opportunities for winning promotion in their chosen careers must be genuine and meaningful (which cannot be said with any confidence of those likely to emerge under the provisions of the 1975 Acts). To cite just one example in the educational field: out of more than 3,000 professors in British universities today, fewer than 50 of them are women.

(6) Any situation or activity in which men retain a dominant role, not through any intrinsic merit or superiority but merely to preserve their accustomed privilege, is totally rejected by members of the Women's Liberation movement. Some American militants advocate all-female communes, the violent overthrow of male domination and, since the human race must continue, the creation of a sperm bank for use by women who want children but do not want men for partners. Others, less militant, believe that marriage is outmoded, that women are exploited by the marital situation and its aftermath in the case of divorce, and that they should be free to choose when and from whom to have babies,

have also led the fight for job re-evaluation which would give proper weight to manual dexterity and other typically female skills, as against men's physical energy and spatial skills.

(4) Typical Women's Lib exaggeration! The legal ruling that a man cannot be convicted of rape if he honestly believes the woman agreed to intercourse, however unreasonable his belief might be, upheld the defence in one specific case. It would not apply generally, and the courts will want particularly convincing evidence before accepting any such plea. There is certainly a good case for the authorities to provide more nursery schools, making it easier for mothers to take paid jobs, if they wish or need to. But the twenty-four-hour centres demanded by Women's Lib would threaten to undermine the whole point of motherhood. Even in communes where children are brought up separately, as in some of Israel's *kibbutzim*, the children spend at least part of each evening with their parents.

(5) Women's Libbers always tend to talk about exciting careers, apparently forgetting that not every man gets fulfilment from his work or has a creative or high-powered job. In real life, only a small minority do. Society does indeed owe women the right to equal opportunities and has at last recognised this in law. But from that point on, it's up to each woman to choose how she is going to use those opportunities. Women themselves must realise – and an ever-increasing proportion of them are doing so – that having a career and a family is not incompatible but, often, merely a question of good organisation (and of true partnership with their husbands). It isn't a case of either-or, between motherhood and a career; in claiming that it is, Women's Libbers give many

if they wish, without being shackled by matrimonial bonds. However, as proof of the breadth of opinions within the movement, there are also some members who warn that Women's Lib must win the support of many more ordinary married women if it is to succeed in its aims and therefore should not antagonise them by appearing to strike at their security.

(7) It is not a question of claiming that women are as good as or better than men – simply that they are (or should be) fully equal as human beings. If they were treated as no more and no less than that, they would not need to demand any special rights. In our present society, though, they remain the 'oppressed majority'. Women's Lib has exposed the blatant inconsistencies of movements which demand freedom, self-determination, or whatever, in the name of human rights, and then exclude more than half of the human race.

(8) Women who make a conscious decision to devote themselves to running their homes and bringing up their children, denying themselves an outside career, should receive proper financial recognition of their sacrifice. It has been estimated that housewives work about 100 hours a week in the home, yet the majority have to rely for money almost solely on what their husbands give them. (And yet another failing of the sex equality laws is that men are still not obliged to tell their wives how much they earn – and many don't.) At a conference in London in 1975, attended by women from the USA and Canada as well as from Britain, one proposal urged was that the State should pay housewives a living wage. It was suggested that £40 a week would be reasonable, for such arduous hours, though the sum would vary depending on such factors as the size of the family. One

ordinary women, quite unjustifiably, a feeling of inadequacy and guilt.

(6) To hear the Women's Libbers talk, one would think the average woman is servile, inefficient, inconsistent, passive and ignorant. Women who, through conscious choice, have made a home and brought up children are made to feel that they have done something wrong. By turning men and women against each other, the Lib movement threatens ultimately to destroy the family – which, whatever the extremists say, is the essential basis of our civilisation.

(7) Few would now contest that parental responsibility should be shared genuinely, that married life should be a partnership in the full sense of the word, and that men ought to shoulder an equal burden of the family and domestic tasks formerly left almost solely to women. But that does not mean leaning too far in the other direction. The sex equality legislation, it should be remembered, is a two-way matter – also giving men opportunities not previously open to them. (For example, men can now become midwives!) The salient point consistently ignored by Women's Lib is that men and women *are* different genetically, irrespective of physical factors and conditioning.

(8) Leaving aside the exaggerated claim that most women do 100 hours of housework each week, and also the fact that many housewives positively enjoy domesticity and pride themselves on running their homes well, the idea of a State wage for housewives is economic madness. No nation on earth, however wealthy, could possibly afford it. (In Britain alone, at the suggested rate, it would cost around £20,000,000,000 annually!) The half-baked character of so many of these Women's Lib-style notions is underlined in this instance by a comparison with the

speaker pointed out that advising housewives to go out to work, so that they could earn a little money and make themselves independent of their husbands, was no answer; a second job was not liberation for any woman – it merely gave her twice as much work to do.

(9) From its earliest stages, education remains riddled with sex discriminatory attitudes and must be radically reformed in this respect. We must rid children's books of their habitual depiction of the sexes in stereotyped roles, with boys always portrayed in adventurous or exciting activities and the girls always steered towards domesticity and motherhood; and this change in attitude must be maintained right up the line. From childhood up to school-leaving age, the present system fails to give girls the full, rounded education that would enable each girl to develop her own potential. Instead, the orientation of girls by their teachers – and, too often, by their mothers – is still almost solely towards biological functions.

(10) In adult as well as school life, even the English language is sexist – masculine-dominated and discriminatory. One of the Women's Liberation movement's achievements has been its successful opposition to the use of words and phrases which have an exclusively male form or connotation, even though they describe functions, activities or job titles which apply to women as well. The Women's Lib agitation on this score has won increasing public acceptance of the need to employ alternative, non-discriminatory terms.

(11) The Women's Liberation movement does not have a top-heavy, bureaucratic organisation, dominating or controlling its national affairs from the centre. It is made up of a large number of small

much more sensible equivalent of 'wages for wives' advocated by the Married Women's Association. Its proposal: 'After the upkeep of the home and family from the joint income, the remainder should be equally shared, and, if invested, the name of both spouses should be documented.' The Association is also demanding that *each* spouse should have the legal right to know the income of the other.

(9) The more experienced women's movements go a great deal of the way with the Libbers in these particular demands. Publishers and teachers have long since accepted the need for sex-stereotyped roles and attitudes to be eradicated from text-books. Even before this, though, bodies like the Fawcett Society were already concentrating as well on trying to secure changes in school curricula, so that girls should be definitely encouraged to continue with mathematics and to take scientific and technical subjects – and, consequently, to think longer-term about their careers and the wider job horizons now opened up for them. The Society is also campaigning for the improvement of careers counselling for girls, which, it says, should start before examination courses are chosen.

(10) Insisting on neutral words like 'chairperson', instead of the usual 'chairman', does not get to the root of the problem. Nor has it made the least contribution, of any real substance, to women's fight for equal rights. Cynics might well say that the only concrete change for which Women's Lib can actually take the (dubious) credit is the spreading usage of 'Ms', as a form of address for women who wish to assert their individuality by refusing to be classed as either 'Miss' or 'Mrs'. If the acceptance of that hideous two-letter abbreviation is regarded as an achievement, how is

cells throughout the country, often only eight or ten strong, the members of which share similar ideals but have complete freedom to discuss and propagate their individual viewpoints on all issues they regard as important. As a result, the movement throws up a continual ferment of new ideas.

(12) Women's Lib may have aggravated and irritated many people, but that is precisely what it has set out to do. However extreme some of its actions and statements may seem to the more conservative-minded, it has succeeded in getting many members of the public to start thinking and talking about issues which had not interested or even occurred to them previously. On the principle that 'any advertising is good advertising', it has had a vanguard role in getting much more attention paid to women's affairs. Without the 'ginger' provided by the Women's Liberation movement, progress towards equality would not have advanced so far or so fast as it has.

it that no one has yet established for sure how it should be pronounced? (The Libbers should take note, too, that there are innumerable women, married and single, who find 'Ms' repulsive and are just as determined in their refusal to let anyone apply it to *them*!)

(11) The Libbers' lack of national organisation is not simply a structural weakness but debilitates their very arguments. While avoiding the pitfalls of the suffragette movement, which was eventually distorted by the over-strong control of those at its top, Women's Lib has stayed too far in the other direction, still almost as scattered and amorphous as when it began. Without some recognised body at its head, responsible for defining agreed policy, a movement will always tend to have the character of an undisciplined rabble. What Women's Lib claims as a virtue is, in the final analysis, proof of its fundamental irresponsibility.

(12) The progress already achieved came about through the work of moderates, men and women, who recognised that it is better to concentrate on securing reforms rather than waste energy in attacking the whole system. Women's Libbers may have helped to stir up public interest in the issues, but they did not make the running. Vociferous, aggressive minorities always get publicity out of all proportion to their actual influence – and, in this case, their jeering and shouting has frequently had a backlash effect. By the intemperate lengths to which they carry their hostility to men, by making ordinary women feel inadequate and guilty, by their unnecessary offensiveness, the Women's Lib extremists have if anything set back the real advance.

(See also the preceding article.)

Written Constitution

Pro: (1) The British constitution is largely at the mercy of the party in power in the House of Commons. Since it is unwritten, there is effectively no legal limitation on what Parliament can enact by ordinary legislation. The Government virtually controls Parliament and there is excessive power in the hands of the Prime Minister; as a result, precedence is always given to the interests of the parliamentary majority – even though that majority may be very small (and, on occasion, has actually gained office with a lower total of votes than those received by the Opposition). A ruling party naturally claims that the measures it carries through are in the national rather than its own interest, but it is highly doubtful if this is always so. A written constitution would reduce the danger of laws being passed for sectional instead of national reasons; it ensures that the exercise of power is kept within due bounds.

(2) One of the main purposes of enacting a constitution is to entrench the principal traditions and conventions relating to the Executive. At present, these can be altered by any party which has a majority of one in Parliament. The Legislature should guarantee the rights of the individual; but under the present British system, as we have indicated, those rights are in the hands of the government of the day, which controls the Legislature. A written constitution would establish a Legislature which had control over the government and thus provide a better safeguard, in all circumstances, for the rights of the individual.

(3) The drafting of a written constitution would provide a unique opportunity for clearing up existing anomalies and for a thorough over-

Con: (1) Britain's unwritten constitution is the result of precedent and tried and tested experience, built up over many centuries. Among its great virtues are that it is extremely flexible and empiric in nature, not based on well-meaning theories. Its replacement by a written constitution, were that possible, would result in a rigidity which, under British conditions, would inevitably hamper the efficient functioning of government. Moreover, who could be sufficiently impartial to draw up a satisfactory written constitution for this country? Ideally, the task would have to be undertaken by the main political parties and all other political groups of any size; yet there could be no hope of them ever reaching full agreement on the subject. And if one majority party tried to do it, there would always be a suspicion (at the least) that some of its provisions favoured that party's own sectional interests.

(2) Under a written constitution, the very rigidity of its statutes renders them more liable to abuse. The establishment of one particular set of laws, intended to cover all eventualities, would probably lead to confusion rather than to better organisation. Under our unwritten constitution, on the other hand, the adaptability of our conventions makes it far easier to give rulings suited to each individual case. In this form, our conventions reflect the evolutionary nature of law, whereby the best remedies have been retained out of the progressive experiences of the past.

(3) Among the most serious drawbacks of a written constitution is that a good number of its provisions are likely to become outdated very

haul of outmoded laws and conventions. Its enactment would fit in with the present codification of other English Law. In the process, it might well simplify the solution of such issues as the powers of the Second Chamber and the national rights of Scotland and Wales. (See *Lords, Reform of the House of*; *Parliament, Reform of.*)

(4) A written constitution can keep pace with the times no less effectively, by the introduction of subsequent amendments as and when new conditions arise which make them desirable. The United States constitution has preserved flexibility in just this manner. Since 1787, more than two dozen amendments have been added to its original written constitution.

(5) Britain is a liberal democracy with, in theory, strict separation of powers (i.e. between the Executive, Legislature and Judiciary). In practice, however, because of the vagueness consequent on having an unwritten constitution, there is blurring at the edges and these three bodies do not in fact retain complete independence from each other. With a written constitution, the separation of powers would be truly effective.

quickly. Britain avoids this because the natural evolution of law keeps pace with the times (more or less!). Public opinion may often be slightly ahead of it, but it does provide a reasonably speedy response to the changing attitudes and needs of society.

(4) Some of the amendments to the American constitution have been the principal sources of abuse. Two other leading nations which also have written constitutions are France and the Soviet Union. In the latter, it is laid down statutorily that women have complete equality with men; yet, apart from the former Minister of Culture, Mrs Furtseva, how many women have been Government Ministers in Soviet history? And in France, how many entire new constitutions have been introduced in the last century?

(5) The separation of powers is secured just as effectively under an unwritten constitution, in practice as well as in theory. The independence of the British Judiciary, for instance, is sacrosanct – and recognised as such throughout the world.

(See also *Cabinet Government.*)

Index

The initial purpose of this Index is to expand on the cross-references, between related subjects, already given in the text. However, a brief explanation is necessary. Many of the individual debating subjects crop up a number of times because, clearly, they are relevant to more than one of the principal themes listed. (As a cardinal example: our lives are touched by politics in so many different ways nowadays that the section for Politics, while already requiring more entries than any other, could logically have embraced almost every subject in the book!) Accordingly, under each main theme, the page numbers are given not only for the obviously related subjects but for others which have a relevance to it that, at first sight, is not always so obvious. Finally, subsidiary references are listed as well for subjects which touch on the principal theme only tangentially or in passing.